J M Turner.
November 1958.

THE EUCHARISTIC WORDS OF JESUS

THE EUCHARISTIC WORDS OF JESUS

by

D.Dr. JOACHIM JEREMIAS

PROFESSOR OF NEW TESTAMENT STUDIES
IN THE UNIVERSITY OF GÖTTINGEN

translated from the second German edition by

ARNOLD EHRHARDT, LL.D., PH.D., B.D.

VICAR OF ST. MARY'S, BIRCH-IN-HOPWOOD, LANCS.

BASIL BLACKWELL
OXFORD
1955

PRINTED IN GREAT BRITAIN

PREFACE

TO

THE SECOND GERMAN EDITION (1949)

This new edition is in very many respects a new book. Numerous questions have been re-examined: the liturgical character of the texts has been taken far more seriously than in the first edition; the problem of literary criticism has demanded more serious consideration (chapter two is completely new); the contribution of astronomy to the chronological problem had to be discussed; and in particular there have arisen a number of questions about the exegesis of the texts (in chapter four). In various respects I have had to reconsider my views: for instance, I no longer think it possible for reasons of textual criticism to hold that the shorter text of Luke (Luke 22. 19a) is original. However, the principal views proposed in the first edition (1935) are reinforced by new material, as for instance in the matter of the paschal character of the Last Supper, the Semitisms in St. Mark's report on the Last Supper, and the interpretation of the words of institution. I have also gladly responded to the frequently expressed demands for a fuller discussion of the objections against the chronology of the Synoptists which are derived from the *Halakha* (pp. 49-53).

My aim has been to give the most precise exegesis possible of the Eucharistic Words. For it is precisely over studies concerning the Last Supper that the uneasy feeling arises that their authors unconsciously read into the text what they want to find. Have we not all to learn more and more how to listen only to the text? Some pages of this book will show that the attempt to recreate the world in which Jesus lived and the language which He spoke provides us with new insights, but also at first confronts us with unexpected and bewildering questions which, however, will deepen our understanding if we face them squarely. Exegesis is really a matter of obedience.

The two indexes were contributed by Pastor Guenter Boehme, Lic. theol. of Kerstlingerode near Goettingen, to whom I offer my heartfelt thanks.

May this study not only serve to promote further research, but also to assist those who work in the ministry of the Word.

JOACHIM JEREMIAS

INTRODUCTION

When the first edition of Professor Jeremias's book appeared in 1935, it did not receive among English-speaking scholars the attention it deserved. There were various reasons for this neglect. The main currents of theological interest in Great Britain were directed towards other things, it was commonly assumed that all that could be said about the origins of the Eucharist had already been said, and in particular the severance of the Last Supper from the Passover was by the vast majority accepted as so axiomatic that argument in a contrary sense was regarded as almost freakish. Moreover, there was some suspicion, not wholly unjustified in the late "Thirties", that German theology was losing much of its objectivity and value. I am ashamed to have to add also that, so far as my experience goes, knowledge of the book's existence was until fairly recently by no means widespread, even among teachers of the New Testament. At any rate, whatever the reasons, whether subservience to the *Zeitgeist* or mere ignorance, the book has hitherto made little impact upon British scholars. I can think of more than one work written in the succeeding decade on this subject in which Jeremias is not mentioned; and when, during the war, I wished to consult him in connexion with a paper I was asked to write, I could find only one copy in Oxford!

It has been different since the end of the war. As German books became more accessible and as interest in the subject revived (much stimulated by Dom Gregory Dix's *Shape of the Liturgy*), more and more of us have come to discover or rediscover what a notable aid Professor Jeremias has put at our disposal. The publication last year of a revised and expanded Second Edition was a welcome and important event, and it is the English translation of this Second Edition which is now before the reader. I am confident that in its English form it will at once be recognized here as a weighty and indispensable contribution in any discussion of the background, nature, and interpretation of the Last Supper.

The author indicates in his own brief foreword the major differences between this and the First Edition. The changes and additions do not make it a significantly different kind of book. As one familiar with and much impressed by the earlier form of the work, I am most struck by the definite change of view with regard to the Shorter Text of Luke, and by the new, interesting, and even startling interpretation of *εἰς τὴν ἐμὴν ἀνάμνησιν*. I am bound to admit I do not find the latter immediately convincing, but perhaps further reflection will soften the shock. The other modifications and slight changes of emphasis in the present form of the work are natural developments of the former. The discussion of the possible contribution which astronomical calculations can make towards determining the chronology is entirely new. The section dealing with the literary criticism of the sources is considerably extended. Greater stress is laid upon the liturgical character of the texts in question. The initial argument for the Passover character of the Last Supper has also been somewhat strengthened, the objections commonly alleged against this identification being more fully dealt with than in the First Edition, in which on a number of points the reader was simply referred to Billerbeck.

This point, the equation of Last Supper and Passover, is the one on which attention is likely to be most focused in the first instance, just because it runs counter to what has been the dominant view among English scholars. It is curious that on this historical point there has been a widespread tendency to forsake the (normally preferred) Synoptic account and to adopt the Johannine dating. It is perhaps still more curious that the dissociation of Last Supper and Passover has been supported by appeals to Jewish law and practice, although the preponderance of leading experts in Judaica and Rabbinica (e.g., Chwolson, Billerbeck, Dalman) has always been in favour of the identification. But the full strength of the case will appear in the author's exhaustive treatment. Whether it appears convincing, as it does to me, or not, it must be taken seriously. It is more important than has always been grasped to get the right answer to this question, for upon it a good deal of our interpretation will depend.

There are things in this book with which I do not agree, and if I were writing a review I might properly give voice to certain queries and reservations, but they would be out of place in this Introduction. I am so grateful to Professor Jeremias, so convinced of the importance of his book, and so much in agreement with its main contention, that I wish simply to express my gratification that it is now made accessible to a wider circle of readers, and then to let the author speak for himself.

JOHN LOWE

THE DEANERY,
CHRIST CHURCH,
OXFORD.
July, 1950.

CONTENTS

CHAPTER I

Was the Last Supper a Passover Meal?[1]

ALL four Gospels agree that the day on which Jesus died was a Friday (Mark 15. 42; Matt. 27. 62; Luke 23. 54; John 19. 31, 42). In view of the fact that at the time of Jesus the day was reckoned from sunset to sunset,[2] this Friday includes—from 6 p.m. on Maundy Thursday to 6 p.m. on Good Friday—the whole of the Passion in its narrower sense: the Last Supper, Gethsemane, arrest and trial, crucifixion and burial, (Mark 14. 17—15. 47; Matt. 26. 20—27. 61; Luke 22. 14—23. 56a; John 13. 2—19. 42). All the Evangelists are at one on this point too.

[1] The spelling "Passah" with final "h" is wrong because it takes its origin from Heb. פֶּסַח whereas Passa is an Aramaic *status emphaticus*. Regarding the pronunciation of the word in Palestine at the time of Jesus, we can affirm: (1) It was pronounced with an initial "ph", as appears from the LXX (2 Chron. 30. 1–18; 35. 1–18; Jer. 38. 8, φασεκ, φασεχ); Philo, only once, *Leg. Alleg.* 3. 30. § 94 (1. 134. 4), φασεκ; and Josephus, *Ant.* 5. 1. 4, etc., φασκα; and the spelling with an initial "p"—in Josephus, Philo, the LXX, and everywhere in the N.T.—is irregular, caused by dissimilation of φ–χ (impossible in Greek) to π–χ; cf. *Theol. Woerterb. z. N.T.* 5 (1954), 895–6. (2) The vocalization with "i" (פיסחא) in the Targ. Onkelos, Jerusalem Talmud, and the Midrash is late, witness the concurrence of the LXX, Philo, Josephus and the N.T.; cf. H. Laible, *Theol. Lit. Bl.* 44 (1923), 115 sq. The correct phonetic spelling of the word as pronounced at the time of Jesus would, therefore, be *phasḥā*.

[2] It has to be noted about every subsequent statement as to time that Jewish chronology at the time of Jesus fixed the beginning of the day at sunset—more precisely at the first appearance of the stars after sunset (b. Ber. 2 ab). It is instructive to notice how the Samaritans fixed the boundary, namely midway between the sun's colouring golden before its setting and the disappearance of the evening red after sunset. Cf. *Finḥas ibn Isḥaḳ, kitab el-ḥulf ben es-samira wel-jahud* (1885), M.S. p. 85, cf. G. Dalman, *Palaestina Jahrb.* 8 (1913), 123; Joach. Jeremias, *Die Passahfeier der Samaritaner und ihre Bedeutung fuer das Verstaendnis der A.T. Passahueberlieferung* (Beih. *Z.A.W.* 59) (Giessen, 1932), 80. *Finḥas* adds that the end of the day is therefore about two minutes after sunset. The

In view of this agreement among the sources, it is all the more surprising to see that the Gospels apparently differ upon another point, viz. whether this Friday or the next day, the Sabbath, was the first day of the Passover, i.e. whether or not the Last Supper was a passover meal. It is important to clear up this point not only for the chronology of the life of Jesus, but in particular—and theologians as well as the Church in general are deeply concerned in elucidating this point—for a better understanding of the meaning of the Eucharist and of its place in the scheme of redemption.[1]

(1) *The Problem*

The Synoptists hold the view that the Last Supper was a passover,[2] and therefore took place in the night of Nīsān 14/15th.[3] It is true that in Mark 14. 12, where the writer refers to the preceding day—i.e., the 14th of Nīsān—and says: *τῇ πρώτῃ ἡμέρᾳ τῶν ἀζύμων ὅτε τὸ πάσχα ἔθυον*, there is a contradiction between the two dates. For normal calculation has it that "the first day of the Feast of Unleavened Bread" is the 15th of Nīsān[4]—only in quite exceptional cases, in learned discussion, is the day of preparation, Nīsān the 14th, called the first day of the feast.[5] However, the

---

fact that in late Judaism the day began in the evening is most clearly shown in that the Sabbath is "sanctified" after sunset, and twenty-four hours later at sunset is "dismissed".

[1] S. Schoeffel, "Gottes Offenbarung im hl. Abendmahl" in *Luthertum* 48 (1937), 340 sq., 355 sq.; 49 (1938), 33 sq.; M. Barth, *Das Abendmahl—Passahmahl, Bundesmahl und Messiasmahl* (1945).

[2] Mark 14. 12, 14, 16 (par. Matt. 26. 17, 18, 19; Luke 22. 7, 8, 11, 13); Luke 22. 15; also Ev. Ebion. in Epiphan. *Haer.* 30, 22, 4.

[3] There are still some amateurs who maintain that in the time of Jesus the Passover was eaten in the night of Nīsān 13/14th; some people even claim that this is still the case amongst the Samaritans. All this is pure invention; cf. Joach. Jeremias, *Die Passahfeier der Samaritaner* (Giessen, 1932), 78.

[4] LXX, Lev. 23. 11; Philo, *Spec. Leg.* 2. § 155–7 (5. 123. 6 sq.); Jos., *Ant.* 3. 10. 5. § 250; Targ. Jerush. I ad Lev. 23. 11; Num. 28. 18, are all agreed on this. D. Chwolson, *Das letzte Passahmahl Christi und der Tag seines Todes* (1892, 2nd ed. 1908), has insisted upon this fact with considerable energy.

[5] P. Billerbeck 2. 812–15; Jacob Mann, "Rabbinic Studies in the Synoptic Gospels", in *Hebrew Union College Annual* 1 (Cincinnati, 1924), 344 sq.

second half—ὅτε τὸ πάσχα ἔθυον—so clearly indicates Nīsān the 14th that only this day can be meant by the writer.[1] Mark 14. 12 is one of the several instances of the rule that, where in the second Gospel two dates are given, one immediately following the other, in what looks like a mere pleonasm, the second is meant to interpret the first, e.g. 1. 32 ὀψίας δὲ γενομένης—ὅτε ἔδυ ὁ ἥλιος (ὀψία may mean the time before or after sunset: the second statement shows that here the period after sunset is meant, for sick people may not be carried before the end of the Sabbath); 15.42 καὶ ἤδη ὀψίας γενομένης—ἐπεὶ ἦν παρασκευή, ὅ ἐστιν προσάββατον (the second statement shows that here the time before the beginning of the Sabbath is meant by ὀψία, i.e. the time before sunset); 1.35 καὶ πρωΐ—ἔννυχα λίαν (πρωΐ may mean the time before or after sunrise: the second statement, therefore, shows that the time before sunrise is meant); 16. 2 καὶ λίαν πρωΐ τῇ μιᾷ τῶν σαββάτων ἔρχονται ἐπὶ τὸ μνῆμα—ἀνατείλαντος τοῦ ἡλίου (the second phrase shows that in this case πρωΐ means the time after sunrise); 14. 30 σήμερον—ταύτῃ τῇ νυκτί (σήμερον comprises the whole day of twenty-four hours, beginning at sunset; the second pointer indicates that the next few hours are contemplated); 4. 35 ἐν ἐκείνῃ τῇ ἡμέρᾳ—ὀψίας γενομένης; 13. 24 ἐν ἐκείναις ταῖς ἡμέραις—μετὰ τὴν θλῖψιν ἐκείνην. The same is true in Mark 14. 12: the date τῇ πρώτῃ ἡμέρᾳ τῶν ἀζύμων, which is most probably due to faulty

---

From the evidence quoted by Billerbeck, Mekh. Ex. 12. 15 and b. Pes. 36a have to be eliminated. Both these passages mean by "the first day of the feast" the 15th of Nīsān, and not the 14th. Evidence for the 14th of Nīsān being called the first day of the feast is therefore only: b. Pes. 5a—school of R. Jischma''ēl (died A.D. 135); j. Pes. 1. 27a—anonymous; j. Pes. 1. 27c—R. Jehūdhā (about A.D. 150); altogether little support. These passages comment on two texts: for in Exod. 12. 15 it is prescribed, "even the first day [i.e. Nīsān the 15th] ye shall put away leaven out of your houses", but since at the time of Jesus the established custom demanded the removal of leaven on Nīsān the 14th (Pes. 1. 1 sq.) there arose a difference between law and general custom, unless "the first day" (Exod. 12. 15) was regarded as Nīsān the 14th. In connexion with this, *bārīshōn*, Exod. 12. 18, was wrongly completed by the addition of "day" (instead of "month"), and thus Nīsān the 14th was found as "the first day" in this verse also.

[1] The killing of the paschal animals took place in the afternoon of Nīsān the 14th. The evidence for this has been collected by me in *Die Passahfeier der Samaritaner* (Giessen, 1932), 79–80.

translation,[1] is unambiguously indicated by the words *ὅτε τὸ πάσχα ἔθυον* in the sense that the preparation of the Upper Room for Jesus and His disciples took place on Nīsān the 14th, the day of preparation. The Last Supper took place, according to Mark 14. 17 par., on the evening, i.e. on Nīsān the 15th, which had begun at sunset. This fact is borne out by Mark 14. 14 par. *ὅπου τὸ πάσχα μετὰ τῶν μαθητῶν μου φάγω* and Mark 14. 16 par. *καὶ ἡτοίμασαν τὸ πάσχα.* Since, however, all these verses come from Mark 14. 12–16, a passage which has to be regarded as an expansion of the original Passion narrative,[2] it is significant that another text which represents an early, independent,[3] separate tradition, Luke 22. 15 *ἐπιθυμίᾳ ἐπεθύμησα τοῦτο τὸ πάσχα*[4] *φαγεῖν μεθ' ὑμῶν,*[5] witnesses to the paschal character of the Last Supper.

St. John, however, differs. Although his statements about the date of the Last Supper, as will be seen,[6] are by no means un-

[1] That has been shown by D. Chwolson, *Das letzte Passahmahl Christi*, 2nd ed. (1908). Nevertheless his suggestion ביומא קמי דפסחא (p. 180) is open to correction, because without any justification he renders *ἄζυμα* by פסחא, in order to support his chronological theory (infra p. 7 sq.). But read: ביומא קמי דפטיריא, meaning (1) the day before the *ἄζυμα* i.e. *πρὸ μιᾶς τῶν ἀζύμων* (cf. below note p. 5 n. 1), i.e. Nīsān the 14th, which is the original meaning, (2) on the first day of the *ἄζυμα*, i.e. *τῇ πρώτῃ ἡμέρᾳ τῶν ἀζύμων*, which is the mistranslation found in Mark 14. 12.

[2] Cf. infra, p. 64 sq. [3] Cf. infra, p. 117 sq.

[4] L. v. Sybel, "Das letzte Mahl Jesu" in *Theol. Stud. u. Krit.* 95 (1923-4), 119, maintains that Luke 22. 15–18 is a free transformation of the Eucharistic formula by St. Luke, who substituted "Passa" for "bread". He is followed by R. Bultmann, *Die Gesch. d. synopt. Tradition*, 2nd ed. (Goettingen, 1931), 286 sq., who—with a certain reserve—asks whether in Luke 22. 15 bread was originally mentioned instead of *pascha*; and the same is stated with greater confidence by A. Loisy, "Les origines de la cène eucharistique" in *Congrès d'histoire du Christianisme* 1, *Annales d'histoire du Christianisme* 1 (Paris-Amsterdam, 1928), 80. Every probability is against this violent emendation of the text: tradition (as is shown e.g. in the story of the miraculous feeding) tends to introduce, but not to obliterate, references to the eucharistic formula.

[5] The suggestion of F. C. Burkitt and A. E. Brooke in *J.T.S.* 9 (1908), 569–72, that Luke 22. 15 should be regarded as an unfulfilled wish, is not only "forced"—"the unsuspecting reader would understand something different", E. Gaugler, *Int. Kirchl. Zeitschr.* 32 (1942), 122—but inconsistent with the vow of abstinence in the following v. 16 (cf. infra, p. 165 sq.).

[6] Cf. infra, p. 55 sq.

equivocal, there is at any rate one passage which differs from the date mentioned by the Synoptists: John 18. 28 *ἀλλὰ φάγωσιν τὸ πάσχα*. Since at the time of Jesus' accusation before Pilate the eating of the paschal lambs had not yet taken place, the crucifixion of Jesus occurred, according to John, on the day of preparation, Nīsān the 14th, and therefore the Last Supper was not a passover meal, but took place twenty-four hours earlier. The same date is to be found in the apocryphal Gospel of Peter.[1]

This is the question to be answered in the first part of our study: John says that the whole Passion in its narrower sense, i.e. all that happened from the Last Supper to the Burial, took place on Nīsān the 14th (ending at sunset); the Synoptists, on Nīsān the 15th. To put it differently, according to John all the incidents mentioned occurred on the day of preparation; according to the Synoptists, on the first day of the Passover, the day which began with the eating of the passover meal. For John it was an ordinary day—although in practice it was observed by refraining from work, to an extent which varied considerably from place to place[2]; for the Synoptists it was a high feast-day. According to John, the Last Supper was an ordinary meal; according to the Synoptists, it was a Passover with all its solemn ritual. Which of the two is right?

One may attempt (as has indeed been done) to harmonize the Synoptic and Johannine datings in three ways:

(1) The Synoptists are right, and John should be interpreted accordingly—the view of the medieval Latin Church, which

[1] 2. 5, ed. E. Klostermann, *Apocrypha* 1, in Lietzmann's *Kl. Texte* 3, 2nd ed. (1921): the trial and crucifixion of Jesus took place *πρὸ μιᾶς τῶν ἀζύμων*, i.e. Nīsān the 14th. On the other hand, the frequently quoted passage b. Sanh. 43a (Bar.), "on the day of preparation Jēshū was hanged", does not refer to Jesus, but to a disciple of R. *Jehōshūaʿ ben Peraḥjā* (about B.C. 100), called Jesus; cf. b. Sanh. 107b (Bar.) par. b. Soṭa 47a.

[2] Pes. 4. 1 distinguishes between places where, on the day of preparation, work was done till noon, and other places where they do not work (as long as that). Pes. 4. 5, "in Judaea they work till noon; in Galilee the Shammaïtes demand that work should be stopped completely, whereas the Hillelites prohibit it from sunrise only". Pes. 4. 6, "tailors, hairdressers and fullers may work on the days of preparation, and according to R. *Jōsē b. Jehūdhā* the cobblers as well".

consequently used unleavened bread, at Holy Communion, and of the Reformers. Those who hold this opinion have to explain the word *πάσχα* in John 18. 28, so that it does not denote the paschal lamb. The translation of *φαγεῖν τὸ πάσχα* should in this case either—on the authority of 2 Chron. 30. 22—read "to celebrate the whole seven days of the Feast of unleavened bread"[1] or, according to Talmudic sayings, "to eat the paschal sacrifices".[2] As the reading of 2 Chron. 30. 22 is uncertain (cf. LXX), only the second possibility is admissible. It is true that the paschal sacrifices (חֲגִיגָה), which were eaten during the seven days of the feast, Nīsān the 15th to 21st, were sometimes called פֶּסַח, in accordance with Deut. 16. 2 and 2 Chron. 35. 7,[3] so that John 18. 28 could be referred to Nīsān the 15th. The meaning in that case would be that the members of the Sanhedrin did not enter the *praetorium* lest they should be defiled and made incapable of eating the paschal sacrifices (*ḥaghīghā*). The date of John would then agree with that of the Synoptists. However, it is very doubtful whether this subtlety would not have been lost upon those Christians from the Gentiles to whom John's Gospel was addressed.[4] They were bound to regard the words *ἀλλὰ φάγωσιν τὸ πάσχα* John 18. 28 in their normal meaning, as for instance in Luke 22. 15, and refer them to the eating of the paschal lamb, i.e. to understand John's report in the sense that Jesus was already buried at the time when the paschal lamb was eaten in the houses of Jerusalem.

(2) John is right, the Synoptists should be interpreted accordingly—the view of the Greek Church, which therefore uses ordinary bread at Holy Communion. If this view be taken, it has to be assumed that Jesus on His own authority anticipated the

[1] This is the view taken by Th. Zahn, *Das Johannesevangelium*, 5th and 6th ed. (Leipzig, 1921), 631–3; cf. his *Einleitung in das N.T.*, 3rd ed., 2. 523, 534–6; C. C. Torrey, "The Date of the Crucifixion according to the Fourth Gospel" in *Journ. of Bibl. Lit.* 50 (1931), 239 sq.

[2] This was held already by John Lightfoot, *Opera Omnia* 2 (Roterodami, 1686), 670 sq.; Chr. Schoettgen, *Horae Hebraicae et Talmudicae* (Dresden-Leipzig, 1733) 400 sq.; C. C. Torrey op. cit., 237–9, and many others.

[3] P. Billerbeck 2. 837 sq.

[4] G. Dalman, *Jesus-Jeschua* (Leipzig, 1922), 81 sq.; P. Billerbeck 2. 839 sq.

passover meal[1] and—perhaps because He foresaw that at the regular time of the Passover He would already be dead—kept it one day earlier than His fellow-countrymen, i.e. on Nīsān the 14th (beginning at sunset). But this point of view fails to account for the wording of Mark 14. 12 par., and moreover any private anticipation of the Passover celebration was an impossibility.[2]

(3) Both the Synoptists and John are correct—a view widely held in post-Reformation times. If this view be taken, it has to be assumed that the contemporaries of Jesus celebrated the Passover on two consecutive days in the year of His death. This view has been taken, on the one hand by D. Chwolson,[3] followed by J. Klausner[4] and J. Zolli,[5] and on the other by Jechiel Lichtenstein,[6] followed by H. L. Strack[7] and P. Billerbeck.[8] Chwolson assumes that in the time of Jesus the paschal lambs were still slaughtered in the twilight of the evening of Nīsān the 14th to the 15th, in accordance with the rule of Exod. 12. 6; Lev. 23. 5; Num. 9. 3, 5, cf. 11. Since Nīsān the 15th in the year of Jesus' death fell on a Sabbath, and since in consequence the Sabbath and the Passover coincided, the killing of the paschal lambs was brought forward to dusk between Nīsān the 13th and the 14th.

[1] So e.g. L. J. Rueckert, *Das Abendmahl* (1850) 45; Frz. Delitzsch, art. "Passah" in Riehm's *Handwoerterb. d. bibl. Altertums* 2 (Bielefeld and Leipzig, 1894), 1161a; A. Merx, *Das Evangelium Matthaeus* (Berlin, 1902) 377 sq.; H. E. D. Blakiston, "The Lucan account of the institution of the Lord's Supper" in *J.T.S.* 4 (1903), 548–55; P. Joüon, "L'Évangile de notre Seigneur Jésus-Christ", *Verbum Salutis* 5 (Paris, 1930), 432; J. Schniewind in *Das N.T. Deutsch* 1. 1 (Goettingen, 1933), 171; K. H. Rengstorf, *Das N.T. Deutsch* 1. 3 (1937), 221 sq.; O. Procksch, *Passa und Abendmahl* (1941), offprint p. 12, and others.

[2] P. Billerbeck 2. 844–5 and 4. 49, who rightly refers to Zebh. 1. 3; Tos. Pes. 3. 8 (162. 2). It should be noted that such a private anticipation of the Passover ceremony would constitute a serious breach of the Mosaic law. G. Dalman, *Worte Jesu*, 2nd ed. (1930), 38, sternly rebuts this attempt at harmonization.

[3] D. Chwolson, *Das letzte Passahmahl Christi und der Tag seines Todes*, 2nd ed. (Leipzig, 1908).

[4] J. Klausner, *Jesus v. Nazareth*, 2nd ed. (1934), 449.

[5] J. Zolli, *Il Nazareno* (1938) 207–9, with inessential modifications.

[6] J. Lichtenstein, *Comm. on St. Matthew* (in Hebrew), 2nd ed. (Leipzig, 1913), 122 sq., on Matt. 26. 18.

[7] H. L. Strack, *Pesaḥim* (Leipzig, 1911), 10*.

[8] P. Billerbeck 2. 847–53.

The Pharisaic section of the people, and Jesus among them, would have eaten the passover meal immediately after the killing, i.e. at the beginning (sunset) of Nīsān the 14th; the Sadducees however, on the usual day, i.e. Nīsān the 15th. So both the Synoptists and John are correct, the former in describing the Last Supper as a Passover, the latter in saying that on the day of the crucifixion the Passover had yet to take place. This brilliant conjecture fails for three reasons: (*a*) it is true that up to the second century B.C. the killing of the Passover took place in the evening twilight, so that a coincidence of Passover and Sabbath, which Chwolson assumes for the year of Jesus' death, could occur. In that event, however, the killing would be brought forward, as is shown by present-day Samaritan practice, which I can substantiate from personal observation, not for twenty-four hours,[1] but only for four to six hours, to the afternoon of Nīsān the 14th;[2] (*b*) however, to bring forward the killing was out of the question at the time of Jesus, for at that time the killing of the Passover no longer took place in the evening twilight of Nīsān the 14th to the 15th, but in the afternoon, from 2 p.m. onwards.[3] There was, therefore, no coincidence of Passover and Sabbath, if Nīsān the 15th fell on a Sabbath in the year of Jesus' death;[4] (*c*) it is unthinkable that the Sadducees should have killed the paschal lamb on the evening of Nīsān the 13th to the 14th, but not have eaten it for twenty-four hours, because Exod. 12. 10 forbids

[1] D. Chwolson, op. cit. 43, "there was no other solution when the 14th fell on a Friday, but to bring forward the killing of the sacrificial lamb to the preceding day, i.e. Thursday the 13th". Chwolson's error is contained in the words "there was no other solution".

[2] Joach. Jeremias, *Die Passahfeier der Samaritaner* (Giessen, 1932) 2, 83 sq., esp. 84. I was present in 1931 at a Samaritan killing of the paschal lambs brought forward because of the Sabbath. The killing took place at 12.30 p.m. on Nīsān the 14th, because Nīsān the 15th (the 2nd of May 1931) fell on a Sabbath, according to the Samaritan reckoning. Besides, the Samaritan practice is by no means the only proof for the advancing of the killing by only four to six hours: this is strongly supported also by the practice among the Jews at the time of Jesus, as has been shown op. cit. 84.

[3] *Jub.* 49. 10. 19, from "the third part of the day" onwards; Philo, *Spec. Leg.* 2. § 145 (5. 120. 18) ἀρξάμενοι κατὰ μεσημβρίαν, and further evidence in *Die Passahfeier der Samaritaner* 79, cf. 83–5.

[4] In such a case the killing was done one hour earlier than usual, in view of the coming of the Sabbath (Pes. 5. 1).

anything to be left over till the next morning. This consideration completely destroys Chwolson's theory.

Lichtenstein, Strack, and Billerbeck are of the opinion that in the year of Jesus' death the Sadducees and the Pharisees had a difference concerning the beginning of the month of Nīsān, which started after the first sighting of the new light.[1] This difference is said to have originated from their stubborn conflict concerning the date of Pentecost, and to have arisen out of their different interpretation of Lev. 23. 11. The Pharisees are said to have put Nīsān the 1st—and consequently Nīsān the 15th, the day of the Passover—one day earlier than the Sadducees, and it is assumed that the conflicting parties had compromised on two killings in that particular year: the Pharisaic party, and among them Jesus and His disciples, had celebrated the killing of the Passover and the passover meal one day earlier than the Sadducees. The Synoptists, therefore, followed the Pharisaic counting of the month, but John that of the Sadducees; and this difference explains the different dates in the Synoptic Gospels and in John. This theory has been advanced, in particular by Billerbeck,[2] with so much circumspection and forethought that its possibility cannot be denied. Its weakness lies in the fact that it is no more than a conjecture: there is no evidence that the paschal lambs were ever killed on two consecutive days in the Temple—and it seems highly improbable that such a thing could ever have happened.[3]

J. Pickl[4] has a less complicated solution: the number of participants at the feast of the Passover, he says, made it impossible that they should all kill their lambs on Nīsān the 14th and follow this with the passover meal, for there was not sufficient room in the houses. So the custom grew up that the Galileans killed their lambs on Nīsān the 13th—and this would account for the day of rest in Galilee on Nīsān the 14th (Pes. 4. 5, cf. supra, p. 5 n. 2.)—and the people of Judaea did so on the 14th. However, when Pickl adduces Josephus as evidence for this, who

[1] Cf. infra, on the next page. [2] P. Billerbeck 2. 847–53.

[3] Certain other objections were raised by J. Krengel in *Monatsschr. fuer Gesch. und. Wiss. des Judentums* 70 (1926), 421 sq.; S. Zeitlin, "The Date of the Crucifixion according to the Fourth Gospel" in *Journ. of Bibl. Lit.* 51 (1932), 263–8. Already in 1898, G. Dalman, *Worte Jesu* 38, had voiced his definite objections to the theory of J. Lichtenstein.

[4] *Messiaskoenig Jesus* (Munich, 1935) 247 sq.

in *Ant.* 3. 10. 5. §249 mentions seven days of *azyma*, and ibid. 2. 15. 1. §317, eight days, he is mistaken—these passages deal with the Jews of the Dispersion, who celebrated each feast one day longer than the Jews in the motherland. There is, therefore, no evidence at all for Pickl's thesis. So this, too, is a pure fabrication.

So none of the attempts at harmonization is convincing, and thus the situation is that the Synoptic and Johannine datings of the Last Supper stand in sharp contradiction, and that means that the question is still open, whether the Last Supper was a Passover or not.

(2) *The Contribution of Astronomy*[1]

In recent times various attempts have been made with the help of astronomical chronology to solve the question of the day of Jesus' death—and incidentally the other question whether or not the Last Supper was a Passover. At the time of Jesus the beginning of each month was fixed empirically by the sighting of the new light. The new moon is of course not visible; what is first visible is the new light, about one or two days after the new moon, a narrow shining sickle appearing over the western horizon shortly after[2] sunset[3]. In the evening of the 29th day of each month, the calendar committee of priests[4] assembled and waited for witnesses who would testify under oath that the new light had appeared. When there were at least two trustworthy witnesses,[5] the new moon was proclaimed. Since the possible dates for sighting the new light can be calculated, astronomers are in a position to calculate the Jewish calendar at the time of Jesus, and to state with some measure of probability the days of the week on which Nīsān the 14th and 15th could have fallen in the years round about A.D. 30.

There remain, however, two uncertain factors. (1) Leap-months: in the course of eighteen years there have to be added no

[1] My esteemed colleague, Professor Bruno Meyermann of the Astronomical Institute of the University of Goettingen, has kindly examined this chapter and has assured me of his assent.

[2] If the astronomical new moon happens at nightfall, shortly before sunset on the next night.

[3] O. Gerhardt, *Der Stern des Messias* (1922) 119.

[4] This was the earlier custom: R. H. 1. 7, cf. B. Zuckermann, *Materialien zur Entwicklung der altjuedischen Zeitrechnung* (1882) 7; A. Buechler, *Die Priester und der Cultus* (1895) 188 n. 1. After the destruction of the temple, the right of fixing the beginning of the month was claimed by the Sanhedrin (R.H. 1. 7).

[5] R.H. 1. 7.

less than seven leap-months to even out the differences between the lunar and the solar year. (2) The actual visibility of the new light: if astronomical calculation shows that the new light could be seen, it does not necessarily follow that it was actually seen, because its actual visibility depends upon factors which cannot now be reconstructed—e.g. whether the atmosphere was clear or misty, the horizon clear or clouded, the dusk light or dark. However, both of these factors of uncertainties are greatly reduced in importance by two unalterable rules of the calendar; the first that the feast of the Passover must not be celebrated before the spring equinox,[1] the second that no month should have less than twenty-nine days nor more than thirty—thus the possible difference amounts to one day at the most.[2]

So the question to be asked of astronomical chronology is this: whether or not in the years before and after A.D. 30 Nīsān the 14th or 15th fell on a Friday. In the first case the Johannine, and in the second the Synoptic chronology would be correct. The answer is shown in the following table.[3]

Year A.D.	
27	Nīsān the 14th either[4] Thursday, April 10th, or **Friday,** April 11th.
	Nīsān the 15th either[4] **Friday,** April 11th, or Saturday, April 12th.
30	Nīsān the 14th probably[5] Thursday, April 6th, perhaps **Friday,** April 7th.
	Nīsān the 15th probably[5] **Friday,** April 7th, perhaps Saturday, April 8th.
(31)[6]	Nīsān the 14th most probably Wednesday, April 25th, hardly[7] Thursday, April 26th.
	Nīsān the 15th most probably Thursday, April 26th, hardly[7] **Friday,** April 27th.

[1] If this contingency threatened, a leap-month was added.

[2] Cf. O. Gerhardt, *Der Stern des Messias* (1922) 119 sq.; E. Schuerer, *Gesch. des Jued. Volkes*, 3rd ed., 1 (1901=5th ed., 1920), 745–60.

[3] O. Gerhardt, op. cit. 124 sq.; K. Schoch in *Biblica* 9 (1928) 48-56; J. Schaumburger, ibid. 62 sq.; O. Gerhardt and K. Schoch, ibid. 464 sq.; O. Gerhardt in *Astron. Nachr.* 240 (Oct. 1930) 137-162; 242 (1931), 127-128, 305-310.

[4] According to atmospheric conditions, which may have precluded the theoretically possible visibility of the new light.

[5] Cf. infra, p. 12 sq.

[6] Only in the case of a leap-month, which, however, is unlikely.

[7] Cf. infra, p. 12.

Year A.D.

33 Nīsān the 14th either[1] **Friday,** April 3rd, or Saturday, April 4th.
Nīsān the 15th either[1] Saturday, April 4th, or Sunday, April 5th.[2]

34 Nīsān the 14th Thursday, April 22nd.
Nīsān the 15th **Friday,** April 23rd.

This table shows that Nīsān the 15th probably fell on a Friday in the years A.D. 30 and 34, and possibly in A.D. 27, and these are therefore the years which agree with the chronology of the Synoptists. Nīsān the 14th possibly fell on a Friday in the years A.D. 27 and 33, and perhaps in A.D. 30, which would agree with John's chronology. The years A.D. 27 and 34, however, must be excluded, because they are not in agreement with the general N.T. chronology of the death of Jesus; the year A.D. 33 is also highly improbable.[3] Since astronomical calculation excludes A.D. 31—the date Nīsān the 15th=April the 27th, cf. the table, "is only of mathematical value", because it rests "only upon the feeblest astronomical foundations"[4]—the question has to be asked:  What were the conditions in A.D. 30? More precisely, did Friday April the 7th A.D. 30 fall on Nīsān the 14th or on Nīsān the 15th? Professor Osw. Gerhardt had shown on the basis of careful observations of the new light made in Palestine during the first World War, and of an extensive study of the rabbinical rules for the proclamation of the new month, that it is most probable that

[1] According to atmospheric conditions, which may have precluded the theoretically possible visibility of the new light.

[2] If a leap-month, which is unlikely, was added, the result would be: Nīsān the 14th=Saturday, May the 2nd or Sunday, May the 3rd; Nīsān the 15th=Sunday, May the 3rd or Monday, May the 4th.

[3] According to Luke 3. 1, John the Baptist began his work in the fifteenth year of Tiberius, which, according to the Syrian calendar, lasted from October 1, A.D. 27 to September 30, A.D. 28; thus the Passover of A.D. 27 is too early a date for Jesus' death. The inscription of Gallio and the chronology of Sabbath years (cf. *Z.N.W.* 27 [1928], 98 sq.) make it clear that the council of the Apostles must have taken place in A.D. 48; the conversion of Paul (according to Gal. 1. 18; 2. 1) took place seventeen years earlier (if the first and the last years are each counted as full: fifteen years plus the months of the first and the last years, altogether about sixteen years) in A.D. 31 or 32, hardly in 33. The year of the conversion of Paul is the last possible for Jesus' death; A.D. 34 is therefore impossible, and A.D. 33 highly improbable.

[4] O. Gerhardt, *Der Stern des Messias* (1922) 140.

Nīsān the 15th was April the 7th A.D. 30;[1] but that as a weaker astronomical possibility the identification of Nīsān the 14th with Friday April the 7th A.D. 30 still remained.[2] His results were questioned by K. Schoch of the "Astronomisches Recheninstitut, Berlin-Dahlem", who pleaded strongly for the equation of Friday April the 7th A.D. 30 with Nīsān the 14th.[3] K. Schoch died shortly afterwards. Professor Gerhardt in a letter dated May the 21st 1944 kindly informed me about the whole course of their debate: "At first Schoch repeatedly wrote to me, expressing his approval of my calculation that April the 7th A.D. 30 was Nīsān the 15th, at a time when identical calculations were being made by other scholars. One day Fotheringham of Oxford read of this in some publication, and informed him that he had made a mistake, as by mathematical formulae April the 7th A.D. 30 must be Nīsān the 14th. Schoch examined his calculation, found an error of $1\frac{1}{2}$ hours, and published all this in *Biblica* 1928. Later both Schoch and Fotheringham, because of an observation of the new light made by many people at Kubebe, were compelled to admit that their formula was inaccurate. Neugebauer, who was an abler mathematician than Schoch, made his calculation in my presence, showing minutely that April the 7th A.D. 30=Nīsān the 15th is correct. And lastly, Fotheringham has publicly taken my side: 'On March 23rd A.D. 30, the sickle of the moon stood a good deal closer to the sun than Prof. Gerhardt demands'—and it was visible, so that April the 7th is Nīsān the 15th."

The result of all this is that astronomical chronology, on the basis of observations and calculations of the new light, makes it probable that Friday April the 7th A.D. 30 fell on Nīsān the 15th. However, the possibility that it fell on Nīsān the 14th cannot be excluded (and if—contrary to all probability—it is assumed that Jesus died in A.D. 33, there is also, but only as one of two possibilities, the equation of Friday April the 3rd A.D. 33=Nīsān the 14th). Astronomical calculation is therefore unable to furnish us with an unquestionable result. It is, however, important that these astronomical calculations lend a certain limited probability to the chronology of the Synoptists, and thus to the paschal character of the Last Supper.

[1] O. Gerhardt, op. cit., 129 sq. [2] Ibid. 134 sq.: a-f; 139.
[3] K. Schoch, *Biblica* 9 (1928), 48 sq.

(3) *The Last Supper—a Passover*

Under these circumstances we can only hope to make progress by the help of some new material. The following exposition seeks to provide it by establishing a number of points previously neglected,[1] but which in my opinion permit a definite conclusion whether or not the Last Supper was a Passover. The fact that the features of the Gospel story, to which we shall draw attention, are to some extent without material importance for the Passion story, and are quite obviously incidental comments only, considerably increases their value as evidence for deciding our question.

(1) According to the unanimous testimony of the Synoptists (Mark 14. 13 par.) and of John (18. 1) the Last Supper took place in Jerusalem. This is by no means a matter of course. In the days before and during the feast of the Passover, Jerusalem was overrun by pilgrims. As I have attempted to show elsewhere,[2] our knowledge of the topography of the Temple area (together with the rabbinical reports on the space allotted in the Temple area to the killing of paschal lambs) permits us to give an approximate estimate of the number of pilgrims before the destruction of the Temple. These seem to have varied between 85,000 and 125,000,[3] to which the population of Jerusalem must be added, between 25,000 and 30,000, reckoning one person to every 43 square yards.[4] There were therefore more than 100,000 participants present in Jerusalem on the days of the Passover. The exceptional overcrowding of Jerusalem after the arrival of the caravans of Passover pilgrims can be shown by a few instances. It was impossible for all the pilgrims to find lodgings in Jerusalem: the majority of them had to sleep in tents[5] all round Jerusalem, and in particular in the Plain,[6] i.e. to the north of the city. Moreover,

[1] A typical view is that taken by M. Goguel, *Das Leben Jesu* (Zürich, 1934), 285, "yet the reports of St. Mark and St. Matthew on it (i.e. on the Last Supper) contain not a single feature which refers to the customs of the Passover".

[2] *Jerusalem zur Zeit Jesu* I (Leipzig, 1923), 90–6.

[3] For the time of Jesus the lower number is the more likely one.

[4] Joach. Jeremias, "Die Einwohnerzahl Jerusalems zur Zeit Jesu" in *Zeitschr. des Deutschen Palaestina-Vereins* 66 (1943), 24–31.

[5] Josephus, *Ant.* 17. 9. 3. § 217, cf. *Jerusalem zur Zeit Jesu* I. 69 sq.

[6] Josephus, *Bellum* 2. 1. 3. § 12.

even in the first century B.C. it had proved impossible to maintain the practice, which had been in use since Josiah's reformation,[1] that all the participants in the feast ate the paschal sacrifice in the temple court;[2] for lack of space the place where the Passover was eaten had to be separate from where it was slain: since the first century B.C. only the killing was done in the Temple area, the paschal meal being transferred to the houses of Jerusalem.[3] It also proved practically impossible that—as was demanded by Deut. 16. 7, according to contemporary exegesis—all the pilgrims spent at least the night of the Passover within the walls of Jerusalem; it was therefore impossible to avoid giving permission for the night to be spent, though not the Passover to be eaten, in the environs of Jerusalem.[4] However, all these measures were quite inadequate. Owing to the great numbers of pilgrims, the overcrowding on the night of the Passover was such that, in spite of the cold season, cf. Mark 14. 54, a considerable proportion of the participants was compelled to eat the Passover meal in the courtyards and even on the roofs of the holy city.[5]

This is in keeping with what is related in Mark 11. 11 par.; 11. 19; 11. 27; Luke 21. 37; Mark 14. 3 par.; Luke 22. 39, that during His last stay in Jerusalem Jesus regularly left the holy city in the evening and went to Bethany (Luke: to the Mount of Olives). Why, contrary to His custom, did He then remain in the overcrowded city for the Last Supper? The answer is, that it was

[1] Before 621 B.C. the Passover had been a domestic solemnity, but after that date it became a cultic celebration; cf. Joach. Jeremias, *Die Passahfeier der Samaritaner* (Giessen, 1932), 66–72.

[2] Deut. 16. 7; 2 Chron. 35. 13 sq.; Jub. 49. 16, 17, 20. The Samaritans have preserved to this day the ancient use according to which the places of killing and eating must be identical; cf. Joach. Jeremias, op. cit. 99.

[3] Pes. 5. 10; 7. 12 sq.; 10. 1 sq., etc.

[4] The way out which was taken was the delimitation of a district of greater Jerusalem, which included Bethphage; cf. my book *Jerusalem zur Zeit Jesu* IIA (Leipzig, 1924), 16 sq.; P. Billerbeck 1. 839 sq., 992; 2. 833 sq. G. Dalman has withdrawn the doubts he stated in *Jesus-Jeschua* (1922) 87–9, in *Orte und Wege Jesu*, 3rd ed. (1924), 338 n. 4, cf. 269 sq., and in *Nachtraege zu Jesus-Jeschua* (1929) 8.

[5] "Although it is written: 'it is to be eaten in one and the same house' (Exod. 12. 46), they nevertheless eat it (the paschal lamb) in their courtyards and on their house-tops" Tos. Pes. 6. 11 (166. 2 sq.). Cf. also j. Pes. 7. 35b. 36, where it is apparently presupposed that the Passover was also eaten on the house-tops of Jerusalem (cf. infra, p. 60 n. 5).

a rule that the paschal lamb which belonged[1] to the category of sacred things of the lower grade[2] had to be eaten within the gates of Jerusalem.[3]

(2) According to 1 Cor. 11. 23; John 13. 30, the Last Supper was held at night,[4] and Mark 14. 17; Matt. 26. 20 agree affirming that Jesus and His disciples came for the Last Supper "when evening had come".[5] Once more, this is by no means a matter of course. Nowhere else in the Gospels do we find that an ordinary[6] meal was held at night; only once are we told that a meal took place in the evening (ὀψίας γενομένης, Matt. 14. 15), at the feeding of the five thousand; but in the same verse it is emphasised that "the time (for a meal) was already past".[7]

[1] b. Zebh. 56a.

[2] *Ḳodhāshīm ḳallīm.*

[3] Siphre Num. 9. 10. § 69 ed. princ. (Venice, 1545) 10b, 29: "Which is the place where it (viz. the paschal lamb) has to be eaten? Within the gate of Jerusalem." Num. R.7. 8 ad 5. 2 (Stettin, 1864), 37a, 8: "Holy things of the lower grade (this category of sacrifices includes the paschal lamb, Zebh. 5. 8) and the second tithe are eaten in Jerusalem." Pes. 7. 9: "The paschal lamb which has been carried out (of Jerusalem) or has been defiled, must be burnt forthwith." Makk. 3. 3: "He who eats sacred things of the lower grade outside the (city-) wall . . . is punished with forty strokes." Cf. also Kel. 1. 8; Tos. Sanh. 3. 4 (418, 22 sq.); Midhr. Tann. ad Deut. 14. 23; 15. 20. Cf. G. Dalman, *Jesus-Jeschua* 99; *Orte und Wege Jesu*, 3rd ed. (1924), 332 sq.; *Arbeit und Sitte in Palaestina* 4 (1935), 112. On the exception in favour of the captives in prison (b. Pes. 91a), cf. my book *Jerusalem zur Zeit Jesu* IIA, 16 and 63.

[4] This has been stressed by A. Oepke, "Ursprung und urspruenglicher Sinn des Abendmahls im Lichte der neuesten Forschung" in *Allgemeine evang.-luth. Kirchenzeitung* 59 (1926), 58: "It has not been taken into consideration so far, that Paul expressly states that the historical Last Supper took place at night" (1 Cor. 11. 23).

[5] The fact that the meal continued into the night follows also from Mark 14. 30 (cf. Matt. 26. 34; Luke 22. 34) σήμερον ταύτῃ τῇ νυκτί, for, since "this day" had begun at sunset, the word must have been spoken during the night. Cf. also John 18. 3 μετὰ φανῶν καὶ λαμπάδων.

[6] Matt. 25. 1–13 seems to presuppose that a wedding meal might begin at midnight; in Luke 11. 5 the exceptional case of a traveller arriving at midnight and demanding a meal is mentioned. In Luke 12. 37 an unreal situation is created through intentional exaggeration when it is said that the master, returning from a party at midnight, will act as host to his watchful servants.

[7] Notice also that it is probable that ὀψία has here the meaning of the time shortly before sunset (cf. supra, p. 3).

It was customary to have two meals a day, a very simple[1] breakfast between 10 and 11 a.m.,[2] and the main meal[3] in the late afternoon.[4] That, for instance, was the custom amongst the Essenes: they had their early meal between 10 and 11 a.m.,[5] after which they continued working until the afternoon (*μέχρι δείλης*), when they had their main meal.[6] Discussions about the blessing of the Sabbath provide ample evidence that in the early times with which we are dealing, the main meal, on the Friday as well as on the Sabbath, took place in the afternoon (בַּמִּנְחָה).[7] Only

[1] P. Billerbeck 2. 204, cf. infra. p. 28.

[2] b. Shab. 10a (Bar.): "... at four (i.e. 10 a.m.) is the meal-time for the labourers; and at five (i.e. 11 a.m.) for all other people"; cf. the parallel in b. Pes. 12b (Bar.), which mentions the sixth hour (noon) as the normal time for a meal; but Josephus, *Vita* 54. §279, says that this applied to the Sabbath only. 10 a.m. is assumed as the normal time for the first meal in b. Pes. 107b and in Targ. Qoh. 10. 16 sq. At the time of the morning prayer (9 a.m.) people are still without a meal, Acts 2. 15.

[3] *Δεῖπνον*, סְעוּדָה, סְעוּדְתָא.

[4] S. Krauss, *Talmudische Archaeologie* 3 (Leipzig, 1912), 29: "in the hours before the evening"; Bauer, *Woerterbuch* s.v. *δεῖπνον*: "held in the early evening"; P. Billerbeck 2. 204, 206; 4. 615: "in the late afternoon". Mekh. Exod. 18. 23, 2nd ed. (Venice, 1545), 22d, 33 sq.: the meal-time comes before the evening (ערב). Shab. 1. 2: shortly before the time of the *minḥā* (the afternoon prayer which, according to Acts 3. 1, cf. ibid. 10. 3, 30, took place at 3 p.m.), you should not sit down at table (so that you do not miss the afternoon prayer). b. Pes. 107b: King Agrippa (I. or II.?) was accustomed to eat at the 9th hour (3 p.m.). The late afternoon is also indicated as meal-time in Luke 24. 29: *πρὸς ἑσπέραν ἐστὶν καὶ κέκλικεν ἡ ἡμέρα*; cf. G. Dalman, *Orte und Wege Jesu*, 3rd ed. (1924), 244; *Arbeit und Sitte in Palaestina* 1. 2 (1928), 613 sq. It is only in this connexion that John 1. 39 *ὥρα ἦν ὡς δεκάτη* (4 p.m.) becomes understandable: Jesus admits the two disciples of John the Baptist to His table.

[5] Josephus, *Bellum* 2. 8. 5. §129: They work *μέχρι πέμπτης ὥρας* (i.e. 10–11 a.m.) and then assemble for their meal.

[6] Ibid. §131 sq.

[7] **Friday:** b. Ber. 48b (Bar.) lays down, in what way the Sabbath-*Ḳiddūsh* (the word of prayer to hallow the Sabbath at the appearance of the first stars after sunset) should be fitted into the after-meal prayer; it is therefore assumed that the meal will be held on Friday in the late afternoon, and may last till sunset. Since there is a reference in R. *'Eli'ezer* (about A.D. 90), the die-hard of the old tradition, to the fitting of the *Ḳiddush* into the after-meal prayer, the custom is very ancient. The

in the case of a special celebration is reference made to a meal lasting into the night, as for instance after a circumcision[1] or at a wedding.[2]

It is therefore certain that the time of the Last Supper did not accord with general custom. How can we explain that it begins "in the evening" and lasts "into the night"? I can see only one answer: the Passover had been eaten at night ever since its institution.[3] "The Passover may only be eaten at night."[4] The meal which began after sunset[5] lasted till late at night.[6]

(3) According to Mark 14. 17—par. Matt. 26. 20—Jesus had the Twelve with Him at the Last Supper. Such a formation of a table fellowship is not found anywhere else in the Gospels.

It seems rather that during His preaching ministry Jesus took

---

same case, that the Friday afternoon meal may last to the beginning of the Sabbath, is found in Tos. Ber. 5. 2 (11. 23 sq.) par. b. Pes. 100a (Bar.) and j. Pes. 10. 37b. 40; Tos. Ber. 5. 3 sq. (11. 28 sq.); b. Pes. 102ab (Bar.), 103b. Only later, at the earliest in the second century A.D. and perhaps not before the third (cf. infra, p. 22 n. 5), the view is proposed that people should not take a meal on a Friday afternoon, so as to enter the Sabbath with a good appetite; Tos. Ber. 5. 1 (11. 22); b. Pes. 99a (Bar.); j. Pes. 10. 37b. 32.—**Sabbath:** Tos. Shab. 12. 16 (128. 15). Ber. 8. 5 reports a discussion of the Shammaïtes and the Hillelites (early first century A.D.) on the question how the after-meal prayer was to be combined with the *Habhdālā* (words of praise, spoken at the end of Sabbaths and feast-days after sunset): this assumes that the meal began in the late afternoon of the Sabbath and finished at sunset. Cf. I. Elbogen, "Eingang und Ausgang des Sabbaths nach talmudischen Quellen" in *Festschr. zu J. Lewy's 70. Geburtstag* (1911) 173–87, esp. 179 sq., 183; and H. Lietzmann, *Messe und Herrenmahl* (Bonn, 1926) 203 sq., 206.

[1] Deut. R. 9. 1 ad 31. 14 (Stettin, 1864), 34a, 1; Qoh. R. 3. 4 ad 3. 2 (81a. 12). [2] Ber. 1. 1.

[3] A. Oepke op. cit. (see p. 16 n. 4) is correct, but his argument receives its full force only from the fact that normally the main meal took place in the late afternoon.

[4] Zebh. 5. 8.

[5] Exod. 12. 8; Jub. 49. 1, 12; Pes. 5. 9; Tos. Pes. 1. 34 (158. 4); j. Pes. 5. 31d. 27; Siphre Deut. 16. 6. §133; Mekh. Exod. 12. 6 (3d. 46).

[6] A rule by which it was intended to forestall any breach of Exod. 12. 8 ("they shall eat the meat in the same night") forbids the eating of the paschal lamb after 2 a.m., Jub. 49. 10, 12, or even after midnight, Pes. 10. 9; Zebh. 5. 8; Tos. Pes. 5. 2 (163. 17), etc. Still more instructive is the report of Josephus, *Ant.* 18. 2. 2. §29, that on the night of the Passover the gates of the temple were opened at midnight.

His meals openly with His audience. This fact is brought out by the warning given to those who confessed Him with their lips only, that it would avail them nothing to appeal to the table fellowship which He had occasionally given them when He had preached near their homes (Luke 13. 26 sq.). Mark (3. 20; 6. 31) says that Jesus was at times so closely surrounded by the crowd that He could not even eat. Often, especially on a Sabbath (Mark 1. 29 sq.; Luke 14. 1), Jesus was invited to a meal, together with other guests (Mark 14. 3 sq.; Luke 7. 36; 11. 37; John 2. 1 sq.); sometimes He entertained His own guests (Luke 15. 2; cf. John 1. 39, and our note 4, supra, p. 17), on one occasion even in large numbers (Mark 2. 15);[1] the description of Jesus as "a gluttonous man and a wine-bibber, a friend of publicans and sinners" (Matt. 11. 19), makes it clear that He frequently took His meals in considerable company. On His journeys Jesus often took His meals in the open (Mark 6. 32 sq.; 8. 14; John 4. 8; 4. 31; 21. 12), surrounded by His disciples and other followers; the size of the circle of His table companions may be gauged by the help of texts such as Luke 8. 1–3; 24. 33; Acts 1. 21 sq.; in one instance the whole Easter pilgrimage formed the table fellowship of Jesus (Mark 6. 32 sq.). We also find Jesus at table with His hosts, when He lodged as a traveller (Luke 10. 38 sq., cf. 10. 7/8).

What surprises us, when Jesus limited the number of His table companions to the Twelve (Mark 14. 17), is the absence of the women, mentioned in Mark 15. 40; Luke 23. 49, 55. Is it just an accident that the small number fits the rule governing the Passover? The Passover *ḥabhūrā* had to consist of at least ten persons,[2] and this was the usual number,[3] as it was assumed that a one-year-old lamb would be sufficient food for about ten people.[4]

(4) Once more the Synoptists, Mark 14. 18; Matt. 26. 20;

[1] Cf. E. Lohmeyer, *Evang. des Markus* (1937) ad h. l.; Joach. Jeremias, *Gleichnisse Jesu*, 2nd ed. (Göttingen-Zürich 1952), 161 n. 1.

[2] Tos. Pes. 4. 3 (163) par. b. Pes. 64b (Bar.) and *Midhr. 'ēkhā r.* 1. 1; Josephus, *Bellum* 6. 9. 3. § 423, 425.

[3] Josephus and the Talmud both witness to this fact.

[4] The Samaritans hold this view even to-day; cf. the pictures of families celebrating the Passover in my book *Die Passahfeier der Samaritaner* (1932), plates 45-47.

Luke 22. 14,[1] agree with John 13. 12, 23 (!), 25, 28,[2] that Jesus and His disciples reclined at table at the Last Supper. This again is not to be taken as a matter of course. In the time of Jesus at an ordinary meal the diners sat down (Heb. *yāshabh*; Aram. *yethēbh*)[3] to eat, as we know from rabbinical sources.[4] Wherever the Gospels mention reclining at meals,[5] they mean either a meal in the open—the feeding of the multitude—or a party (Mark 12. 39 par.;

[1] Provided *ἐστρωμένον* in Mark 14. 15; Luke 22. 12 means: laid with carpets or mats, these two texts will have to be added.

[2] Cf. also John 21. 20.

[3] G. Dalman, *Arbeit und Sitte in Palaestina* 7 (1942), 220: "the term does not exclude squatting".

[4] E.g. j. Ber. 7. 11c. 48 ישבו ואכלו, and the same in Aramaic sources, b. Sanh. 38a יתבו בסעדתא; j. Ber. 7. 11b. 62 and (verbatim the same) 11c. 42 הוו יתבין אכלין; also Ber. 6. 6; b. Ber. 42a; b. Sanh. 38a. Cf. Franz Delitzsch, *Ein Tag in Kapernaum*, 2nd ed. (Leipzig, 1873), 152 n. 1: "at a noble and solemn banquet people lay at table in the Graeco-Roman fashion. So did Jesus and His disciples at the Last Supper . . . ; but the ancient custom of Israel was to sit at table. Such was the case here, in the house of the Galilean fisherman." P. Billerbeck 4. 617–8: "at the daily family meal people were seated". G. Beer, *Pesachim* (Giessen, 1912) 189; S. Krauss, *Talmudische Archaeologie* 3 (Leipzig, 1912), 43 sq.; H. L. Strack, *Berakhoth* (Leipzig, 1915) 14 n.f.; G. Dalman, *Arbeit und Sitte in Palaestina* 7 (1942), 222. In the earliest time the Israelites squatted on the floor for their meals; in later times they sat at an elevated table (1 Sam. 20. 5, 24–5, cf. also Gen. 27. 19; Exod. 32. 6=1 Cor. 10. 7; Judges 19. 6; 1 Kings 13. 20; Prov. 23. 1; Ecclus. 31. 12, 18, etc.), cf. G. Beer op. cit. 188; J. Benzinger, *Hebraeische Archaeologie*, 3rd ed. (Leipzig, 1927), 105 sq. Amos the prophet protested against the custom imported from Mesopotamia, that the nobles lay at table (Amos 6. 4; 3. 12). Ecclus. 41. 19 possibly—the passage is ambiguous—raised a similar protest against the identical custom, this time taken over from Hellenism. In everyday life the common people and their families never adopted this foreign attitude, but observed the ancient use of sitting down for an ordinary meal.

[5] *Ἀνακεῖσθαι*, Mark 6. 26; 14. 18; 16. 14; Matt. 9. 10; 22. 10–11; 26. 7, 20; Luke 22. 27; John 12. 2; 13. 23, 28. *Συνανακεῖσθαι*, Mark 2. 15; 6. 22; Matt. 9. 10; 14. 9; Luke 7. 49; 14. 10; 14. 15. *Κατακεῖσθαι*, Mark 2. 15; 14. 3; Luke 5. 29; 7. 37. *Ἀναπίπτειν*, Luke 11. 37; 14. 10; 17. 7; 22. 14; John 13. 12. *Ἀνακλίνειν*, Luke 12. 37; pass.: Mark 6. 39; Matt. 8. 11; 14. 19; Luke 13. 29. *Κατακλίνειν*, Luke 9. 14–15; pass.: Luke 7. 36; 14. 8; 24. 30. *Πρωτοκλισία*, Mark 12. 39; Matt. 23. 6; Luke 14. 7–8; 20. 46. Cf. *κόλπος*, John 13. 23; 1. 18; Luke 16. 22–3. Cf. also supra, note 1.

14. 3 par.; Luke 7. 36/7, 49; 11. 37; 14. 15; John 12. 2), or a feast (Mark 2. 15 par., esp. Luke 5. 29), be it a royal feast (Mark 6. 26 par.), or a wedding feast (Matt. 22. 10/11; Luke 14. 8, 10), or the feast of the Kingdom (Matt. 8. 11; Luke 13. 29, cf. ibid. 16. 23).[1] There are only two exceptions, Luke 24. 30 and pseudo-Mark 16. 14, but the first is in typically Lucan idiom (*κατακλίνειν* is found only in Luke in the New Testament), and the second represents a strand of tradition which is too late to serve as evidence for Palestinian table manners at the time of Jesus. It is absolutely impossible that Jesus and His disciples should have been reclining at table at their ordinary meals. Why then did they recline at table at the Last Supper?

This question would be satisfactorily answered if it could be proved that the Last Supper was a "*Ḳiddūsh*-meal". Certain scholars have indeed tried to prove this. As it must be admitted that hardly any matter of biblical exegesis has given rise to so many errors as the *Ḳiddūsh*, some explication is necessary.[2] (1) What is a *Ḳiddūsh*?[3] *Ḳiddūsh* means sanctification. The *Ḳiddūsh* is a Blessing which was said at the beginning of each Sabbath or feast-day. It was quite simple: R. *'El 'āzār bar Zādhōq* (born between A.D 35 and 40 at Jerusalem[4]) said: "My father . . . used to say over the cup, '(blessed be He) who has sanctified the Sabbath day'. He did not add a closing benediction."[5] This benediction marks off the sacred from the profane period at its beginning, just as the *Habhdālā* (the blessing of separation at the close of the Sabbaths and feast-days) marks it off at its close: a separation of the *Ḳiddūsh* or the *Habhdālā* from the sacred time is quite

[1] Even Luke 22. 27 does not speak of an ordinary meal, as appears from the servant waiting at table, but either—probably—of a party, or of a meal in a wealthy household. The same is true of Luke 12. 37, where the master on his return serves his servants. This meal too is a banquet.

[2] A. Berliner, *Randbemerkungen zum taeglichen Gebetbuch* 1 (1909), 43, 73 sq.; I. Elbogen, "Eingang und Ausgang des Sabbaths" in *Festschr. zu I. Lewy's 70. Geburtstag* (1911) 173 sq.; id., *Der juedische Gottesdienst in seiner geschichtlichen Entwicklung*, 2nd ed. (1924), 107 sq.; G. F. Moore, *Judaism in the first centuries* 1 (1927), 36.

[3] Or else *Ḳedhushshā* (fem.).

[4] Cf. A. Schlatter, *Die Tage Trajans und Hadrians* (1897), 80 sq.

[5] Tos. Ber. 3. 7 (6. 22 sq.). Another, somewhat longer, wording of the Sabbath-*Ḳiddūsh*: b. Ber. 49a, which also gives the feast-day *Ḳiddūsh*.

3

unthinkable and without example. (2) How is the *Ḳiddūsh* performed? When the first stars appear after sunset,[1] the Paterfamilias (on the Sabbath: after lighting the Sabbath candle) says the blessing[2] at table over a cup of wine,[3] in the midst of all the family and his guests. Then he himself drinks and is followed by all the other people present. If the meal began on a Friday afternoon and went on till the beginning of the Sabbath, or even longer, the meal was first brought to an end,[4] and the *Ḳiddūsh* was added to the grace after the meal.[5] At the Passover, which was the only meal[6] of the year which began after the setting of the sun, the sanctification of the feast took place at the beginning of the meal. The *Ḳiddūsh* is therefore neither a meal,[7] nor a sacrament,[8] nor a sacrifice,[9] nor has it

[1] Cf. supra, p. 1, n. 2.

[2] The drinking of wine calls for a benediction of the wine. The sequence of the two blessings (the *Ḳiddūsh* and the blessing of the cup) was a matter of conflict between the Shammaïtes and the Hillelites, i.e. in the early first century A.D. This shows that the rite was not yet stereotyped: Ber. 8. 1; Pes. 10. 2, more explicitly Tos. Ber. 6. 1 (13. 6); Tos. Pes. 10. 2 sq. (172. 14).

[3] The cup is first mentioned c. A.D. 50 (R. *Zādhōq*): Tos. Ber. 3. 7 (6. 24 sq.), cf. the passage quoted above, p. 21.

[4] So R. Jōsē (c. A.D. 150) who in this case—as often—stands certainly for the earlier tradition: Tos. Ber. 5. 2 (11. 23) par b. Pes. 100a (Bar.); 102ab (Bar.); j. Pes. 10. 37b. 45, also Tos. Ber. 5. 3–4 (11. 29).

[5] Cf. supra, p. 17 n. 7, esp. R. *'Eli'ezer*, the consequent representative of early tradition, b. Ber. 48b (Bar.). When at a later date (according to I. Elbogen, *Der jued. Gottesdienst*, 2nd ed. [1924], 107, 263, in the period of the Amoraïm) in Babylonia first, and afterwards in Palestine also, the custom of holding a service at the beginnings of Sabbaths and special feast-days arose, the meal was interrupted for the purpose of attending the service (Tos. Ber. 5. 3 [11. 28], held to be the advice given by R. *Jehūdhā* [c. A.D. 150]), and at a still later period it was postponed till after sunset (Tos. Ber. 5. 1 [11. 22], also held to be the view of R. *Jehūdhā*) so that the *Ḳiddūsh* was now said at the beginning of the meal. This is the modern use.

[6] Cf. supra, p. 18.

[7] M. Dibelius, *Jesus* (1939), 113.

[8] F. C. Burkitt, quoted after E. Lohmeyer in *Theol. Rundschau* 9 (1937), 200.

[9] K. G. Goetz, "Abendmahl und Messopfer" in *Schweiz. Theol. Zeitschr*. 35 (1918), 15–24: the Eucharist is a *Ḳiddūsh*, therefore a sacrifice; for *Ḳiddūsh* means nothing else than sanctification, dedication: that is to say, sacrifice (!!).

sacrificial meaning,[1] but it is just a simple blessing. "*Ḳiddūsh* meals"—the term is of modern invention—never existed if anything more is meant by them than meals at which the normal grace was combined with a special blessing on account of the Sabbath or a feast-day starting during the meal or as the meal began.

F. Spitta,[2] Foxley,[3] G. H. Box,[4] P. Batiffol,[5] and R. Otto[6] have maintained that the Last Supper is to be identified with the rite of Sabbath-*Ḳiddūsh*, i.e. the ritual "sanctification" of the Sabbath. This has found much favour, because nowadays at the Sabbath-*Ḳiddūsh* the blessing of the wine is followed by the breaking of the bread at the beginning of the meal. However, we have seen (cf. p. 22 n. 5) that this combination of the blessing of the wine and the breaking of the bread, arose only in the late Tannaite—or, perhaps, in the early Amoraean—period as the result of the introduction of the Friday Evening Service in Babylonia, and therefore does not belong to the time of Jesus; and, above all, the sanctification of the Sabbath took place on the Friday

[1] J. M. Nielen, *Gebet und Gottesdienst im N.T.* (1937), 264: "In view of the uncertainty not only of the sacrificial meaning of the *Ḳiddūsh* as such(!!), but also of its equation(!) with the Last Supper, this alone(!) cannot be regarded as sufficient proof for the sacrificial character of the *δεῖπνον κυριακόν* of primitive Christianity."

[2] *Zur Geschichte und Litteratur des Urchristentums* I (1893), 247.

[3] *Contemporary Review* (February 1899).

[4] "The Jewish antecedents of the Eucharist" in *J. T. S.* 3 (1902), 357–69. "I venture to suggest then, that the real Jewish antecedent to the Lord's supper was the weekly Kiddûsh" (p. 363).

[5] *L'Eucharistie* (Paris, 1905). Batiffol says in the first editions of his book that the Last Supper exhibits similarities to the Jewish meals of the Sabbath-eve (*Ḳiddūsh*); in the later editions, however, Batiffol has shown more caution.

[6] "Vom Abendmahl Christi" in *Christl. Welt* 31 (1917), 246. Otto arrived, independently of these other scholars (when taking part in a Jewish sanctification of the Sabbath), at the conclusion that "Jesus prayed the *Ḳiddūsh* with His disciples and then, by way of interpretation, gave it a new and peculiar meaning" (p. 246). At a later time Otto realized that this view was untenable (*Reich Gottes und Menschensohn* [1934], 241) but, unwilling to abandon it altogether, he derived the Eucharist from rites similar to the *Ḳiddūsh* "which were known and practised independently from it" (ibid.), and which were given a new meaning by Jesus. These rites similar to the *Ḳiddūsh*, for which Otto offers not an iota of proof, are of his own invention.

evening, after the setting of the sun,[1] whereas all the four Gospels are agreed that the Last Supper was on a Thursday night.[2] How should Jesus have arrived at the idea of performing the Sabbath ritual on a Thursday night? W. O. E. Oesterley[3] has accordingly explained the Last Supper as a Passover-*Ḳiddūsh*, a ritual "sanctification" of the feast, which is supposed to have taken place on the eve, i.e. twenty-four hours before it began.[4] G. H. C. Macgregor,[5] H. Huber,[6] F. Gavin,[7] T. H. W. Maxfield,[8] and M. Dibelius[9] have adopted his view without realizing that this Passover-*Ḳiddūsh*, which is thought to have taken place twenty-four hours before the beginning of the feast, is a product of fancy, for which there is no evidence.[10] It should have been enough that F. C. Burkitt, in 1916, had already made it quite clear that "*Ḳiddūsh* immediately precedes the actual celebration of the day, e.g. *Ḳiddūsh* for the Sabbath is done on what we call Friday evening, not twenty-four hours earlier";[11] the Passover-*Ḳiddūsh* was ac-

[1] That the Sabbath-*Ḳiddūsh* should ever have been severed "from its formal connexion with the weekly Sabbath" (Box, op. cit. 363) is an entirely unfounded assumption.

[2] Supra, p. 1.

[3] *The Jewish Background of the Christian Liturgy* (Oxford, 1925), 167 sq., esp. 175.

[4] A similar view was held, before Oesterley, by K. Bornhaeuser, "Zeiten und Stunden in der Leidens- und Auferstehungsgeschichte", *Beitraege zur Foerderung christl. Theologie* 26. 4 (Guetersloh, 1921), 8 sq.: the Last Supper was an "opening meal", which took place on the day before the killing of the paschal lambs. But the source for this, quoted by Bornhaeuser p. 8, Mekh. Exod. 12. 16, "honour it (the first day) with eating, drinking and a clean robe", refers to the 15th and not the 14th of Nīsān.

[5] *Eucharistic Origins*, (London, 1928), 37–49.

[6] *Das Herrenmahl im N.T.*, Diss. Berne (Leipzig, 1929), 21, 70.

[7] *The Jewish Antecedents of the Christian Sacraments*, 2nd ed. (London, 1933), 65 sq.

[8] *The Words of Institution* (Cambridge, 1933), 22 sq.

[9] *Jesus* (1939), 113.

[10] The thesis of W. O. E. Oesterley, op. cit. 175, that the Passover-*Ḳiddūsh* anticipated the Sabbath-*Ḳiddūsh* in the year of Jesus' death, is a conjecture which piles one impossibility upon another: (*a*) it is unthinkable that the "sanctification" of the Sabbath should be moved forward, and (*b*) it is impossible that the Passover should be "sanctified" twenty-four hours before it began.

[11] "The Last Supper and the Paschal Meal" in *J.T.S* 17 (1916), 294.

cordingly the beginning of the passover meal and was said over the first of the four paschal cups. When will that wholly illusory Passover-*Ḳiddūsh* on the eve of the feast vanish from discussion? And finally, when H. Lietzmann, who is followed by K. G. Goetz,[1] R. Otto,[2] and Dom Gregory Dix,[3] refers to "the Jewish meals endowed with a religious benediction, which might always be held with a group of friends (חבורה), whenever they desired to do so",[4] here too there has been an *ad hoc* conjecture of a custom for the existence of which evidence is totally lacking. "Religious benediction" was given to every meal—irrespective of whether it was taken alone or in company or of whether it was a mere snack or a formal meal—by saying grace. Mention is indeed made occasionally of "fellowships", when ritual meals are referred to; but these "fellowships" were חֲבוּרוֹת מִצְוָה,

[1] *Der Ursprung des kirchlichen Abendmahls* (Basel, 1929), 27 sq. Goetz here refers to his book *Die Abendmahlsfrage* (Leipzig, 1904, 2nd ed. 1907), 243 sq., where on p. 245 he quotes a tractate Joanith 2. 5 (sic!)—he means *Ta'anith* 2. 5, although in this passage no mention is made of the "amen" after "grace", but only of the "amen" in the service of the synagogue—and on p. 245 sq. he holds that it was customary at Jewish meals to save fragments of the "consecrated" (sic!) bread for the poor, quoting Sanh. 11, where, however, what is discussed is crimes punishable by strangulation! Cf. my article "Das Paulinische Abendmahl—eine Opferdarbringung?" in *Theol. Stud. u. Krit.* 108 (1937), 124–41.

[2] In his valuable study on the Eucharist in: *Reich Gottes und Menschensohn* (Munich, 1934), 235, Otto finds the type of the Eucharist in "the 'religious celebration of a meal' of a *cheber* or a *chaburah*, with a sacred character" (sic!) "and with religious peculiarities". He quotes verbatim a sentence from A. Geiger, *Urschrift und Uebersetzungen der Bibel* (Breslau, 1857), 123, "generally speaking, any meals which were eaten in common, were meritorious, sanctified and of a religious character"; but this statement is erroneous, for Sanh. 8. 2—the passage quoted by Geiger—treats of a חֲבוּרַת מִצְוָה (cf. what follows supra, p. 25 sq.), and not of meals in general, and with this erroneous statement the consequences which R. Otto draws from it also fall to the ground; cf. also supra, p. 23 n. 6.

[3] *The Shape of the Liturgy* (1944), 50 sq., but cf. infra, p. 183.

[4] *Messe und Herrenmahl* (Bonn, 1926), 210, cf. p. 228. H. Lietzmann follows G. Loeschcke in *Zeitschr. f. wiss. Theologie* 54 (N. F. 19, 1912), 202, who found evidence for "semi-cultic meals" in b. R.H. 29a and in b. Ber. 46a. Actually, both these passages treat of the grace said over the bread at every meal.

i.e. "fellowships to perform some special duty".[1] and as for the meals in which they took part, the point is that they were duty meals, as at a betrothal or a wedding, or at the celebration of a circumcision or at a funeral,[2] where participation was considered meritorious. That these fellowships, which moreover were of a charitable nature,[3] or other "communities of friends" met at any time "when they deemed it necessary" to hold a ritual—let alone a sacral[4]—meal, cannot be proved.[5]

Thus the solemnities of the Last Supper cannot be explained by theories about the *Ḳiddūsh* or the *Ḥabhūrā*. The question has to be asked again, therefore, how did it come about that at the Last Supper Jesus and His disciples did not sit, but ceremoniously reclined at table? There is only one answer: at the Passover, as a symbol of liberty,[6] it was the ritual duty of the people present to recline at table even—as is expressly stated—for "the poorest man in Israel".[7]

(5) According to Mark 14. 22; Matt. 26. 26, Jesus breaks the bread during the course of the meal. It is probably true that the words *ἐσθιόντων αὐτῶν* are no more than an editorial transition to the institution of the Eucharist,[8] but even the editor—and in particular Mark, who hailed from Jerusalem[9]—must have been conscious of the fact that with the words *ἐσθιόντων αὐτῶν* he was

[1] Sanh. 8. 2; b. Pes. 113b.

[2] Tos. Megh. 4. 15 (226. 13) par. *Semaḥoth* 12 (Babylon. Talmud ed. Frankfurt a. M., 1721, fol. 16a).

[3] P. Billerbeck 4. 607 sq.; Joach. Jeremias, *Jerusalem zur Zeit Jesu*, IIB (Leipzig, 1929), 118 sq. There I have given reasons which suggest that these charitable fellowships were connected with the Pharisaic fellowships, an hypothesis which is probable, but cannot be fully established.

[4] So H. Lietzmann, *An die Korinther*, 3rd ed. (Tuebingen, 1931), 56; R. Otto, op. cit. supra, p. 25 n. 2.

[5] "Constant repetition of the *Ḥabhūrā* theme does not constitute proof", is quite correctly stated by C. W. Dugmore in *J.T.S.* 47 (1946), 109.

[6] j. Pes. 10. 37b. 56: "R. *Lēwī* (about A.D. 300) has said: 'whereas the slaves eat standing, here (at the Passover) people should recline when they eat, to signify that they have gone out from bondage into liberty'." Exod. 12. 11 was regarded as having been a binding rule only on the actual day of the exodus.

[7] Pes. 10. 1; Tos. Pes. 10. 1 (172. 12).

[8] Cf. infra, p. 108.

[9] Acts 12. 12.

describing a sequence which differed completely from that of everyday. There is no question but that ordinary meals began with the breaking of bread. The one exception to this was at the festival meals among the upper classes, where, following Hellenistic custom, a preliminary course was first served outside the dining room, and the meal proper was started with the breaking of bread after the guests had entered the dining room and taken their places, reclining at table.[1] But such a preliminary course served in an ante-room cannot be meant by *ἐσθιόντων αὐτῶν*,[2] which can apply only to a meal already begun. But then it is most unusual that Mark 14. 22 describes a meal in which the breaking of bread follows the service of a dish (Mark 14. 20). How unusual this was is shown by the following fact. In order literally to fulfil the command of Exod. 12. 26 sq. to explain the Passover ritual to the children in answer to their questions, the Paterfamilias, according to an unbroken tradition, began his Passover devotions in such a way as to stimulate the children to ask about the special actions of that evening. One of these children's questions was, "How is it that on every other evening we dip bread into the dish, but on this evening simply dip into the dish?" i.e. without bread.[3] This children's question shows conclusively that the Passover was the only meal of the year at which the service of a dish preceded the breaking of bread.

(6*a*) Jesus and His disciples drank wine at the Last Supper, Mark 14. 23, 25 par.[4] Once more, this is far from being an ordinary occurrence. Wine was drunk only on festal occasions.[5] First and foremost: at family celebrations wine was drunk when entertaining guests,[6] at a meal given to celebrate a circumcision,[7] or an engage-

[1] P. Billerbeck 4. 616.

[2] The reason being that at such a preliminary course the people were seated—P. Billerbeck 4. 616—whereas, according to Mark 14. 18, Jesus and His disciples were already reclining at table.

[3] j. Pes. 10. 37d. 4–5. Cf. infra, p. 58 sub. A.

[4] V. Zapletal, "Der Wein in der Bibel," *Biblische Studien* 20. 1 (1920); G. Dalman, *Arbeit und Sitte in Palaestina* 4 (1935), 291 sq.; 6 (1939), 124 sq.

[5] b. Pes. 109a (Bar.).

[6] P. Billerbeck 4. 613 sq. The name of *Mishtītā* is usually given to such a solemn meal.

[7] Qoh. R. 3. 2 (Stettin, 1864), 81a. 9, etc.

ment,[1] or a wedding;[2] it was also customary for wine to be served in the house of the bereaved during the seven days of mourning.[3] Secondly, the annual feasts offered an occasion for the drinking of wine, and in particular the three feasts of pilgrimage (Passover, Pentecost, and the Feast of Tabernacles); the drinking of wine was specially prescribed for Passover[4] and for Purim,[5] and was customary at meals for the "sanctification" and the "dismissal" of the Sabbath.[6] Otherwise in everyday life wine was used, generally speaking, for medical purposes only;[7] it was regarded as an excellent medicine.[8]

On week-days water was drunk. The daily breakfast consisted of "bread and salt and a tankard full of water",[9] and even at the main meal bread and water were the chief ingredients,[10] not only for the poor, who even in the evening had to do without other additions to their diet and be satisfied with salt and bread.[11] The scribes were specially expected to lead a Spartan life: "This is the way (to gain knowledge) of the Torah, eat bread and salt and 'drink also water by measure' (Ezek. 4. 11), sleep on the ground, lead a life of self-denial and take pains over the Torah."[12] One special instance may serve for many: *Rabbān Gamlī'ēl* had only two dates and one jug of water brought to his tabernacle.[13]

The reports of the Gospels agree with what we have said. Only twice elsewhere is it mentioned that Jesus took wine: in Matt. 11. 16–19 par., where there is a reference to special receptions

[1] P. Billerbeck 2. 394.

[2] John 2. 1 sq.; cf. P. Billerbeck 1. 514u, 517ee.

[3] S. Krauss, *Talmudische Archaeologie* 2 (Leipzig, 1911), 70. P. Billerbeck, 4. 594, 600, 602 sq. G. Dalman, *Arbeit und Sitte in Palaestina* 4 (1935), 396; cf. already Jer. 16. 7, "the cup of consolation".

[4] According to Pes. 10. 1, four cups are regarded as the minimum.

[5] S. Krauss, op. cit. 243.

[6] Ibid. 242.

[7] Cf. e.g. Luke 10. 34; 1 Tim. 5. 23; Shab. 19. 2; Nedh. 9. 8, P. Billerbeck, 1. 428, 3. 654 sq.; G. Dalman, *Arbeit und Sitte* 4 (1935), 261, 263, 375 sq., esp. 398.

[8] "In a place where there is no wine, medicines are needed", b. B. B. 58b.

[9] b. B. M. 107b (Bar.).

[10] S. Krauss, *Talmudische Archaeologie* 3 (1912), 29; G. Dalman, *Arbeit und Sitte* 6 (1939), 123 sq.

[11] b. Ber. 2b.

[12] P. A. 6. 4.

[13] Sukka, 2. 5.

arranged by His grateful followers which Jesus attended; and in the story of the marriage at Cana, John 2. 1–11. Apart from this it may be assumed, although it is not expressly stated, that Jesus and His disciples drank wine when they were invited to a festal occasion, for instance by a Pharisee on a Sabbath (Luke 14. 1), and assuredly if there were here a Sabbath "dismissal". It is however, quite unthinkable that Jesus and His disciples drank wine at their daily meals. The simplicity of their ordinary meals is shown in Mark 6. 38 par.: they have with them no more than some bread and two fishes for their ordinary lunch.[1] How is it that at the Last Supper wine is drunk? The answer is: at the passover meal it was the duty of everyone who took part in it to drink wine—at least four cups, according to Pes. 10. 1—"even if it is from the poor-dish".[2]

(6*b*) Jesus and His disciples drank red wine at the Last Supper. That follows clearly from the comparison made between wine and blood. There was in Palestine in the Talmudic period red,[3] white,[4] and black[5] wine. For the passover meal red wine was usual.[6]

[1] An observation by A. Schlatter is instructive with regard to the rarity of the drinking of wine on week-days: in 1 Cor. 11. 25, at the command to repeat the ceremony it is added with regard to the wine ὁσάκις ἐὰν πίνητε, which has no analogy in the case of the bread; Luke 22. 19 sq. omits altogether the command of repetition with regard to the wine. A. Schlatter, *Das Evangelium des Lukas* (Stuttgart, 1931), 422, therefore surmises with reason that both these instances find their explanation in the fact that "the wine cup was only rarely found at the meals of the congregations". On the celebrations *sub una* cf. A. v. Harnack, *T.U.* 7. 2 (1891); C. Clemen, *Religionsgeschichtliche Erklaerung des N.T.s*, 2nd ed. (1924), 174 sq.; H. Lietzmann, *Messe und Herrenmahl* (Bonn, 1926), 239 sq., 248; W. Goossens, *Les origines de l'Eucharistie* (1931), 161, 164 sq.; A. Greiff, "Brot, Wasser und Mischwein, die Elemente der Taufmesse" in *Theol. Quartalschr.* 13 (1932), 11 sq.; A. Arnold, *Der Ursprung des christl. Abendmahls* (1937), 10–53; G. Gentz, art. *Aquarii* in *Real-Lexikon f. Antike und Christentum* 1 (1942), 574 sq.; G. Dix, *The Shape of the Liturgy* (1944), 61.

[2] Pes. 10. 1. The consumption of wine at the Passover is an established custom already in the pre-Christian period, cf. Jub. 49. 6, 9, where it is treated as an ancient custom.

[3] S. Krauss, *Talmudische Archaeologie* 2 (1911), 241 No. 18.

[4] Ibid. No. 14 and 16.

[5] Ibid. No. 15, 17 and 19.

[6] Cf. infra, p. 145.

(7) According to John 13. 29, the disciples assume that Jesus had commissioned Judas, who left the table after the meal (v. 26), to give something to the poor. "And it was night" (v. 30). It is hard to imagine that it was Jesus' custom to arrange for the distribution of alms at night; but unless this was His custom, the disciples would not have explained the sudden, nocturnal disappearance of Judas in this way. It was, however, customary to assist the poor on the night of the Passover. Even the poorest had a right to four cups of wine, "even if it were from the poor-dish".[1] An old Aramaic Passover formula, spoken by the Paterfamilias,[2] said: "See, this[3] is the bread of misery, which our fathers had to eat when they left Egypt. Whosoever hungers, let him come and eat, and whosoever is in need, let him come and keep the Passover (with us)."[4] That this invitation to the poor to come to the passover table was not only theoretical may be seen from an incidental remark in the *Mishna*, that it was not unusual to "invite somebody from the street"[5] to the Passover. So when Josephus' report that on the night of the Passover the Temple gates were opened at midnight[6] leads Billerbeck[7] to the conclusion that there would be no lack of beggars around the Temple on that night, no one with any knowledge of Palestinian conditions can do other than agree.

(8) The Last Supper ends, as is mentioned incidentally (Mark 14. 26; Matt. 26. 30), with the singing of a hymn. Since "the *Hallēl* at the end of the ordinary meal", mentioned in several modern studies of our subject, is a mere product of fantasy—the thanksgiving after the meal (Mark 14. 23 εὐχαριστήσας) cannot be described by ὑμνεῖν—this can refer only to the second

[1] Literally "from the bowl", i.e. from the daily distributions of meals as opposed to "from the box", the weekly distribution of relief in cash.

[2] I. Lewy, "Ein Vortrag ueber das Ritual des *Pesach*-Abends", *Jahresbericht d. jued. theol. Seminars* (Breslau, 1904), 11: spoken at the open door of the house. However, this report is late, coming from a certain *Gaon* of *Pumbeditha* (about A.D. 860), who refers to earlier sources.

[3] The *Mazzoth*.

[4] This saying still belongs to the passover ritual today, cf. infra, p. 33 n. 2.

[5] Pes. 9. 11.

[6] *Ant.* 18. 2. 2. §29 sq.

[7] 2. 842 sq.

half[1] of the Passover *Hallēl*,[2] which in rabbinical literature, as Billerbeck[3] has shown, is sometime called הִימְנוֹן.[4]

(9) After the meal Jesus did not return to Bethany, although He had regularly spent the preceding nights there.[5] Rather he went to the Mount of Olives (Mark 14. 26 par.) into a garden (ibid. v. 32 par.) which was situated east of the brook Kidron (John 18. 1). Why? The night of the Passover had to be spent in Jerusalem (contemporary exegesis derived this command from Deut. 16. 7). In order to make possible the observation of this commandment, the city district had been enlarged to include Bethphage.[6] Bethany, however, lay outside the enlarged city district, and therefore must not be entered by Jesus during the night of Nīsān the 14th to the 15th, whereas the Kidron valley and the western slope of the Mount of Olives, and consequently the garden of Gethsemane, were within the permitted district of greater Jerusalem.[7]

(10) Lastly, there is one quite decisive fact: Jesus announces His impending Passion at the Last Supper by interpreting the meaning of the bread and of the wine. What was the reason for this very strange way of announcing His Passion? I can see only one answer to this question: interpreting the elements of the meal is a fixed part of the Passover ritual. The custom, which is still

[1] The first half of the *Hallēl* (according to the Shammaïtes, Ps. 113, to the Hillelites, Ps. 113–14) was sung after the *Passa-Haggādhā* (Pes. 10. 6; Tos. Pes. 10. 9. 173, 2), the second half (Ps. 114–18 or 115–18) after the ending of the meal (Pes. 10. 7). The Shammaïtes probably here, as often elsewhere, represent the older use, for the response with the Halleluja (cf. infra, p. 172 sq.) suggests that both parts of the *Hallēl* began with this word.

[2] Aug. Wuensche, *Neue Beitr. z. Erlaeuterung der Evangelien aus Talmud und Midrasch* (Goettingen, 1878), 334; J. Wellhausen, *Das Evangelium Marci*, 2nd ed. (Berlin, 1909), 119; G. Dalman, *Jesus-Jeschua* (Leipzig, 1922), 120 sq.; J. Mann, "Rabbinic Studies in the Synoptic Gospels" in *Hebrew Union College Annual* 1 (Cincinnati, 1924), 341 sq.; P. Billerbeck 4. 75 sq.; A. Schlatter, *Der Evangelist Matthaeus* (Stuttgart, 1929), 745.

[3] P. Billerbeck 4. 76.

[4] The same in Philo, *Spec. Leg.* 2. §148 (5. 121. 19), saying that the Passover is celebrated "*μετ' εὐχῶν τε καὶ ὕμνων*".

[5] Cf. supra, p. 15.

[6] Cf. supra, p. 15, n. 4.

[7] Cf. E. Lohmeyer, *Das Evangelium des Markus* (1937), 311.

continued to-day, arose from the exegesis of Exod. 12. 26 sq.; 13. 8. It took place after the preliminary course and the mixing of the second of the four prescribed cups. The liturgical interpretation of the elements of the passover meal was introduced by the son's question about the peculiar features of the passover meal. This was answered by the Paterfamilias telling the story of the exodus based on Deut. 26. 5–11, and combining with it the interpretation of the elements (Pes. 10. 4). Three of the ingredients of the meal had to be specially mentioned: "*Rabbān Gamlī'ēl* (probably II, about A.D. 90) said: Whosoever does not mention (in his interpretation) the following three things at the passover meal has failed in his duty: the paschal lamb, the unleavened bread, and the bitter herbs; cf. Exod. 12. 8" (Pes. 10. 5).[1] The form in which the interpretation was couched appears from the later part of the same passage, "the paschal lamb (should be interpreted as follows): because God passed over (*pāsaḥ*) in mercy the houses of our fathers in Egypt, Exod. 12. 27; the bitter herbs: because the Egyptians made bitter the life of our fathers in Egypt, Exod. 1. 14; the unleavened bread: because our fathers were delivered out of Egypt (in such haste, that there was no time left to wait for the leavening of the dough), Exod. 12. 39" (Pes. 10. 5).

Of special interest is the interpretation given to the unleavened bread. The one just quoted, referring to the haste in which the exodus took place (Exod. 12. 34, 39), from Pes. 10. 5,[2] recurs in Philo.[3] A related, but different, account is based upon Deut. 16. 3, where the unleavened bread is called "the bread of affliction": Josephus, explaining the custom of eating unleavened bread at the Passover, refers to the thirty days after the exodus from Egypt, when the Israelites passed through the desert and in their need had to feed on unleavened bread for lack of other food.[4] "Therefore, in memory of that misery, we celebrate the feast of unleavened bread for eight days."[5] From the same text, Deut. 16. 3, there also comes an ancient Aramaic formula of interpretation,

[1] It was customary to elevate the *mazzoth* and the bitter herbs when interpreting them, b. Pes. 116b.

[2] Mekh. Exod. 12. 39.

[3] Philo, *Spec. Leg.* 2. §158 (5. 124. 6 sq.).

[4] Josephus, *Ant.* 2. 15. 1. §316.

[5] Ibid. §317. Cf. Siphre Deut. 130 ad Deut. 16. 3 (43d. 31): R. *Shim'ōn* said, "Why is it called bread of affliction? Because of the affliction they had to endure in Egypt."

which still serves to introduce the *Passa-Haggādhā*[1] and is of special importance here, as its beginning is formally related to Jesus' Words of institution: "Lo, this is the bread of sorrow (cf. Deut. 16. 3), which our fathers ate when they left Egypt."[2]

But the explanation of the unleavened bread was not necessarily limited to an historical retrospect. In Philo we find no less than three allegorical interpretations.[3] The first, that the unleavened bread is unfinished (ἀτελής), and thus reflects Nature before the time of harvest—unleavened loaves are intended to raise man's hopes for the gifts of harvest;[4] the second, that the unleavened bread is a gift of Nature, whilst leavened bread is an artificial product—the unleavened loaves are meant to exhort man to return to primitive life, a life without artificial demands or needs;[5] the third, that the unleavened loaves are the "bread of affliction", Deut. 16. 3—they should remind man that a great task can be accomplished only by labour and self-denial.[6]

Just as Philo gave several explanatory allegories, so also did Palestinian scholars in the homeland give numerous explanations of the meaning of לֶחֶם עֹנִי, Deut. 16. 3.[7] Alongside the widespread interpretation of the "bread of affliction" already mentioned, which refers to Israel's sufferings in Egypt, or on her journey from Egypt and afterwards, the following explanations occur:

[1] The Passover prayer of the Paterfamilias, cf. supra, p. 32, and infra, p. 58.

[2] Quoted after the Yemenite *Siddūr* by G. Dalman, *Jesus-Jeschua* (Leipzig, 1922), 127 sq. These are not words of distribution, as is so often alleged; they are not said at the breaking of the bread by which the main meal is opened (cf. infra, p. 58 sq.), but earlier on, as an introduction to the interpretation of the elements during the *Passa-Haggādhā*.

[3] A source analysis of these interpretations has been given by I. Heinemann, *Philos griech. u. jued. Bildung* (Breslau, 1932), 121 sq.

[4] *Spec. Leg.* 2. §158 (5. 124. 9 sq.).

[5] Ibid. 2. §159 sq., 161 (5. 124. 16 sq.).

[6] *De Congressu eruditionis gratia* §161–7 (3. 105. 23 sq.). Cf. also *Quaest. in Exodum* 1. §15, describing the unleavened bread as a warning against conceit.

[7] This one example bears out the correctness of P. Billerbeck's remarks about the differences between the allegories of the Alexandrian and the Palestinian scholars: in the former the letter of Holy Scripture is seen only as the outer shell of its spiritual content, in the latter it retains its full validity (P. Billerbeck 3. 397 sq.).

(1) "bread of affliction", i.e. bread that lacks something (bread or cake that has not been kneaded);[1] (2) (reading לֶחֶם אוֹנִי)[2] "bread which may (also) be eaten during mourning";[3] (3) "bread over which (at the Passover) many words are spoken" (עוֹנִין);[4] (4) "bread of the poor" (reading לֶחֶם עָנִי), i.e. fragments of bread,[5] or bread for the baking of which the Paterfamilias himself has to heat the oven.[6] It appears that, in the homeland, too, the interpretation of the unleavened bread was by no means limited to an historical retrospect. Rather, the following quotation shows how very much the interpretation of the elements of the Passover was related to the contemporary world: "in each generation it is a duty to regard oneself as though one had oneself been brought up out of Egypt".[7]

If the interpretation of the elements in the Passover ritual was concerned mainly with the three ingredients of the meal mentioned in Exod. 12. 8, the paschal lamb, the unleavened bread, and the bitter herbs, it was by no means limited to them. Important for our investigation is the fact that we find in the Jerusalem Talmud a witness to the allegorical interpretation of the four cups: "R. *Jōḥānān* (*bar Nappāḥā*, died A.D. 279) said in the name of R. *Bannājā* (about A.D. 200): [the four cups] correspond to the fourfold description of redemption in Exod. 6. 6 sq.[8] R. *Jehōshūaʿ b. Lēwī* (about A.D. 250) said: [they] refer to the four cups of Pharaoh, Gen. 40. 11, 13. R. *Lēwī* (about A.D. 300) said: [they] refer to the four world empires. The doctors said: [they] refer to the four cups of punishment which the Holy One, praise be to Him, will one day give to the nations of the world to drink. . . . And similarly the Holy One, praise be to Him, will give four cups of comfort[9] to Israel to drink."[10] This passage is significant, be-

1 Siphre Deut. §130 ad Deut. 16. 3 (43d. 29, 31), cf. b. Pes. 36a.

2 Cf. Deut. 26. 14.

3 b. Pes. 36a (Bar.).

4 b. Pes. 36a, 115b.

5 Cf. infra, p. 43 sq.

6 b. Pes. 115b–116a.

7 Pes. 10. 5. The sentence is missing in the Mishna codices Kaufmann, de Rossi ed. Lowe, and Vatic. Hebr. 109.

8 "Bring you out"; "rid you out"; "redeem you"; "take you to me".

9 Mentioned in Ps. 16. 5, 23. 5 and 116. 13 (in the plural, meaning two cups).

10 j. Pes. 10. 37b. 64 sq. par.: Gn. R. 88 ad 40. 9–11; Midhr. Ps. 75. §4.

cause not only does it bear witness to the allegorical interpretation of the four cups of the Passover, but proves at the same time that these interpretations of the elements of the meal combined looking back to God's salvation in the past with looking forward to future salvation in the Messianic age.[1]

But of special importance is that along with the historical and the contemporary interpretation of the unleavened bread there can also be found an eschatological one: " 'Go thy way forth to the ends[2] of the flock (of Israel)', Cant. 1. 8. . . . R. *'Eli'ezer* (*ben Hyrkanos*, about A.D. 90) said: of the ash-cake (i.e. the unleavened bread) which Israel took out of Egypt, they have eaten thirty-one days (from Nīsān the 15th to 'Ijjār the 15th) . . . from this you may learn,[3] what I shall do at last in the end; so Ps. 72. 16: 'there shall be plenty of corn in the land'."[4] So already in the first century A.D. we can trace the eschatological interpretation of the unleavened bread on which God had miraculously fed Israel during their journey through the desert, and had thus given a type of the abundance of bread in the Messianic period. It is no accident that in the New Testament the unleavened loaves are also eschatologically interpreted in 1 Cor. 5. 7–8. This passage is probably based upon a Pauline *Passa-Haggādhā*. Its theme is: on Good Friday the great Passover has begun. To be a Christian means to live in Passover-time, in the deliverance from the bondage of sin. This theme is elaborated by Paul, who interprets the elements of the meal thus: the paschal lamb is the symbol of the Messiah who was sacrificed as the immaculate Lamb; the leaven which is removed from all the houses during the night of Nīsān 13/14 is the symbol of the evil and wickedness of the nature of the old world order. The unleavened loaves are interpreted eschatologically in two ways: as pure dough, they are the symbol of purity and truth, of the nature of the new world (1 Cor. 5. 8); and as the new dough, they are the symbol of the redeemed community (ibid. 5. 7).[5]

[1] Cf. infra, p. 137 sq.

[2] Thus the Midhrash, instead of "by the footsteps".

[3] With Aug. Wuensche, *Der Midrasch Schir-ha-Schirim* (1880), 37, and P. Billerbeck 1. 86, we follow the reading of *Mattenōth Kehunnā*.

[4] Midhr. Cant. 1. 8.

[5] A similar eschatological interpretation of the unleavened bread may underlie the eucharistic prayer in Did. 9. 4: the bread, the grains

When we add that Jesus' interpretation of the bread, *τοῦτό ἐστιν τὸ σῶμά μου*, bears a formal likeness to the ancient Aramaic interpretation of the unleavened bread הָא לַחְמָא עַנְיָא, quoted above,[1] we may conclude that the ritual interpretation of the elements of the passover meal which we have described gave Jesus the opportunity for His new interpretation of the elements of the Last Supper. This conclusion is supported by the fact that the annual interpretation of the elements at the Passover became a model for other occasions. The following tradition[2] may be mentioned, referring to the meal on *'Ābh* the 9th, the day on which the destruction of Jerusalem by the Babylonians and by the Romans was remembered: "when *Rabh* (died A.D. 247) had finished his meal, he took a damaged loaf, poured ashes over it and said, 'This is the meal of the ninth of *'Ābh.*' "[3] The difference between the interpretation of the elements in the passover ritual and their interpretation by Jesus lies in the fact that the former refers mainly to past, and that of Jesus mainly to present acts of salvation. The circumstances of the Last Supper account for this difference; which is the less surprising, since, as we have seen, eschatological explanations are not lacking in the rabbinical interpretations of the Passover, and the expectation of the Messianic future was indissolubly connected with the Passover.[4] The other difference, that Jesus did not combine His interpretation with the *Passa-Haggādhā* at the end of the preliminary course, but with the saying of grace before and after the main meal which immediately followed it, may have arisen from His desire to combine His new interpretation with the distribution of the elements.[5]

---

of which were gathered from the mountains, signifies the gathering of the dispersed congregation of God at the end of time. 1 Cor. 10. 17 testifies to the antiquity of this eschatological interpretation of the bread. The fact that it represents an old tradition follows, as R. Hupfeld (*Die Abendmahlsfeier* (1935), 74) has remarked, from the omission, in both Did. and 1 Cor., of a similar allegory for the wine, referring to the multiplicity of grapes from which the one wine is produced.

[1] Cf. supra, pp. 30, 33.

[2] Cf. G. Dalman, *Jesus-Jeschua* (Leipzig, 1922), 127.

[3] Midhr. *'ēkhā rabb.* ad Lament. 3. 16 (ed. Stettin, 1864), 51b. 18.

[4] G. Dalman, *Nachtraege zu Jesus-Jeschua* (Leipzig, 1929), 9 sq.; P. Billerbeck 2. 256. Cf. the text of the present-day Passover ritual.

[5] Cf. infra, p. 152 sq.

These ten observations are concerned not only with the framework of the report but also with its substance. It cannot be held, therefore, that only later embellishment has turned the Last Supper into a Passover. It is much rather the case that the paschal character of the Last Supper is unanimously supported by—

(1) the ancient liturgical formula itself: No. 2, 6a, b, 10;
(2) the Eschatological Saying: Luke 22. 15;
(3) the description of both the beginning and the end of the meal: No. 2, 3, 4, 8, 9;
(4) the report about the arrangement of the room: No. 1 and Mark 14. 12, 14, 16;
(5) the redactor's explanatory remark, Mark 14. 22a: No. 5.

One last remark: the report of the Synoptists that the Last Supper was a Passover does not agree with the rite of the early Church. The early Church did not celebrate the Eucharist according to the Passover ritual; nor yet only once a year, but daily or on each Lord's day. Therefore, if the Synoptists nevertheless describe the Last Supper as a Passover, with no attempt at concealment, the reason is obviously that the recollection of the fact was so firmly established that it could not be removed even by the established ritual.[1]

(4) *Objections*

We now turn to those considerations which have caused scholars to question the Synoptic assertion (Mark 14. 12, 14, 16 par.; Luke 22. 15) that the Last Supper was a Passover. The main objections are as follows:[2]

(1) Ever since J. Wellhausen's[3] short study in 1906 scholars have held that the Last Supper could not have been a Passover,

[1] K. Voelker, *Mysterium und Agape* (1927), 19.

[2] Those objections which are obviously erroneous I shall not discuss, as for instance the statement of M. Goguel, *L'Eucharistie des origines à Justin Martyr* (Paris, 1910), 62, that the Last Supper could not have been a Passover, because the distribution of the bread at the Passover took place only "après le repas proprement dit".

[3] *Z.N.W.* 7 (1906), 182. The same had been proposed already by earlier scholars, as for instance B. G. W. Pieritz, *The Gospels from the Rabbinical Point of View* (Oxford-London, 1873), 30, and still earlier by John of Damascus, *Migne Gr.* 94, 367 sq.

because Mark 14. 22 par. speaks of ἄρτος, whereas only the word ἄζυμα (Heb. מַצָּה, Aram.[1] פַּטִּירָא) could properly be used in describing a passover meal. It would thus be impossible to call the unleavened bread ἄρτος. Unfortunately, none of the many scholars[2] who have repeated Wellhausen's thesis has made any attempt to test its accuracy, although as early as 1912 G. Beer[3] seriously challenged it. As a matter of fact, the thesis that unleavened bread cannot be called ἄρτος is incorrect. Quite apart from the possibility of a mere inaccuracy of the report when Mark 14. 22 par. speaks of ἄρτος,[4] or from the fact that the eucharistic practice of the earliest churches which used ordinary leavened bread[5] may have given rise to some inaccuracy of expression, it has to be stated that לֶחֶם as well as ἄρτος may mean leavened as well as unleavened bread.[6] See Exod. 29. 2: לֶחֶם מַצּוֹת; Targ. Jer. I, Targ. Onk., Targ. Samar. ad Exod. 29. 2: לְחֵים פַּטִּיר; LXX Exod. 29. 2; Lev. 2. 4; 8. 26; Num. 6. 15, 19; Philo, *Spec. Leg.* 2. §158 (5. 124. 6); *De congressu eruditionis gratia* §168 (3. 107. 13); *De Vita contemplativa* §81 (6. 68. 13); Josephus, *Ant.* 3. 6. 6. §142: ἄρτος ἄζυμος. What is more, it can be shown that it was quite common usage to call unleavened bread simply לֶחֶם or ἄρτος. Absolutely conclusive in view of the quite extraordinary abundance of testimony is the description of the twelve pieces of shewbread which were arranged upon their special table in the sanctuary of the Temple.[7] We know for certain that the shewbread was unleavened; a fact not mentioned—probably by accident—in the Old Testament, but reported unanimously by Philo, Josephus, and the

[1] E.g. Targ. Jer. I ad Exod. 12. 15.

[2] The latest is J. Finegan, *Die Ueberlieferung der Leidens- und Auferstehungsgeschichte Jesu* (Giessen, 1934), 62.

[3] *Pesachim* (Giessen, 1912), 96.

[4] R. Bultmann, *Geschichte der synopt. Tradition*, 2nd ed. (Goettingen, 1931), 285 n. 4.

[5] Unleavened bread was hardly available on an ordinary day.

[6] G. Beer, *Pesachim* (Giessen, 1912), 96; A. Oepke in *Allg. Evang.-Luth. Kirchenzeitung* 59 (1926), 58; P. Fiebig in *Theol. Lit. Zeitg.* 59 (1934), 416.

[7] Cf. the catalogue of the names given to the shewbread in P. Billerbeck 3. 719, together with the numerous Talmudic testimonies collected ibid. 3. 719–28; 1. 618–19, of quotations referring to the shewbread.

Talmud.[1] Nevertheless, the name for the shewbread in the Old Testament as well as in the Mishna is always לֶחֶם, in the Targum always לַחְמָא, in the Talmud always the one or the other, in the LXX and in Aquila[2] always *ἄρτοι*, as for instance Exod. 25. 30 (LXX v. 29): לֶחֶם פָּנִים; Targ. Onk. לְחֵים אַפַּיָּא; Targ. Jer. לַחְמָא גַוָּאָה; LXX *ἄρτοι ἐνώπιοι*; Aquila *ἄρτοι προσώπου*. The New Testament use is no different: *οἱ ἄρτοι τῆς προθέσεως* Mark 2. 26; Matt. 12. 4; Luke 6. 4, *ἡ πρόθεσις τῶν ἄρτων*, Heb. 9. 2. Most significant is the fact that the name of the shewbread may be simply הַלֶּחֶם (Lev. 24. 7, or—without the article—in Exod. 40. 23).[3] The same usage is found in Philo, Josephus, and the Mishna. For Philo calls the shewbread (*a*) by its Old Testament names, as for instance *ἄρτοι τῆς προθέσεως*,[4] (*b*) in some passages *ἄρτοι ἄζυμοι*,[5] (*c*) elsewhere simply *ἄρτοι*;[6] Josephus has *ἄρτοι ἄζυμοι*,[7] *ἄρτοι τοῦ θεοῦ*,[8] or also just *ἄρτοι*;[9] the Mishna calls the shewbread by its Old Testament name[10]

[1] Philo, cf. *Spec. Leg.* 2. §161 (5. 125. 6); *de Vita contemplativa* §81 (6. 68. 13). Josephus, *Ant.* 3. 6. 6. §142, *ἄρτων δώδεκα ἀζύμους*; 3. 10. 7. §255, *σῖτος ὀπτὸς ζύμης ἄμοιρος*. Talmud: Siphra ad Lev. 2. 11 ed. princ. (Venice, 1545), 7c, 15: " 'no meat offering which you offer unto Yahwe may be made with leaven' (Lev. 2. 11). R. *Jōsē* the Galilean (about A.D. 110) said: (this has been said) to include the shewbread". According to Men. 5. 1, all flour offerings were unleavened with the exception of ten of the forty cakes of the salvation thank-offering (cf. on these cakes infra, p. 40), and the two loaves of the first-fruits at Pentecost (Lev. 23. 16 sq.); b. Men. 77b.

[2] There is no mention of the shewbread in the existing fragments of Symmachus and Theodotion.

[3] The shewbread eaten by King David at Nob, 1 Sam. 21. 1–7, is also called just לֶחֶם or *ἄρτος* in 1 Sam. 21. 7 (LXX 1 Kings 21. 6). That at a later time they were believed to have been unleavened, follows from b. Men. 5b, where the rules of the Jerusalem Temple are applied to 1 Sam. 21. 1–7, and the same is shown by b. Men. 29a, 96b.

[4] *De fuga et inventione* §185 (3. 150. 15).

[5] Cf. the instances quoted supra, p. 38.

[6] *Spec. Leg.* 1. §172 (5. 42. 1); ibid. §175 (5. 42. 20); *de Vita Mosis* 2 (3) §104 (4. 225. 8); cf. Spec. Leg. 2. §161 (5. 125. 6).

[7] *Ant.* 3. 6. 6. §142.

[8] Ibid. 8. 3. 7. §89.

[9] Ibid. 3. 6. 6. §143; 8. 3. 7. §90; *Bell.* 5. 5. 5. §217.

[10] E.g. Men. 6. 2, 6; 11. 7; Tam. 3. 3; Mid. 1. 6, and elsewhere.

לֶחֶם הַפָּנִים, but in one place,[1] three times repeated, simply הַלֶּחֶם. It therefore appears that the Old Testament, Philo, Josephus, and the Mishna do not hesitate to describe the unleavened shewbread as *ἄρτοι* or לֶחֶם without any additional qualification.

This unqualified description of unleavened bread as לֶחֶם or *ἄρτος* is not confined to passages referring to the shewbread. According to Exod. 29. 31 sq.; Lev. 8. 31 sq., the consecration of priests is followed by a sacrificial meal for them. The unleavened bread (Exod. 29. 2–3) eaten by the priests on this occasion is called simply הַלֶּחֶם in Exod. 29. 32, 34; Lev. 8. 31-2, לַחְמָא in Targ. Onk. and Jer. I, and *οἱ ἄρτοι* in the LXX.[2] Along with the thank-offering for salvation four kinds of cakes are to be offered, three of which are unleavened (loaves, wafers and cakes of meal mixed with oil, Lev. 7. 12), only the fourth (ibid. v. 13) being leavened. The three unleavened kinds, חַלּוֹת מַצּוֹת, are called *ἄρτους ἐκ σεμιδάλεως* in the LXX Lev. 7. 2 (12), in the Tosephta[3] לַחְמָהּ שֶׁל תּוֹדָה; the Mishna[4] comprises all four under the name

[1] Men. 11. 8.

[2] At the consecration of the priests it was also the rule to burn three unleavened loaves, among them, according to Exod. 29. 23: כִּכַּר לֶחֶם אַחַת וְחַלַּת לֶחֶם שֶׁמֶן אַחַת; Targ. Onk. and Jer. I פִּיתָּא דִלְחֵים חֲדָא וּגְרִיצְתָּא דִלְחֵים מְשַׁח חֲדָא (Jer. I: חַד); LXX (only one loaf instead of these two) *καὶ ἄρτον ἕνα ἐξ ἐλαίου*. In Lev. 8. 26 these two unleavened loaves are called חַלַּת מַצָּה אַחַת וְחַלַּת לֶחֶם שֶׁמֶן אַחַת; Targ. Onk. and Targ. Jer. I גְּרִיצְתָּא פַּטִּרְתָּא (Jer. I: פַּטִּירָא) חֲדָא וּגְרִיצְתָּא דִלְחֵים מְשַׁח חֲדָא; LXX *ἄρτον ἕνα ἄζυμον καὶ ἄρτον ἐξ ἐλαίου ἕνα*. In these passages simple לֶחֶם, לְחֵים, or *ἄρτος* are used without further qualification to signify unleavened bread. Only in LXX Lev. 8. 26 do we find, along with *ἄρτος*, the more definite description *ἄρτος ἄζυμος*.

[3] Tos. Sheq. 1. 11 (174. 24) puts side by side (*a*) *minḥath tōdhā* and (*b*) *laḥmāh shel tōdhā*; according to b. Men. 77b, the former is leavened, therefore the latter is unleavened. The *'al* in Lev. 7. 13 (meaning: in addition to) caused the leavened bread to be regarded as *minḥa*, and the unleavened bread as its complement.

[4] Men. 2. 3; 7. 3–5; Tem. 3. 2.

of הַלֶּחֶם; the Talmud[1] the three kinds of unleavened bread under the term לחמי תודה. Lastly, the sacrifice of the "Nazirite", Num. 6. 15, contains the offering of a basket filled with unleavened cakes and wafers. The LXX (Num. 6. 15) calls the former *ἄρτους ἀναπεποιημένους ἐν ἐλαίῳ*, whilst the Mishna once more includes the unleavened cakes and wafers of this offering under the term לֶחֶם without any further qualification.[2]

The evidence already given, which is complete for the Hebrew Old Testament, the LXX, Philo, and the Mishna, and which can easily be enlarged with the help of the Tosephta, the Midhrashim, and the two Talmuds, proves that it is wrong to maintain that *ἄρτος* in Mark 14. 22 par. cannot possibly mean unleavened bread. Moreover, direct evidence exists that the unleavened bread which was eaten during the feast of the Passover could be described as לֶחֶם or *ἄρτος*. In this respect reference has to be made to Deut. 16. 3, where the unleavened bread is called the "bread of affliction" (לֶחֶם עֹנִי; Targ. Onk. לְחֵים עֲנִי; Targ. Jer. I. לַחְמָא עַנְיָא; LXX *ἄρτος κακώσεως*). Dependent upon Deut. 16. 3 is the ancient Aramaic formula of the Passover liturgy, quoted above,[3] in which the unleavened bread is called לַחְמָא עַנְיָא, and the comments in b. Pes 36a, b; 37a; 38a; 115b-116a, where the Passover unleavened bread, following Deut. 16. 3, is called לֶחֶם. But the same usage is found, independent of Deut. 16. 3, in the Passover liturgy, in the blessing said over the unleavened bread, which begins with the words of the ordinary blessing of bread:[4] ברוך המוציא לחם מן הארץ. Philo calls the unleavened bread for the Passover *ἄρτος ἄζυμος*, *Spec. Leg.* 2. §158 (5. 124. 6), and Josephus once describes the unleavened bread which the Israelites ate when leaving Egypt simply as *ἄρτοι*, *Ant.* 2. 15. 1. §316. Finally, it has to be noted that in Luke 24. 30, 35 *ἄρτος* must mean unleavened bread: the Emmaus incident took place during Passover week.

Thus, the word *ἄρτος* in Mark 14. 22 par. by no means excludes

[1] b. Pes. 37a; b. Men. 78b.

[2] Me'ila 3. 2; Naz. 4. 4; Zebh. 10. 2.

[3] Cf. supra, pp. 30, 33, 36.

[4] Maimonides, *Hilkhoth ḥamez umazza* 8. 6. 8 (Berlin, 1862), 103a.

the possibility that this account of the Last Supper is really of a Passover meal.

(2) Mark 14. 22–25 par. contains no explicit reference to the Passover rite, in particular none to the paschal lamb and the bitter herbs. This is true; but this silence is no longer surprising, when we reflect that Mark 14. 22–24 is a cultic formula, not purporting to give a description of the Last Supper, but recording the constituent elements of the celebrations of the primitive Church. Since this celebration was not a repetition of the Last Supper with all its historical accompaniments, but the daily assembly of the disciples of Jesus in the table fellowship of the Messiah,[1] it is but natural that only the rites which continued to be performed by the Church should be mentioned in the liturgical formula. A striking analogy is found in the elaborate description of the Passover meal in Mi. Pes. 10, which only mentions the eating of the paschal lamb (the central act) in an aside: "and in the time of the temple, they put the paschal lamb before him",[2] although the killing and preparing of the paschal lamb had formed the subject of an extensive description in the earlier chapters, Pes. 5 sq. The reason for this strange neglect of the paschal lamb is to be found in the fact that Pes. 5 sq. gives a description of the passover sacrifices while the Temple still stood, whereas in Pes. 10 there follows the ritual for the contemporary, annual celebration of the feast at which, since the destruction of the Temple, no paschal lamb was eaten. Thus we have in the Mishna treatise *Pesāḥīm* the same combination of historical report and cultic ritual as in the passages which describe the Last Supper; and on each occasion the same thing happens: the cultic ritual overshadows the historical facts and concentrates upon the continuing rites.[3] All the more important is the direct mention made of the paschal lamb in Luke 22. 15, and the indirect reference to the bitter herbs in Mark 14. 20 par. (*ἐμβαπτόμενος*).[4]

[1] Cf. infra, p. 136 sq.

[2] Pes. 10. 3 fin.

[3] "On s'étonne qu'une différence si claire dans les genres littéraires semble échapper à des critiques qui ont fait tant de justes observations sur les rapports entre la vie de la communauté primitive et la formulation des péricopes évangéliques", is the just criticism of P. Benoit in *Rev. Bibl.* 48 (1939), 385.

[4] On the possibility that Jesus compared Himself to the Easter Lamb in the Passover ceremony, cf. infra, p. 144.

(3) A third objection consists in the thesis that the description of the Last Supper is inconsistent with the Passover ritual. On the one hand it is held that at the Passover—in distinction from normal custom—the bread was broken first and the blessing said afterwards.[1] Since the reverse sequence is presupposed in Mark 14. 22 par. (*εὐλογήσας ἔκλασεν*), many[2] have drawn the conclusion that, because of this difference, the Last Supper could not have been a Passover. On the other hand, it is claimed that by the time of Jesus individual cups were used at the Passover; and since, according to Mark 14. 23 par., all the people present at the Last Supper drank from the same cup, this too is alleged as a reason why the Last Supper could not have been a passover meal.[3] Finally, it is claimed that each participant in the Passover was supposed to have his own dish before him, and that this is contrary to the eating from one dish, as is presupposed by Mark 14. 20.[4]

(*a*) As regards the first thesis, that at the Passover the bread was broken first and the blessing said afterwards, I have elsewhere[5] attempted to show that this is simply incorrect. The error has been caused by misunderstanding a saying of Maimonides (died in 1204). Maimonides[6] says that in his time the general

[1] So Haller, "Das heilige Abendmahl und das Passahmahl" in *Theol. Studien aus Wuerttemberg* 8 (1887), 69; F. Spitta, *Beitraege zur Gesch. und Litt. des Urchristentums* 1 (Goettingen, 1893), 238; C. Clemen, *Der Ursprung des heiligen Abendmahls* (Leipzig, 1898), 25; K. G. Goetz, *Die Abendmahlsfrage*, 2nd ed. (Leipzig, 1907), 132; P. Batiffol, L'Eucharistie, 8th ed., *Études d'histoire et de théologie positive*, 2nd ser. (Paris, 1920), 72; A. Greiff, *Das aelteste Paschorituale der Kirche, Did.* 1–10, *und das Johannes-Evangelium* (Paderborn, 1929), 149 n. 2.

[2] E.g. Haller, Spitta and Goetz.

[3] G. H. Box, "The Jewish antecedents of the Eucharist" in *J.T.S.* 3 (1902), 359; G. Beer, *Pesachim* (Giessen, 1912), 97–9; K. G. Goetz, *Das Abendmahl, eine Diatheke Jesu oder sein letztes Gleichnis?* (Leipzig, 1920), 18 n. 3; W. O. E. Oesterley, *The Jewish Background of the Christian Liturgy* (Oxford, 1925), 163.

[4] R. Bultmann, *Die Geschichte der synopt. Tradition*, 2nd ed. (Goettingen, 1931), 284; J. Finegan, *Die Ueberlieferung der Leidens- und Auferstehungsgeschichte Jesu* (Giessen, 1934) 66.

[5] "Das Brotbrechen beim Passahmahl und Markus 14. 22 par." in *Z.N.W.* 33 (1934), 203 sq.

[6] *Ḥilkhoth ḥamez umazza* 8. 6 (Berlin, 1862), 103a.

custom (which first appears in b. Pes. 115b-116a) was to say the blessing over a piece of bread, part of which was broken off. This custom was meant to symbolise—following Deut. 16. 3, where the unleavened bread is called "the bread of affliction"—how poor the Israelites were when they left Egypt. The poor man does not possess a whole loaf. The first, as far as I can see, to mistake this breaking (חלק, is used by Maimonides, not פרס) before the blessing for the actual breaking of bread after the blessing was John Lightfoot, *Opera Omnia* 2 (Roterodami, 1686), 379, ad Matt. 26. 26, and his mistake has been repeated down to this day. The truth is that at the Passover, just as at any other meal, the blessing was said first, and afterwards the unleavened bread was broken and the fragments distributed. The sequence blessing—breaking of the bread (Mark 14. 22 par.: *εὐλογήσας ἔκλασεν*) is in full accord with the Passover ritual.

(*b*) What then is the force of the argument that at the time of Jesus the individual cup was used at the Passover? The fact is that from the second century A.D. onwards there were objections on hygienic grounds to the practice of drinking from one cup.[1] However, these very protests prove that it was not uncommon for several people to drink from one cup; and it is a fact that R. *Jehōshūa' b. Lēwī*, who lived in the middle of the third century, still allowed for both possibilities, the individual cup and the common cup, at the common meal;[2] and on festal occasions it remained the general custom that the cup of blessing, after the person who had blessed it had drunk from it, was handed to all the people present.[3] Thus, as G. Dalman has shown,[4] it is extremely probable that the earlier custom prescribed that the cup over which grace after meal had been said should be handed round in order to let everyone present share in the benediction. This view is supported by the analogous treatment of the bread: the bread over which the blessing had been said was broken into fragments, so that every guest could share in the blessing by eating a piece.

[1] Tos. Ber. 5. 9 (12. 9); *Derekh 'erez* R. 8, cf. P. Billerbeck 4. 59*a*. Evidence dating from a later period in H. L. Strack, *Pesaḥim* (Leipzig, 1911), 11*.

[2] j. Ber. 6. 10a. 58, cf. P. Billerbeck 4. 58 sq., 62.

[3] G. Dalman, *Jesus-Jeschua* (Leipzig, 1922), 140.

[4] Ibid., cf. *Allgemeine Evang.-Luth. Kirchenzeitung* 64 (1931), 798; *Arbeit und Sitte in Palaestina* 4 (1935), 393.

As regards the Passover in particular, the words of Pes. 10. 2, 4, 7 ("the first cup has been mixed for him", 10. 2—who is that? the Paterfamilias?[1] or each guest?[2]) leave room for some doubt whether the common or the individual cup is meant, although the context is in favour of the former alternative.[3] However, even if the Mishna should presuppose the individual cup, it would be difficult to use its testimony as valid evidence for conditions in Jesus' time. For the Mishna describes the celebration of the Passover as it was held after A.D. 70, when it was no longer celebrated by the whole nation, in Jerusalem, but by individual families in their own homes. More significance may be attached to the fact that b. Pes. 108b states that the Paterfamilias in some cases invited his children and other members of the family to share his cup with him, for this may be the survival of an earlier custom. However, for the time of Jesus a simple, technical consideration seems to be decisive: was there enough crockery in that overcrowded holy city for everyone of the celebrants who filled its houses, its courtyards and roof-tops in tens of thousands, and celebrated the Passover, to have his own cup? Anyone who knows something of oriental households will certainly have to answer in the negative.

It seems highly probable, therefore, that the sharing of one common cup at the Passover—at least in the case of the cup of blessing, the third of the four cups drunk at the Passover, but more probably during the whole meal—was the earlier custom, and that Mark 14. 23 is therefore in agreement with the conditions obtaining at the Passover in the time of Jesus.

[1] G. Beer, *Pesachim* (Giessen, 1912), ad h. l.

[2] P. Billerbeck, 4. 59 and 61; H. L. Strack, *Pesaḥim* (Leipzig, 1911), ad h. l; E. Baneth, *Mischnaioth* 2 (Berlin, 1920), ad h. l., pages 238 n. 8, 239 n. 11.

[3] Pes. 10. 2: "the first cup has been mixed for him; now, according to the Shammaïtes, he pronounces the benediction on the day". The subject of the second clause is without any doubt the Paterfamilias, and therefore he should also be the subject of the first, since there is no sign that the subject of the sentence changes. The same applies to Pes. 10. 7: "the third cup has been mixed for him; now he says the prayer after meat". Here, too, the subject of the second clause is the Paterfamilias. It is assumed, therefore, that his cup is handed round.

(*c*) Finally, we come to the thesis that at the Passover each participant had his own dish—contrary to the assertion of Mark 14. 20. This is derived from a statement of Billerbeck,[1] which refers to the main course alone and not to the preliminary course, and which moreover is in need of certain further modifications. It is indeed true that evidence from the period of the Amoraïm shows that at the Passover each participant had a little table at his side on which the additional fare (fruit jelly, unleavened bread, and bitter herbs) was placed, while the main dishes were put on the common table. Conclusive evidence for this custom is forthcoming only from Babylonia and only in the fourth and fifth centuries;[2] a remark by Palestinian scholars may, however, suggest that this custom was already in existence by the third century.[3] But that, in overcrowded Jerusalem, individual tables should have been already in general use at a feast celebrated under such entirely different circumstances—in part on the roof-tops!—cannot be proved and is utterly improbable.

Thus, there is not one single point on which any contradiction between the description of the Last Supper and the Passover ritual of the earlier period can be demonstrated.

(4) Another, fourth objection refers to Mark 14. 2. The Sanhedrin attempted to arrest Jesus by a ruse: *ἔλεγον γάρ· μὴ ἐν τῇ ἑορτῇ, μήποτε ἔσται θόρυβος τοῦ λαοῦ.* The common translation is, "not during the feast", with the widely accepted conclusion that the decision of the Sanhedrin not to arrest Jesus "during the feast" excludes the Synoptic chronology, according to which Jesus was arrested during the night of the first day of the feast (which began at sunset).[4] But, even assuming this translation to

[1] I. 989; 4. 65 sq., 71 sq.

[2] b. Pes. 115b, *Rabh Shīmī b. 'Āshī* (after A.D. 400). It is likely that the event, reported in the same place as having occurred in the house of *Rabbā bhar Naḥmānī* (died A.D. 330), has to be understood in this sense.

[3] b. Pes. 115b: scholars of the school of R. *Jannai*, who flourished between A.D. 220 and 250.

[4] So J. Wellhausen, *Das Evangelium Marci*, 2nd ed. (Berlin, 1909), 108, 114 sq., followed by E. Schwartz, "Osterbetrachtungen" in *Z.N.W.* 7 (1906), who on p. 23 states with aplomb, "the earliest report which was still free from corrections, Mark 14. 1–2, says explicitly that He (Jesus) was arrested two days before the Passover"; C. G. Montefiore, *The*

be correct, the conclusion rests upon precarious foundations. How do we know that the decision of the Sanhedrin was implemented? For it was taken before Judas had offered to play the traitor, which provided an unexpected opportunity of arresting Jesus at the very time of the feast.

But quite apart from this, the interpretation of the words μὴ ἐν τῇ ἑορτῇ as a definition of time, which has called forth a whole library of comment, is untenable since it makes no sense. If they are interpreted—in line with the majority of scholars—"not during the feast, but before",[1] they make no sense, because the great mass of pilgrims had already arrived several days before the feast for the performance of the rite of purification, John 11. 55. Therefore, a θόρυβος was threatening on the two days preceding the feast (Mark 14. 1) as much as during the feast itself. If, however, these words are to be understood as "not during the feast, but afterwards",[2] that interpretation is no more satisfactory, since the return of the pilgrims was permitted from the second feast-day, Nīsān the 16th, onwards;[3] and was there

---

Synoptic Gospels, 2nd ed., 1 (London, 1927), 309; M. Dibelius, *Die Formgeschichte des Evangeliums*, 2nd ed. (1933), 181; J. Finegan, *Die Ueberlieferung der Leidens- und Auferstehungs-Geschichte Jesu* (Giessen, 1934), 61 sq., and several others.

[1] F. Spitta, *Beitraege zur Gesch. und Litt. des Urchristentums* 1 (1893), 223; J. Wellhausen, op. cit. 108; id., *Einleitung in die drei ersten Evangelien*, 2nd ed. (Berlin, 1911), 133; K. Bornhaeuser, *Das Wirken des Christus durch Worte und Taten* (Guetersloh, 1921), 195; E. Klostermann, *Das Markus Evangelium*, 2nd ed. (Tuebingen, 1926), 157; H. Lietzmann, *Messe und Herrenmahl* (Bonn, 1926), 212; O. Holtzmann, *Das N.T. nach dem Stuttgarter griechischen Text* 1 (Giessen, 1926), 61; C. G. Montefiore, *The Synoptic Gospels*, 2nd ed., 1 (London, 1927), 309 sq.; M. Dibelius, "Das historische Problem der Leidensgeschichte" in *Z.N.W.* 30 (1931), 194 sq.; M. Goguel, *Das Leben Jesu* (Zuerich, 1934), 290; J. Finegan, op. cit. 3, and many others.

[2] H. J. Holtzmann, *Die Synoptiker*, 3rd ed. (Tuebingen-Leipzig, 1901), 171; Th. Zahn, *Das Evangelium des Matthaeus*, ad Matth. 26. 5; G. Dalman, *Jesus-Jeschua* (Leipzig, 1922), 91; A. Schlatter, *Der Evangelist Matthaeus* (Stuttgart, 1929), 701; E. Lohmeyer, *Das Evangelium des Markus* (1937), 290 sq.; and others.

[3] P. Billerbeck 2. 147 sq. According to Luke 24. 13 sq., two followers of Jesus left Jerusalem on Nīsān the 17th, cf. infra, p. 53 n. 3, and they regard Jesus as yet another returning pilgrim, cf. ibid. 24. 18, παροικεῖς.

any guarantee that Jesus would be in Jerusalem after the seven days of the feast were over? Lastly, any temporal interpretation of the words *μὴ ἐν τῇ ἑορτῇ* is excluded by the preceding *γάρ*, which is meant to prepare for the words *ἐν δόλῳ*, Mark 14. 1. Jesus has to be arrested by a ruse, so that no tumult be caused among the crowd—this precaution makes sense only if He is supposed to be arrested during the feast.

All these difficulties disappear when it is recognized that *ἑορτή* in our passage has the meaning of "festal assembly, festal crowd".[1] This meaning is found especially in John 7. 11 *ἐζήτουν αὐτὸν ἐν τῇ ἑορτῇ*, the Jews sought Jesus among the festal crowd,[2] and ibid. 2. 23.[3] The same usage is found also in Plotinus (ed. A. Volkmann, Leipzig, 1883-4), *Enn.* 6. 6. 12 *ὄχλος καὶ ἑορτὴ καὶ στρατὸς καὶ πλῆθος*, a passage in which *ἑορτή* is clearly established as meaning the festal crowd by the three co-ordinated nouns,[4] cf. H. G. Liddell—R. Scott, *A Greek-English Lexicon I* (1925), 601b: "*ἑορτή* . . . 4. assembled multitude at a festival." *'Εν τῇ ἑορτῇ* Mark 14. 2, therefore, need not be temporal, but may also be meant locally, in the presence of the multitude, cf. for this frequent use of *ἐν* P. Petrie 2. 4 (6). 16 (B.C. 255/4) *δινὸν γάρ ἐστιν ἐν ὄχλῳ ἀτιμάζεσθαι*, i.e. in the presence of a crowd.[5] Only in this way can an intelligible meaning be given to Mark 14. 1-2: secretly, by craft, Jesus will have to be arrested, for "they said, not at the feast (i.e. in the presence of the crowd), lest there be an uproar of the people". *Μὴ ἐν τῇ ἑορτῇ* corresponds exactly in substance to *ἄτερ ὄχλου* Luke 22. 6 "in the absence of the multitude".[6] If, however, Mark 14. 2 does not fix the time, no conclusion can be

[1] Recognized by G. Bertram, *Die Leidensgesch. Jesu u. d. Christuskult* (Goettingen, 1922), 13, cf. J. Pickl, *Messiaskoenig Jesus* (1935), 62 sq.

[2] So also R. Bultmann, *Das Evangelium des Johannes* (1941), 222 n. 2.

[3] A. Loisy, *Les Évangiles synoptiques* 2 (1908), 491.

[4] "The passage is particularly telling, because it intends to give a definition, and this definition is accounted generally accepted and self-evident," G. Bertram, op. cit. 13 n. 2.

[5] *The Flinders Petrie Papyri*, ed. Mahaffy and Smyly (1891-1905). Cf. W. Bauer, *Woerterbuch* s. v. *ἐν* I 3.

[6] Cf. also Mark 11. 32 *ἐφοβοῦντο τὸν λαόν* par., and Jesus' rebuke, Mark 14. 49 par.

drawn from it for the chronology of the day of Jesus' death or the character of His Last Supper.[1]

(5) The two most important objections, however, have still to be dealt with. The first maintains that many of the incidents reported in Mark 14. 17—15. 47 could not possibly have taken place on Nīsān the 15th, which, as the first feast-day of the Passover, had the character of a holy day and a Sabbath.[2] Among them are (1) Jesus' retreat to Gethsemane on the night of the Passover; (2) the carrying of arms by the Temple guards and some of the disciples on that night; (3) the meeting of the Sanhedrin and the trial and condemnation of Jesus during the night of the Passover; (4) the tearing of the robe at the session of the court; (5) the participation of the Jews in the session of a Roman court on the morning of the feast-day; (6) the coming of Simon of Cyrene ἀπ' ἀγροῦ on the morning of Nīsān the 15th; (7) the execution of Jesus on the high feast-day; (8) the purchase of the shroud for the body in the evening of the feast-day; (9) the taking down of the body of Jesus, His burial, and the rolling of the stone; (10) the preparation of spices and ointments. This much discussed objection was examined simultaneously but independently[3] by G. Dalman in *Jesus-Jeschua* 86–98, and P. Billerbeck 2. 815–34, who both had an exceptionable knowledge of the material, and both agree in rejecting it.

[1] Equally erroneous is the conclusion drawn from 1 Cor. 11. 23 *ὅτι ὁ κύριος Ἰησοῦς ἐν τῇ νυκτὶ ᾗ παρεδίδοτο* . . . , that this remark makes it impossible to regard the Last Supper as a Passover. The scholars holding this view claim that if the Last Supper had been a Passover Paul would have mentioned it in preference to the colourless phrase "in the night that He was betrayed". This *argumentum e silentio* overlooks altogether the liturgical character of the passage. "The night that He was betrayed" is no more a chronological statement than *μὴ ἐν τῇ ἑορτῇ* (Mk. 14. 2), but these words which are derived from an earlier tradition and echo Is. 53, have a ring of "history of salvation", cf. for a detailed argument infra, p. 107 sq., and E. Lohmeyer, *Theol. Rundschau* 9 (1937), 185. In their present place they are meant to remind the Corinthians of the seriousness of the Eucharist, in view of the abuses which they had admitted into their celebrations.

[2] Exod. 12. 16; Lev. 23. 7; Num. 28. 18. Still, the cooking of food was permitted on Nīsān the 15th: Exod. 12. 16; Beza 5. 2.

[3] Dalman's book appeared in 1922, at the time when P. Billerbeck had already given the last touches to his *magnum opus*.

The ten objections mentioned are not of equal importance, but vary greatly in weight. (*a*) Some of them rest upon ignorance of the *Halakha* and should not be brought forward again. That applies to (1): certainly Jerusalem could not be left during the night of the Passover; but while the paschal lamb had to be eaten within its walls, a district of greater Jerusalem had been created, where it was permitted to spend the night of the Passover. Gethsemane lay within the boundaries of this district, cf. supra, p. 15 n. 4, 31 no. 9. (2) According to the earlier *Halakha*, which was in force at the time of Jesus, the carrying of arms on a Sabbath (or a feast-day) was permitted, Shab. 6. 4 (according to R. *'Eli'ezer ben Hyrkanos*, the constant champion of the earlier tradition). (4) The tearing of the robe at the session of the court was not contrary to the rules: "he who tears his robe in indignation or because of a death (on a Sabbath) . . . is free of guilt", Shab. 13. 3. (9) The express rule of the Torah, Deut. 21. 23, "his body shall not remain all night upon the tree, but thou shalt in any wise bury him on that day", was of course also applicable on a feast-day. (10) "It is permitted (on a Sabbath or a feast-day) to do anything necessary for a dead person, (e.g.) to anoint and to wash him; only that no limb of his must be moved", Shab. 23. 5. (Notice also that the preparing [perhaps, laying out] of spices and ointments is mentioned in Luke 23. 56 alone, whereas Mark 16. 1 records that they were purchased after the Sabbath.) (*b*) Two objections refer to measures which could not be taken by the Jewish authorities, but only by the Roman governor. This applies to (5), which moreover arises from the popular acclamation on the occasion of the use of the Passover amnesty (Mark 15. 6 par.), so that Pilate may not even have intended originally to sit in court, and (7): Polycarp of Smyrna too was executed by the Romans σαββάτῳ μεγάλῳ,[1] on (February the 23rd, A.D. 155 or) February the 22nd, A.D. 156,[2] and the Jews were not prevented by the Sabbath from making a notable contribution to the carrying of wood and sprigs to the pile.[3] (Notice also that Luke 4. 29 takes place on a Sabbath and John 10. 22 sq. on the feast of the Dedication of the Temple. Cf. also an analogous case from an earlier time:

[1] *Mart. Polyc.* 21, cf. 8. 1, ὄντος σαββάτου μεγάλου.

[2] W. Bauer, *Das Johannesevangelium*, 3rd ed. (1933), 215.

[3] *Mart. Polyc.* 13. 1.

Jōsē bhen Jō'ezer from *Zerēdhā* suffered martyrdom[1] in 162 B.C. (or 88 B.C.) on a Sabbath[2]). It is arguable that the crowds at the feast may have appeared to the Romans to provide an opportunity for using the three executions as an impressive deterrent. (*c*) One of the objections rests upon arbitrary assumptions: (6) The report that Simon of Cyrene came *ἀπ' ἀγροῦ* (Mark 15. 21) contradicts the chronology of the Synoptists only on the assumption that he had been working in the fields. This, however, is most unlikely so early in the morning, Mark 15. 25; whereas it was quite in order for Simon to go to his field within the distance permitted on a Sabbath (2,000 cubits, i.e. 1,000 yards, from the circumference of a built-up urban district), if for instance he wanted to fetch some wood or the parts of an animal which had had to be destroyed.[3] Furthermore, it is not even certain whether *ἔρχεσθαι ἀπ' ἀγροῦ* has to be translated as "to come from the field": *ἀπ' ἀγροῦ* may mean "from the farm" or "from the village",[4] or even "from outside the town".[5] Simon may have lived outside the city walls,[6] and may have been on his way to the Temple for morning prayer at 9 a.m. (cf. Acts 3. 1)[7]—if he were a Jew. But was Simon of Cyrene a Jew? No word is said about this. Simon was a common name among Greeks as well. If he were not a Jew the feast-day was no concern of his. (*d*) Only two objections remain to be considered seriously. (8) According to Mark 15. 46, Joseph of Arimathaea purchased the shroud on Good Friday (*ἀγοράσας σινδόνα*). The report, which is found only in Mark, seems to contradict the rule forbidding buying and selling on the Sabbath. However, the necessities of life had led to certain relaxations of the rule: merchants were allowed to hand out foodstuffs to their

[1] Ber. R. 65 ad Gen. 27. 27, edited with variants in G. Dalman, *Aramaeische Dialektproben*, 2nd ed. (1927), 35.

[2] So the editions of Constantinople (1512), Venice (1545), and Saloniki (1593).

[3] Cf. the evidence in P. Billerbeck 2. 828 sq.

[4] The disciples of Emmaus went *εἰς ἀγρόν* (to their village), Ps.-Mark 16. 12.

[5] Cf. the evidence in G. Dalman, *Jesus-Jeschua* (1922), 94.

[6] On the inhabitants of the immediate neighbourhood of Jerusalem in N.T. time, cf. my article "Die Einwohnerzahl Jerusalems zur Zeit Jesu" in *Zeitschr. d. Deutsch. Palaestina-Vereins* 66 (1943), 28–31. Inside the city walls there lived about 20,000 and outside 5–10,000, pp. 28, 31.

[7] G. Dalman, op. cit. 94.

customers if no remarks were made about measurements, weight, or price.[1] The Passover in particular is discussed in Shab. 23. 1: "if the day of preparation for the Passover (Nīsān the 14th) in Jerusalem fell on a Sabbath, he (the purchaser) leaves his cloak (as a pledge) with him (the vendor),[2] and eats[3] his paschal lamb, and settles his debt after the feast-day". A coffin and a shroud could belong to the essentials of life as much as foodstuffs, especially if—as in the year of Jesus' death—two days of rest came together. In the Palestinian climate an early funeral, at latest on the day after the actual death, was essential. About the coffin and the shroud it is said, "and (on the Sabbath) he tells him: If you cannot have it at the arranged place fetch it from such and such a place; and if you cannot have it for one Mina (100 *denarii*) then get it for 200 (*denarii*); *R. Jōsē bhen Jehūdhā* (about A.D. 180) added: Only he must not mention the exact price".[4] Adding to this that the rule prohibiting work on the feast-day was less stringent than that for the Sabbath[5] and that an express command of the Torah required the burial of Jesus on the same day as His death (Deut. 21. 23), cf. supra p. 50, then the report about the purchase of the shroud on the first day of the Passover should not be regarded as a difficulty at all. The only serious difficulty is (3): could the sitting of the Sanhedrin and the condemnation of Jesus take place on the night of the Feast? "No trials on feast-days" was a valid law.[6] And it must be emphasized that this objection applies to the Johannine as well as to the Synoptic account: for neither could criminal trials be held on the day of preparation for a feast.[7] That is to say, if the objection holds, it does not favour the Johannine date of Nīsān the 14th for Good Friday as over against the Synoptic dating, as is commonly but erroneously supposed, but it weighs equally against both

[1] P. Billerbeck, 2. 832.

[2] This is preceded by rules about the borrowing of wine, oil, and bread.

[3] Read with the majority of ancient MSS. ואוכל (and not ונוטל), as appears from the critical apparatus of H. L. Strack, *Schabbath* (1890), 51.

[4] Tos. Shab. 17. 13 (137. 14); b. Shab. 151a.

[5] Cf. supra, p. 49 n. 2.

[6] Beza 5. 2; Tos. Yom ṭobh 4. 4 (207. 15); Philo, *De migr. Abr.* §91 (2. 286. 10), cf. P. Billerbeck, 2. 815–20.

[7] Sanh. 4. 1; b. Sanh. 35a.

the Synoptic and Johannine chronology of Jesus death.[1] The decisive text is Deut. 17. 12, which prescribes the death penalty for anyone who opposed the decisions of the priests and judges of the High Court in Jerusalem. As a deterrent such a case was to be made public: "and all the people shall hear and fear and do no more presumptuously", Deut. 17. 13. Because "all the people" were assembled in Jerusalem only on the three feasts of pilgrimage, it was concluded from Deut. 17. 13 and its parallels (ibid. 21. 21; 13. 12) that the execution in these cases which had been singled out by the Torah—despite the prohibition of executions on a feast-day—had to take place בָּרֶגֶל, "during the feast". "The son who dishonours and molests (his parents), Deut. 21. 18 sq.; the scribe who rebels against the (supreme) court, Deut. 17. 8 sq.; the seducer (to idolatry), Deut. 13. 7 sq.; he who turns (a whole village to idol worship), Deut. 13. 13 sq.; the false prophet and the false witnesses are not executed at once, but they shall be brought to Jerusalem to the Sanhedrin and be kept in prison until the Feast, and their sentence shall be executed at the Feast. For it is said: And all the people shall hear and fear and do no more presumptuously, Deut. 17. 13."[2] Here was such a case. Jesus was regarded by His adversaries as a false prophet. Therefore He had to be tried at once, so that the execution could take place, according to the rule of Deut. 17. 13, before "all the people", i.e. on Nīsān the 15th, for on Nīsān the 16th[3] the Passover pilgrims were already at liberty to go home.[4] We see, therefore, that there is nothing in the Passion narrative which is inconsistent with the date of Nīsān the 15th.

[1] It cannot be argued either that John's Gospel does not know of any condemnation of Jesus by the Sanhedrin, but only of a "purely personal" ruling of Annas and Caiaphas—so G. Dalman, *Jesus-Jeschua* (Leipzig, 1922), 92. With R. Bultmann, *Das Evangelium des Johannes* (1941), 500, I feel sure that John 18. 19 means to describe an official hearing in the presence of the High Council, as in Mark 14. 53 par.

[2] Tos. Sanh. 11. 7 (432. 1) par.: b. Sanh. 89a (Bar.), *R. 'Aqībhā* (died about A.D. 135). Luke 13. 33 makes it evident that the rule to execute the false prophet in Jerusalem was actually in force at the time of Jesus.

[3] If this day fell on a Sabbath: on Nīsān the 17th. So Luke 24. 13 sq.

[4] Cf. supra, p. 47 n. 3. This disproves Lietzmann's suggestion, *Messe und Herrenmahl* (Bonn, 1926), 213 n. 1, that *bāreghel* might refer to all the subsequent days "on which 'all people' would still be in Jerusalem". And the preceding days did not belong to the Feast.

(6) We now come to the chief objection which is raised against the Synoptic representation of the Last Supper as a Passover: the report of the Fourth Gospel. We have seen (p. 5) that the phrase *φαγεῖν τὸ πάσχα*, John 18. 28, implies that Jesus was crucified before the evening of the Passover. But the following has to be borne in mind:

(*a*) John 13. 1 *πρὸ δὲ τῆς ἑορτῆς τοῦ πάσχα* can hardly be used in support of this chronology, for the time-reference here clearly belongs to *εἰδώς*,[1] and it simply asserts that Jesus already knew before the feast of the Passover that His death was imminent. Caution is again required in interpreting the words *ἦν δὲ παρασκευὴ τοῦ πάσχα* in John 19. 14. For it is not at all certain that *παρασκευὴ τοῦ πάσχα*—a Greek formulation of an Aramaic thought—should represent an Aramaic *status constructus* עֲרוּבַת פַּסְחָא, i.e. the day of preparation for the Passover,[2] because such a *status constructus* cannot be found in early Aramaic.[3] Rather, as C. C. Torrey[4] in discussing a view of P. Billerbeck[5] has shown, the expression *παρασκευὴ τοῦ πάσχα* can also be the translation of an Aramaic genitive= עֲרוּבְתָּא דִי פַּסְחָא, i.e. the Friday of the Passover week.[6] For even if such a genitive cannot be cited from early

[1] So already the Greek commentators, cf. Th. Zahn, *Das Evangelium des Johannes*, 5/6 ed. (Leipzig, 1921), 531; W. Bauer, *Das Johannes-evangelium*, 3rd ed. (1933), 167; R. Bultmann, *Das Evangelium des Johannes* (1941), 352.

[2] Analogous to ערובת ריש שתא, meaning the day before the New Year; ערובת צומא רבא, meaning the day before the Feast of Reconciliation.

[3] Whilst Hebrew עֶרֶב פְּסָחִים or עֶרֶב הַפֶּסַח, meaning the day of preparation for the Passover, Nīsān the 14th, is common already in the time of the Mishna, e.g. Pes. 10. 1, and often elsewhere, the analogous Aramaic *status constructus* עֲרוּבַת פַּסְחָא is not found anywhere in earlier times. The expression first occurs in the Midhrash to the book of Ruth 1. 17 (10b. 5), one of the most recent Midhrashim. In early Aramaic the day of preparation for the Passover is either called מעלי יומא דפיסחא, i.e. "the beginning of the Passover day", Targ. Jer. I. ad Gen. 14. 13, or יומא דמיקמי חגא, i.e. "the day preceding the Feast", ibid. ad Exod. 12. 15, as appears from the usage of the Targum.

[4] "The Date of the Crucifixion according to the Fourth Gospel" in *Journ. Bibl. Lit.* 50 (1931), 232 sq.

[5] P. Billerbeck, 2. 834–7.

[6] Cf. שבת בפסח, Sifra Lev. 23. 15, meaning the Sabbath of the Passover week.

Aramaic sources, it is a fact that עֲרוּבְתָּא, meaning Friday, is a well-known usage in earlier Aramaic as well as in earlier Syriac.[1] No certain verdict is possible.

(*b*) There are traces of a Synoptic dating in the Fourth Gospel, and indeed in the account of the Last Supper, John 13. 2 sq. The fact that John refers to the same meal as that which is described in Mark 14. 17 sq. par. is shown by the betrayal scene (cf. John 13. 18 sq. with Mark 14. 18 sq. par.) as well as by the ensuing walk to Gethsemane (John 18. 1 sq. as compared with Mark 14. 26 sq. par.).[2] Some of John's remarks presuppose that this was a passover meal.[3] He tells us that the Last Supper took place in Jerusalem, in spite of the overcrowding of the city by the pilgrims who had come to celebrate the Passover, cf. John 11. 55; 12. 12, 18, 20. John too records that the Last Supper was held at an unusual hour: it lasted right into the night. John also tells us that Jesus ate it along with the closest circle of His disciples. Moreover, John witnesses to the fact that the Last Supper was a ceremonial meal: those who took part reclined at table. John too reports the fact that Jesus did not return to Bethany after the meal, but went to a garden on the other side of the valley of Kidron. Lastly, John 13. 29b also belongs here: the supposition of some of the disciples that Judas was sent to distribute alms to the poor during the night may very well refer to the night of the Passover.

[1] The protest of S. Zeitlin, "The Date of the Crucifixion according to the Fourth Gospel" in *Journ. Bibl. Lit.* 51 (1932), 268–70, is utterly unconvincing, because Zeitlin in the most incredible way pays no attention to the N.T. usage in his statements on παρασκευή and πάσχα. Zeitlin's first thesis that παρασκευή is an expression used exclusively by Gentile writers for the eve of Sabbaths and feast-days may be supported by the decree of Augustus in Jos., *Ant.* 16. 6. 2. §163, but is invalidated by John 19. 14, for here the evening is not meant, but the sixth hour, from 11 a.m. to noon, and by Did. 8. 1, for here παρασκευή means the whole Friday. How untenable his second thesis is, that πάσχα (or פסח, פסחא) could only have the meaning of the paschal lamb, not of the seven days of the Feast, should have been made evident to Zeitlin by one glance at Mark 14. 1 par.; John 2. 13; 11. 55; 12. 1; 18. 39; Acts 12. 4, and the Gospel of the Ebionites 8a ed. E. Preuschen, *Antilegomena*, 2nd ed. (Giessen, 1905).

[2] Cf. also the announcement of Peter's denial, John 13. 36–8; Mark 14. 29–31 par.

[3] Cf. supra, pp. 14–31.

The other assumption that Jesus sent Judas away to make some last-minute (τάχιον John 13. 27) purchases for the feast may also be explained, if it happened on the night of the Passover; for in that case there was great urgency, because the next day was a feast-day followed by the Sabbath.[1] Otherwise the urgency would be inexplicable, as another whole day would have been available for the purchases.[2]

The Johannine report, therefore, is not uniform. Rather does it show, alongside the dating of the Last Supper on the eve of the Passover—which is only unambiguously stated in John 18. 28—traces of another tradition, according to which the Last Supper was a Passover.[3]

(*c*) The connexion between the Passion and the Passover seems to be severed by John's dating of the Last Supper on the night before the Passover; but in actual fact this connexion becomes even more impressive.[4] For by putting the events of the Passion twenty-four hours earlier, the crucifixion of Jesus is made to coincide with the killing of the paschal lambs. While there were hundreds and thousands of paschal lambs being killed in the Temple, the true Paschal Lamb, of whom according to the will of God no bone should be broken (John 19. 36, cf. Exod. 12. 46–LXX: 12. 10–; Num. 9. 12), died unrecognised outside the gates of the city. This comparison between Jesus and the Paschal Lamb is very old (cf. 1 Cor. 5. 7; 1 Pet. 1. 19, and also Rev. 5. 6, 9, 12; 12. 11; John 1. 29, 36). Paul already presupposes its existence, as appears from the way in which he argues in 1 Cor. 5. 7.[5] It was probably an established part not only of the Pauline but also of the early Christian *Passa-Haggādhā* in general. It was possibly the popularity and vividness of this comparison

[1] On the possibility of purchasing something during the night of the Feast cf. supra, p. 51 sq., sub (*d*).

[2] P. Billerbeck 2. 843, 852 sq.; C. C. Torrey op. cit. 230.

[3] "13. 21–30. Jesus and His disciples are here still at table and in fact at the passover meal, i.e., the Holy Supper of the Synoptists; in contradiction to 13. 1; 18. 28; 19. 14—it is idle to shut one's eyes to this contradiction", so J. Wellhausen, *Das Evangelium Johannis* (1908), 60.

[4] E. Gaugler in Daluz-Ramseyer-Gaugler, *La Sainte-Cène* (1945), 58 sq.

[5] J. Weiss, *Der erste Korintherbrief* (1910), ad h. l.

which—perhaps all unconsciously—affected the recollection of the events of the Passion and caused them to be antedated by twenty-four hours in that part of the tradition to which the Gospels of John and Peter belong.

(5) *The Eucharistic Words of Jesus within the framework of the Passover*

If then we are entitled to regard the Last Supper as a Passover, we must now set the words which Jesus used within the framework of such a meal. The ritual of the meal, which consisted of the preliminary course and the main meal, is known;[1] it will, therefore, suffice to outline it briefly. It has to be said, however, that the more recent commentaries on St. Mark's Gospel commit grave errors in their descriptions of the Passover ritual. These we shall correct without comment.[2] Nevertheless we must emphasize, for it is essential to our purpose, that unleavened bread was not eaten in the preliminary course[3]—modern commentaries on Mark's Gospel almost unanimously maintain the opposite.[4] Furthermore, let it be noted that for the Pater-

[1] An excellent collection of the sources is found in P. Billerbeck 4. 41–76. H. L. Strack, *Pesaḥim* (1911), 36 sq., may be consulted for information about the present *Sedher* rite. On the history of the rite cf. B. Italiener, etc., *Die Darmstaedter Pessach-Haggadah* (1927).

[2] Even the description of the celebration of the Passover in A. Merx, *Die vier kanonischen Evangelien* 2. 2 (1905), 416 sq., which of late has been frequently referred to, is in need of correction in several places, cf. infra, p. 58 n. 2.

[3] The clearest evidence (j. Pes. 10. 37d. 4–5) may be consulted supra, p. 26 sq. under (5); cf. also the very full commentary on it given by E. Baneth, *Mischnaioth* 2 (Berlin, 1920), 242–5 n. 27. Another clear proof is found in Tos. Pes. 10. 9 (172. 27): "R. *'Eli'ezer* (about A.D. 90, a representative of the old tradition) says: *Ḥōṭephīn* (literal translation: 'to make haste', then 'to do in advance', 'to break bread without benediction,' cf. M. Jastrow, *Dictionary*, 1903=1926, s.v.) the unleavened bread for the small children, lest they fall asleep (during the *Passa-Haggādhā*)."

[4] J. Wellhausen, too, is mistaken when he states, in *Das Evangelium Marci*, 2nd ed. (Berlin, 1909), 111, that the blessing of the bread, Mark 14. 22, belongs to the beginning of the whole meal. J. Finegan, *Die Ueberlieferung der Leidens- und Auferstehungs-Geschichte* (Giessen, 1934), 67 sq., even maintains that Mark 14. 22, "in a way which is impossible in Jewish custom", puts "the breaking of the bread right in

familias to distribute half an unleavened loaf among the guests after the meal, but before saying grace, is a custom of late origin.[1] Any description of the Last Supper which refers to this custom[2] will therefore be incorrect.

A. The preliminary course:[3]

Word of blessing (the blessing of the feast-day [*Ḳiddūsh*] and of the cup)[4] spoken by the Paterfamilias over the first cup.[5]

The preliminary dish, consisting amongst other things of green herbs, bitter herbs, and a sauce made of fruit purée.[6]

The meal proper (cf. C.) is served but not yet eaten; the second cup is mixed and put in its place but not yet drunk.

B. Passover-Liturgy:

Passa-Haggādhā by the Paterfamilias (in Aramaic).

First part of the Passover *Hallēl*[7] (in Hebrew).

The second cup is drunk.

C. The main meal:

The Grace spoken by the Paterfamilias over the unleavened bread.

---

the middle of the meal". More fatal still than these misstatements themselves are the drastic manipulations of the text of the Passion story by literary criticism, which have again and again been based upon them.

[1] This usage first arose together with the late custom, mentioned above, p. 43 sq., of saying the opening prayer over a broken piece of unleavened bread.

[2] So A. Merx, op. cit. 428; R. Eisler, "Das letzte Abendmahl" in *Z.N.W.* 24 (1925), 161–92, cf. the devastating criticism of H. Lietzmann, ibid. 25 (1926), 1–5; P. Fiebig in *Neues Saechsisches Kirchenblatt* 42 (1935), 376.

[3] The sources for the post-biblical Passover tradition have been collected by me in *Die Passahfeier der Samaritaner* (Giessen, 1932), 54.

[4] This was the custom among the Shammaïtes. The Hillelites prescribed the reverse order, Pes. 10. 2; Tos. Pes. 10. 2 (172. 14).

[5] This was the cup of the *Ḳiddūsh*, fully discussed supra, p. 21 sq.

[6] Pes. 10. 3; Tos. Pes. 10. 9 (173. 6), cf. the cry of the Jerusalem spice pedlars, infra, p. 59. The fruit purée (*ḥarōseth*) was a mixture of squashed and grated fruits (as figs, dates, raisins, apples and almonds), with spices and vinegar. The preliminary dish was meant to stimulate the appetite.

[7] Cf. supra, p. 31 n. 1.

The meal consisting of the paschal lamb,[1] unleavened bread, bitter herbs (Exod. 12. 8) with fruit purée and wine.

A prayer (*birkath hammāzōn*) over the third cup.

D. The close:

The second part of the Passover *Hallēl*[2] (in Hebrew).

The praise over the fourth cup.[3]

The fact that the ritual outlined here was substantially that of the time of Jesus can be shown with the help of numerous individual observations. With regard to the food and drink mentioned, the eating of the paschal lamb, the unleavened bread and the bitter herbs was prescribed already in the Old Testament, Exod. 12. 8, etc. The fact that fruit purée was added to them in New Testament times is shown by the cry of the Jerusalem spice pedlars, noted by R. *'El'āzār b. R. Zādhōq* (born in Jerusalem between A.D. 35 and 40):[4] "come and buy spices for your commanded duty (of the fruit purée)";[5] and the drinking of wine is presupposed as an ancient custom in the book of Jubilees,[6] which dates from about 120 B.C.[7] As regards the liturgical rites, the sequence of the blessings of the feast-day and of the cup at the initial benediction was already a subject of discussion between the

[1] Before the paschal lamb it was permissible to eat a voluntary sacrifice, (an ox or a head of small cattle), Pes. 6. 4 sq.

[2] Cf. supra, p. 31, n. 1.

[3] The earliest witnesses for the four cups are: Pes. 10. 1; Tos. Pes. 10. 1 (172. 13); b. Pes. 108b (Bar.). A. Merx, *Das Evangelium des Matthaeus* (Berlin, 1902), 386; *Die Evangelien des Markus und Lukas* (Berlin, 1905), 151 has expressed doubts with regard to the early date of the fourth cup. They arise from Mark 14. 25. There Jesus says before the second part of the *Hallēl* that He would drink no more wine upon earth. This argument is, however, without weight if Mark 14. 25, as we believe, cf. infra, p. 165 sq., refers to a vow of abstinence on the part of Jesus. G. Dalman, *Die Worte Jesu*, 2nd ed. (1930), 402; *Allgemeine Evang.-Luth. Kirchenzeitung* 64 (1931), 797 sq., has also expressed doubts whether the rabbinical rule for the drinking of wine at the Passover (the four cups of obligation) was generally enforced at the time of Jesus. For our investigation this question is of no import.

[4] Cf. A. Schlatter, *Die Tage Trajans und Hadrians* (Guetersloh, 1897), 80 sq.

[5] b. Pes. 116a, cf. P. Billerbeck 4. 65; the same is found anonymously in j. Pes. 10. 37d. 9.

[6] Jub. 49. 6, 9.

[7] On the date cf. S. Klein, "Palaestinisches im Jubilaeenbuch" in *Zeitschr. des Deutsch. Palaestina-Vereins* 57 (1934), 16 sq.

Shammaïtes and the Hillelites.[1] A remark of *Rābbān Gamlī'ēl II.*[2] is preserved about the *Passa-Haggādhā*, which grew out of Exod. 12. 26 sq.; 13. 8, and the antiquity of the *Hallēl* is guaranteed by another discussion between the Shammaïtes and the Hillelites,[3] by Philo,[4] and by a Jerusalem proverb from the time before the destruction of the temple.[5]

The preceding arguments leave no doubt that, if the Last Supper was a Passover, the Word of institution over the bread was spoken by Jesus in connexion with the grace at the beginning of the main meal. This was the only occasion on which the thanksgiving for the bread was said, since no bread was eaten with the preliminary course at the passover meal. As regards the Word of institution spoken over the wine, this can only have been said in connexion with the Grace (Mark 14. 23 εὐχαριστήσας) after the meal, since Mark says that it was spoken after the breaking of the bread (14. 22) and before the Passover *Hallēl*, 14. 26. This is twice endorsed by Paul, first by *μετὰ τὸ δειπνῆσαι*, 1 Cor. 11. 25, and secondly by the expression used ibid. 10. 16, *τὸ ποτήριον τῆς εὐλογίας*.[6] Jesus, therefore, used the prayers before and after the main course of the passover meal to add His Words of institution over the bread and the wine.[7]

[1] Pes. 10. 2, cf. Ber. 8. 1, and supra, p. 22 n. 2.

[2] Pes. 10. 5, cf. supra, p. 32.

[3] Pes. 10. 6, cf. supra, p. 31 n. 1.

[4] In *Spec. Leg.* 2. §148, *μετ' εὐχῶν τε καὶ ὕμνων*, the word "hymns" might refer to the *Hallēl*, cf. Mark 14. 26 *ὑμνεῖν*, and supra, p. 31 n. 4.

[5] j. Pes. 7. 35b. 36, "the Passa is only like an olive, and yet the *Hallēl* breaks through the roofs", meaning that although each guest received a piece of meat no bigger than an olive, the jubilation of the celebrants on the roofs made the roofs collapse—much ado about nothing. The Passover *Hallēl* may be mentioned already in Is. 30. 29; 2 Chron. 30. 21; Jub. 49. 6 and Wisd. 18. 9 ("praises of the fathers" in the night of the Passover).

[6] For *kōs shel berākhā* is the technical term for the cup of wine over which the thanksgiving after the meal has been said, cf. P. Billerbeck 4. 628, 630 sq., and ibid. 58, 72.

[7] So also P. Billerbeck, 4. 75. The fact, therefore, that the Words of institution over the bread and the wine occur together in both Matthew and Mark must not lead to the conclusion that they were said the one immediately after the other. Rather, this reflects the development of the Christian liturgy of the Eucharist, cf. infra, p. 133.

CHAPTER II

The Account of the Last Supper within the Framework of the Passion Story

The investigation of our Lord's eucharistic words themselves is best begun by discussing the problems of literary criticism: what is the position of the account of the Last Supper within the whole framework of the Passion story? This question leads us first to

(1) *A Comparison of Mark's Account of the Passion with that of John*

This comparison is meant to provide standards for assessing the reports on the Last Supper by means of literary criticism. It leads to three conclusions of fundamental importance for the literary criticism of the Passion story.

(1) While John shows only infrequent parallels to the Synoptists in his description of Jesus' ministry,[1] the picture is completely changed from the time of His entry into Jerusalem, i.e. with the beginning of the Passion story. By far the greater part of the account given by Mark 11. 1–16. 8, beginning with the Entry and ending with the empty tomb, is also found—at least in substance, though not with the same detail nor in the same words—in John. The Passion story is thus clearly shown to belong to a very early cycle of tradition.

Mark's Gospel itself supports this view: in chapters 1–10 we

[1] Apart from individual Sayings and points of contact in the subject-matter, John and the Synoptic Gospels have no more than four pericopes in common up to the Passion story: (1) the Baptist and the baptism of Jesus, Mark 1. 2–11 par. and John 1. 19–34; (2) the miraculous draught of fish, Luke 5. 1–11 and John 21. 1–11; (3) the centurion at Capernaum, Matt. 8. 5–13 (Luke 7. 1–10) and John 4. 46–53; (4) the feeding of the multitude and the walking on the water, Mark 6. 30–52 par. and John 6. 1–21. Close similarities exist between (5) the healing of the blind man, Mark 8. 22–6 and John 9. 1–7; and (6) the confession of Peter, Mark 8. 29 (33) and John 6. 69 (71).

find, not, as is frequently maintained, individual stories and sayings, but separate blocks of traditional material (cf. infra, p. 63 sq.), loosely connected without continuous chronological or topographical coherence. Chapter 11 starts a close-packed, purposeful, and coherent narrative with precise geographical and temporal reference, which has only one remote analogy in Mark, in the block of material in Mark 1. 16–38. After their previous divergences this doubly surprising agreement between John and the Synoptists from the story of the triumphal entry into Jerusalem onwards, as well as the integration of Mark's Passion story into the whole framework of Mark's Gospel, proves that the Passion narrative constitutes a coherent and a very early block of the Gospel tradition.

(2) But we can go one step further by observing which items in Mark's Passion narrative, as we now have it, have nothing even approximately corresponding to them in John. John omits three sections, (*a*) the cursing of the fig-tree (Mark 11. 12–14) with its subsequent discussion (11. 20–25); (*b*) the great collection of polemical discussions (chapter 12) and the little apocalypse (chapter 13); (*c*) the account of the preparation of the Passover (14. 12–16). The account of the Last Supper itself (14. 22–25) and of Gethsemane (14. 32–42) do not belong here. For, although they are not found in John, John 18. 1; 12. 27; 18. 11; 14. 31 shows that the Gethsemane tradition was known to him, and the same applies to the Last Supper,[1] which is omitted for special reasons.[2]

It can hardly be an accident that these three items missing from John can be clearly recognized as additional matter in their Marcan setting:

(*a*) The cursing of the fig-tree (Mark 11. 12–14) and the subsequent discussion (vv. 20–25). With regard to these the different place which Matthew gives them in distinction from Mark must be noted, even if it is not so very significant in view

[1] John 6. 51-8. Many scholars find in the story of the washing of the disciples' feet (John 13. 1–20) a reference to the Last Supper: thus just lately O. Cullmann, *Urchristentum und Gottesdienst*, 2nd ed. (1950), 103. E. Lohmeyer, *Z.N.W.* 38 (1939), 90 sq., even regards the passage as a substitute for the Synoptic account of the Last Supper.

[2] Cf. infra, p. 72 sq.

of the numerous changes of place which Matthew makes in the material he takes over from Mark. More important is the fact that both passages are missing from Luke as well as from John. Furthermore, the observations of various literary critics have established traces of editorial work before the cursing of the fig-tree and before and after the subsequent discussion: Mark 11. 11 is a Marcan connecting link;[1] Matthew and Luke are right in making the triumphal entry end with the cleansing of the Temple. Mark 11. 18b–19 shows itself in form[2] and content as one of the many Marcan summaries. Finally, v. 27a is a connecting link:[3] John 2. 18 supports the original connexion between the cleansing of the Temple and the inquiry as to Jesus' authority, a connexion which alone provides a reference for the twice repeated *ταῦτα* (Mark 11. 28), which in its present position has no reference at all. The decisive reason for the view that the cursing of the fig-tree and the subsequent discussion did not belong originally to the Passion narrative is that they separate what clearly hangs together. For the triumphal entry, the cleansing of the Temple and the inquiry into Jesus' authority form an indivisible whole. Not only is it a fact that in the East the enthronement of the king and the restoration of the cult are closely connected as symbols of the new era and of Messianic authority,[4] but also in this particular situation, when Jesus is proclaimed king on His way to the Temple, everything presses towards a conclusion on His arrival at the holy place, which to this day is the goal of all pilgrimages. All these observations lead to one and the same conclusion, that the original sequence—the triumphal entry, the cleansing of the Temple, the inquiry about Jesus' authority—has been disturbed in Mark at some later date by including the story of the cursing of the fig-tree and the subsequent discussion.

(*b*) With regard to chapters 12 and 13, we have to start from the fact that the whole of Mark's Gospel has arisen out of the

[1] Mark 11. 11a is repeated in 15a; *περιβλεψάμενος* is one of Mark's favourite words, and the time given in 11b belongs to the editor, as do the times in 12 and 19 (on v. 19 in particular cf. the next note).

[2] Two favourite expressions of Mark's occur: *διδαχή* and *ἐκπορεύεσθαι*.

[3] In 11. 27 the plural *ἔρχονται* in 27a disagrees with the singular *αὐτοῦ*, *αὐτόν*, *αὐτῷ* in 27b and 28, and *πάλιν* in 27a is one of Mark's favourite words.

[4] Joach. Jeremias, *Jesus als Weltvollender* (1930), 35–44.

combination of a number of blocks of traditional material—a conclusion of fundamental importance for the understanding of its composition.[1] One of these blocks is to be found in the series of polemical discussions in chapter 12, and another in the little apocalypse in chapter 13. It is characteristic of all the various blocks of traditional material in Mark that they are only loosely connected in one whole. In this case the polemical discussion of Jesus' authority, Mark 11. 27b to 33, clearly attracted the great complex of polemical discussions in 12. 1–40,[2] to which is added the little apocalypse of chapter 13.[3] The fact that these two blocks did not originally belong to the Passion narrative is borne out by observing the way in which they interfere with the close-knit structure of the story, which proceeds immediately from 11. 27–33 to 14. 1–2, for it was the cleansing of the Temple which had as its direct result the plot to kill Jesus.

(*c*) In Mark 14. 12 the time given comes as a surprise. Whereas in 14. 1 *ἦν δὲ τὸ πάσχα* (i.e. Nīsān the 14th) *καὶ τὰ ἄζυμα* (i.e. Nīsān the 15th to 21st) *μετὰ δύο ἡμέρας*, a perfectly correct time-statement was offered,[4] the same cannot be said in the case of 14. 12 *καὶ τῇ πρώτῃ ἡμέρᾳ τῶν ἀζύμων, ὅτε*

[1] If Mark 1. 1 (like Matt. 1. 1, "the genealogy of Jesus Christ") is the heading of the chapter, *εὐαγγέλιον Ἰησοῦ Χριστοῦ* is meant as a subjective genitive, "how Jesus Christ began to preach the Gospel"; this heading would therefore cover Mark 1. 1–15. The first obvious block of tradition is Peter's report 1. 16–38, characterized by the constant use of the name *Σίμων* 1. 16 (twice), 29, 30, 36. There follows the collection of polemical debates of increasing violence, 2. 1 to 3. 35; the parables 4. 1–34; the cycle of miracles enacted on the shores of the Galilean sea 4. 35 to 5. 43; the persecution by Herod 6. 14–32. In 6. 34 to 7. 37 and 8. 1–26, two parallel blocks of tradition are added. 8. 27 to 9. 1 has been combined from the catechetical point of view "confession of faith and suffering with Him". 9. 30–50 is the great "catchword complex" of Sayings, introduced by the prediction of the Passion. In 10. 1–31 three Sayings regarding the attitude to marriage, children, and possessions are combined for the purpose of instruction.

[2] The verses 41–4, *ad vocem χήρα* (vv. 40/42) are added as a pendant to 12. 40.

[3] The addition of chapter 13 was probably caused by the identity of place, for 11. 27 takes place *ἐν τῷ ἱερῷ*; 12. 35 the same; 12. 41, Jesus is seated *κατέναντι τοῦ γαζοφυλακίου*, and in 13. 1 He leaves the sanctuary.

[4] Num. 28. 16 sq.; 2 Chron. 35. 17. Post-canonical evidence in P. Billerbeck 1. 988c.

τὸ πάσχα ἔθυον. Here Nīsān the 14th is included in the *ἄζυμα* (cf. supra, p. 2 sq.). Even admitting that G. Dalman's verdict "no Jew who had any knowledge of the law would have spoken of the first day of the Feast when he actually meant the day of preparation for the feast"[1] is too harsh (for in learned discussions on Exod. 12. 15, 18, the description of Nīsān the 14th as "the first day of the Feast" can be found occasionally),[2] still he is substantially correct. For these learned discussions should not be cited in support of Mark 14. 12; rather should it be admitted that this is either a mistranslation[3] or else the faulty expression of a non-Jewish author. It is not only this date but also the description of the disciples that shows Mark 14. 12–16 as coming from a different cycle of tradition than that of 14. 1: in verses 12, 13, 14, 16 they are called *οἱ μαθηταί*, as opposed to *οἱ δώδεκα* in verse 17 (cf. verses 10 and 20). Moreover, verse 17, as shown by *οἱ δώδεκα*, knows nothing about the despatching of the two disciples who, as verse 16 suggests, probably had to see to the killing of the lamb, its transport to the Upper Room and its preparation (otherwise it should read *μετὰ τῶν δέκα*).[4]

All this brings us to an important result. Both the comparison between John's and Mark's Passion narratives and the literary criticism of the Marcan text lead to the conclusion that there was a stage in the development of the Passion story when it contained in brief succession perhaps[5] no more than the triumphal entry, the cleansing of the Temple, the inquiry about Jesus' authority, the announcement of the betrayal, the Last Supper, Gethsemane, the arrest, and so on.

[1] G. Dalman, *Jesus-Jeschua* (1922), 97.

[2] Cf. supra, p. 2 n. 5.

[3] Cf. supra, p. 4 n. 1.

[4] E. Lohmeyer, *Evangelium des Markus* (1937), 300.

[5] An exact determination, let alone a reconstruction of a written source, is quite impossible. It is simply a stage in the development of growing oral traditions, which probably showed very marked local differences. Another example of the same process of growth of traditions may be found in the story of the anointing of Jesus in Bethany, Mark 14. 3–9. On the one hand, it belongs to the material which the Passion-stories of Mark and John have in common, and therefore must be of a comparatively early age; on the other hand, it can be shown to be an accretion, first because it disrupts the connexion between Mark 14. 1 sq. and 10 sq., and secondly because its place is not fixed: in Mark it follows the triumphal entry, whereas in John it precedes it.

(3) Finally, if the sequence of the various incidents in the Passion stories in Mark and John is carefully compared, a third result may be reached. Up to and including the Gethsemane story the arrangement of the material varies greatly:

Mark	John
Mark 11. 1–10	John 12. 12–16
15–17	2. 13–17[1]
24	14. 13 sq.; 16. 23
28	2. 18[1]
14. 1–2; 3–9	11. 47–53; 12. 1–8
10–11	cf. 13. 2
18–21	13. 21–30
26–31	18. 1a; 16. 32; 13. 36–8
32–42	18. 1b; 12. 27; 18. 11; 14. 31

By contrast, however, from the arrest of Jesus onwards (Mark 14. 43–50; John 18. 2–11), John agrees with the Synoptists in the arrangement of the material. The fact that the arrest of Jesus marks a break in the tradition is supported by other evidence as well. For, whereas up to His arrest large portions of the material are not shared by Mark and John, the picture changes completely from that moment onwards: apart from some lesser incidents, dialogues, particular episodes and the like, the Synoptists' report and that of John run parallel with very little extra material in either. The Fourth Gospel in particular keeps its own character, defined by Christ's discourses, even in the Passion narrative right up to the High Priestly prayer (chap. 17); but from 18. 1 sq., i.e. from the arrest of Jesus, there follows a continuous narrative quite in the Synoptic manner.

These observations all show that at a very early stage the Passion story began with the arrest of Jesus.[2] We can adduce evidence for the existence of such a short report: the ancient summary of the Passion in the so-called third announcement of the Passion has as the first of its eight parts the delivering up of

[1] The surprising fact that John tells us of the cleansing of the Temple and the inquiry about Jesus' authority already in the second chapter may be due to an exchange of leaves. On such exchanges of leaves in the Fourth Gospel and other contemporary books cf. E. Schweizer, *Ego Eimi* (Goettingen, 1939), 109–11, and my article "Johanneische Literarkritik" in *Theol. Blaetter* 20 (1941), 41 sq.

[2] The same result has been reached by R. Bultmann, *Geschichte der synopt. Tradition*, 2nd ed. (Goettingen, 1931), 297–308, although on the basis of entirely different considerations.

Jesus to the chief priests and the scribes.[1] This agrees with the evidence from all the other early summaries of the Passion-kerygma. Apart from the betrayal of Jesus, they mention Jesus' condemnation by the Sanhedrin,[2] His transference to Pilate,[3] the proceedings before Pilate,[4] the mocking and scourging,[5] the crucifixion[6] and the burial[7]—there is not one of these old Passion summaries which begins with an incident preceding Judas' betrayal.[8] Finally it must be noticed that the traitor is introduced in Mark 14. 43 with the words *Ἰούδας εἷς τῶν δώδεκα*, as if he were as yet wholly unknown, although he has been already described in Mark 14. 10 as *Ἰούδας Ἰσκαριώθ, ὁ εἷς τῶν δώδεκα* (in this case with reason, since he had been mentioned only once before in the list of the Apostles, Mark 3. 19).

This comparison between the Passion narratives of John and Mark gives us some insight into the living growth of the tradition. If 1 Cor. 15. 3–5 is added to mark the initial stage, the following appear to have been stages of the growth of the tradition:

(1) First to claim our attention is the primitive kerygma of 1 Cor. 15. 3–5, which was originally Aramaic.[9]

(2) The second recognisable stage is a short narrative beginning with the arrest of Jesus.

(3) The third stage (the long narrative) is represented by the material which all four Gospels have in common. The material is now filled out right back to the triumphal entry. Further, the tradition about Peter (Mark 14. 26–42, 53 sq., 66–72), known to all four Gospels, is inserted. This long narrative contains therefore in close succession the triumphal entry, the cleansing of the Temple, the inquiry about Jesus'

[1] Mark 10. 33 sq., cf. ibid. 9. 31; Matt. 26. 2.

[2] Mark 8. 31; 10. 33; Luke 17. 25; Acts 4. 11; 13. 27.

[3] Mark 10. 33; Luke 24. 7, 20; Acts 2. 23; 3. 13; 7. 52.

[4] Acts 3. 13 sq.; 13. 28.

[5] Mark 10. 34; 1 Pet. 2. 23.

[6] Matt. 20. 19; 26. 2; Luke 24. 7, 20; Acts 2. 23, 36; 4. 10; 5. 30; 10. 39; 13. 29; 1 Cor. 1. 17 sq., 23; 2. 2; Gal. 3. 1; 1 Pet. 2. 24.

[7] 1 Cor. 15. 4; Acts 13. 29.

[8] 1 Cor. 11. 23 *ὁ κύριος Ἰησοῦς ἐν τῇ νυκτὶ ᾗ παρεδίδοτο*, the words introducing the report of Paul about the Last Supper, provide us with yet another testimony for the fact that the betrayal at night belonged already at an early time to the Passion-kerygma.

[9] Cf. infra, p. 130.

authority, the announcement of the betrayal, the Last Supper, the prophecy of the denial, Gethsemane, the arrest of Jesus, His trial before the Sanhedrin, Peter's denial, the story of Barabbas, the condemnation by Pilate, the crucifixion, the empty tomb. There is no reason to assume that this third stage of the tradition ever attained written form.

(4) The Passion narrative was expanded by the addition of particular incidents and blocks of traditional material into the forms which we have today in the four Gospels.[1]

It goes without saying that these four stages are only the milestones of a much more colourful and complicated development.

(2) *The Accounts of the Last Supper*

The picture which we have just drawn on a large canvas is repeated on a smaller scale when the narratives of the Last Supper (Mark 14. 12–26; Matt. 26. 17–30; Luke 22. 7–39; John 13. 1–30) are subjected to the detailed scrutiny of literary criticism. They are blocks of tradition consisting of very diverse elements.

This fact is most conspicuously evident in Mark, whose account is closely followed by Matthew. The three sections of Mark's report belong to three totally different strata of tradition. (1) We have just seen that the preparation of the Upper Room (Mark 14. 12–16 par.) is a late section. (2) The announcement of the betrayal at the Last Supper (Mark 14. 17–21 par.) is common to all four Gospels, and must therefore be regarded as part of what we have called the longer narrative (supra, p. 67, No. 3). Since Mark, Luke, and John give independent accounts of this announcement, the tradition that it took place at the Last Supper must be an old one. (3) When Mark and Matthew introduce the account proper of the Last Supper (Mark 14. 22–25 par.) with a resumptive introduction (Mark 14. 22 *καὶ ἐσθιόντων αὐτῶν* is a duplicate of 14. 18 *καὶ ἀνακειμένων αὐτῶν καὶ ἐσθιόντων*), when this account is unconnected with what precedes it in that it contains no reference to the preparations mentioned in verses

[1] The way in which this filling-out process took place can best be seen by means of a comparison of Matthew chapters 21–28 with Mark chapters 11–16.

12–16, and when Mark's usually plain style gives place to a solemn, stylised speech[1]—all this can be explained quite simply by the fact that every account of the Last Supper had to revert at this point to a liturgical formula, the wording of which had been fixed long before and had become common property through its use in the cult. This reversion to a liturgical formula was a matter of course for Luke as well, and Paul confirms its independent existence and its great antiquity.

It is very likely that Luke's account (22. 7–39) follows the special Lucan source from verse 15 onwards. For wherever Luke follows Mark in his Gospel he also keeps to Mark's arrangement of the material most faithfully, and thus we find only two insignificant deviations, Luke 6. 17–19; 8. 19–21,[2] until we come to the Passion narrative. Luke, therefore, in contrast to Matthew was an enemy of rearrangement. The result is that any deviations in order must be regarded as indications that Luke is not following Mark. In Luke's account of the Last Supper there is a large number of such deviations from Mark: the Eschatological Saying comes before the words of institution (Luke 22. 15–18); on the other hand, the announcement of the betrayal follows them (22. 21–23); the lament over the traitor precedes the speculations of the disciples (22. 22); the announcement of the denial is made before the departure to Gethsemane (22. 33 sq.). These deviations show that Luke's report from 22. 15 onwards is not an extension of Mark's but comes from his special source; only the preceding story of the preparation of the Upper Room (22. 7–13) appears to be taken from Mark and inserted into Luke's own material (when Luke incorporated Mark's account into his own independent narrative).[3] In the middle

[1] Mark 14. 22a, for instance, appears almost as if it were a liturgical rubric, cf. infra, p. 108.

[2] K. Grobel, *Formgeschichte und synoptische Quellenanalyse* (1937), 87.

[3] I feel certain that Luke incorporated Mark's material into his own and not vice versa. For this hypothesis at least one reason may be mentioned here: wherever Luke reports a story in a form different from that of Mark, e.g. the Nazareth sermon in 4. 16–30; the calling of Peter in 5. 1–11; the anointing of Jesus in 7. 36–50; the greatest commandment in 10. 25–8; the story of the fig-tree in 13. 6–9, etc., he has it in another context than Mark (only the story of the temptation in 4. 1–13 takes the same place). In all these cases Luke was in possession of two

of Luke's account of the Last Supper there is the conjunction of the two eschatological Sayings (22. 15–18) with the two eucharistic words (22. 19–20). The different origin of these two sections is evident, e.g. in the change from the indefinite *ποτήριον* (22. 17) to *τὸ ποτήριον* (v. 20): the Saying about the Passover comes from Luke's special source, the eucharistic words from the liturgical tradition. The fact that the subsequent Sayings are also diverse in origin (22. 24–38) is made evident, for example, by the change from the (older) name of *Σίμων* used in v. 31 to the (later) *Πέτρε* in v. 34, and also by a comparison with their various parallels.[1]

Finally, John's account of the Last Supper consists of two elements, the washing of the disciples' feet (13. 1–20) and the announcement of the betrayal (13. 21–30). The latter, as we know, formed part of the longer narrative; the former, a special tradition of John's, is twice explained by Jesus in verses 6–11 and 12–20, which shows that this section had already had a fairly long history.[2] Its early date is also shown by numerous Semitisms.[3]

We therefore arrive at the following conclusions:

(1) The so-called words of institution (Mark 14. 22–24 par.) are the earliest part of the account of the Last Supper, and they may be very nearly as old as the primitive kerygma.

different forms of the same subject-matter, the one in Mark and the other in his own special source, and each time he preferred the latter and abandoned that of Mark. The really significant fact is that Luke did not put his story in the same place where it is found in Mark, but produced it in an entirely different context. In view of the fact that Luke, as we have said, was opposed to rearrangement, it must be assumed that the passages in question already had their fixed positions when he came to know Mark's Gospel. On the problem of Proto-Luke cf. B. H. Streeter, *The Four Gospels*, 5th ed. (1936), chap. 8, "Proto-Luke", p. 201 sq., and M. Dibelius' review of Streeter's first edition (1924) in *Theol. Lit. Zeitg.* 51 (1926), 74–7.

[1] Luke 22. 24–7, 33–4, have parallels in Mark and Matthew; vv. 28–30 only in Matthew; vv. 31–2 and 35–8 are not found elsewhere.

[2] Cf. the searching analysis by R. Bultmann, *Das Evangelium des Johannes* (1941), 351 sq.

[3] The evidence for these given by R. Bultmann, op. cit. 352 n. 3, can be enlarged, e.g. *βάλλειν ὕδωρ* (v. 5) = *hiṭṭīl mayim* (to throw water); *τὸν νιπτῆρα* (*status emphaticus* with the sense of an indefinite article).

(2) The announcement of the betrayal (Mark 14. 17–21 par.) is an original part of the longer narrative. It is common to all four Gospels, and in the Synoptists is firmly embedded in its context.[1]

(3) Everything else is old special tradition (for example, the vow of abstinence, Luke 22. 15–18; Mark 14. 25; Matt. 26. 29, and the washing of the disciples' feet, John 13. 1–20) or is a collation (for example, the conversation in Luke 22. 24–38) or an expansion (as the report of the preparation of the passover meal in Mark 14. 12–16 par., which has its analogy in Jesus' miraculous foreknowledge in Mark 11. 1–6).

For our purposes the most important result gained in this second section is that the early date of Jesus' words of institution is brought out by a process of literary criticism, a result which will receive conclusive support from other considerations. Another significant result is that the accounts of the Last Supper, as we have them it in the four Gospels today, are seen to be the outcome of a living process of growth in the tradition.

[1] Mark 14. 1–2, 10–11 par., cf. John 13. 2.

CHAPTER III

The Earliest Text of the Words of Institution

THE words which Jesus used at the Last Supper have come down to us in three forms: (1) the earliest account we owe to Paul (1 Cor. 11. 23–25), written in all probability in the spring of A.D. 54;[1] (2) Mark 14. 22–25, and in the same form with only slight alterations and additions: Matt. 26. 26–29; (3) Luke 22. 15–20.[2]

Before, however, these three texts are compared, two preliminary questions must be dealt with:

(1) *The Silence of the Fourth Gospel*

The omission of the words of institution in the Fourth Gospel is the more remarkable in that John 13. 2 sq. certainly describes the same meal as Mark 14. 17 sq.: the Last Supper with the ensuing journey to Gethsemane by night. The usual explanations

[1] I have attempted to show in my article "Sabbath-Jahr und neutestamentliche Chronologie" in *Z.N.W.* 27 (1928), 98–103, that it is suggested by the chronology of the Sabbath years that the date of the imprisonment of the Apostle Paul is the year A.D. 55. The zeal with which Paul on his so-called third missionary journey worked for the collection on behalf of the Jerusalem Church makes it probable that the disastrous experiences of the Sabbath year of A.D. 47–8 had caused great anxiety with regard to that of A.D. 54–5. This view is supported in particular by 2 Cor. 8. 13 sq. (cf. 9. 12), showing that the collection was called for by an actual emergency which had arisen in the Jerusalem Church. It should also be noticed that, apart from this collection which was taken on the third missionary journey, only one other is mentioned (Acts 11. 27–30), and that this was taken in order to remedy the famine which had been increased by the Sabbath year of 47–8. The imprisonment of Paul is dated A.D. 55, also by (among others) K. Lake in his careful contribution to F. J. F. Jackson-K. Lake, *The Beginnings of Christianity* I, vol. 5, 445–74.

[2] Justin Martyr's account, 1 *Apol.* 66. 3, does not constitute a separate tradition, cf. infra, p. 86.

for the omission of the words of institution in John are quite unsatisfactory. Or is it seriously maintained that the Apostle John "wrote his account of this night before it was possible to speak of a Christian Eucharist"?[1] Was there ever such a time? What features in John 13. 1 sq. justify such an early date? It is no better to hold that the Fourth Gospel rejected the Eucharist or regarded it as superfluous[2]—where in the history of the Apostolic age do we find the slightest support for so weighty a thesis? Finally, the opinion that John did not connect the institution of the Eucharist with the Last Supper, but with the feeding of the five thousand,[3] is too artificial to be convincing. Besides, John 6. 51c–58 does not originally belong to the discourse on the bread of life,[4] but comes from a pre-Johannine eucharistic homily. All difficulties disappear, however, when it is realized that the author of the Fourth Gospel consciously omitted the account of the Last Supper because he did not want to disclose the sacred formula to the heathen.[5]

But is it possible to think that such a practice of secrecy had already begun by the end of the first century? The answer has to be given in the affirmative. The whole environment of primitive Christianity knew such disciplines

[1] So Gottfr. Kittel, "Die Wirkungen des Abendmahls nach dem N.T." in *Theol. Stud. und Krit.* 96–7 (1925), 224.

[2] R. Bultmann, *Das Evangelium des Johannes* (1941), 360.

[3] H. Windisch, *Johannes und die Synoptiker* (Leipzig, 1926), 78; E. Lohmeyer, *Journ. of Bibl. Lit.* 56 (1937), 249.

[4] E. Schwartz, *Nachr. Goettingen* (1907), 363 n. 2; A. Merx, *Das Evangelium des Johannes* (1911), 25, 136–40; A. Andersen, *Z.N.W.* 9 (1908), 163 sq.; J. Wellhausen, *Evangelium Johannis* (1908), 32; F. Spitta, *Das Johannes-Evangelium* (1910), XXII, 145–56; Thompson, "The Interpretation of John 6" in *The Expositor*, ser. 8, vol. 11 (1916), 345 sq.; A. Loisy, *Le Quatrième Évangile*, 2nd ed. (1921), 233; J. E. Carpenter, *The Johannine Writings* (1927), 428 and note 2; E. v. Dobschuetz, in *Die Evangelische Theologie* 2 (1927), 62; id. in *Z.N.W.* 28 (1929), 163, 166; E. Hirsch, *Studien zum Vierten Evangelium* (1936), 14; R. Bultmann, op. cit. 162.

[5] R. Eisler, "Das Letzte Abendmahl" in *Z.N.W.* 24 (1925), 185; H. N. Bate, "The 'Shorter Text' of Luke 22. 15–20" in *J.T.S.* 28 (1927), 367 sq.; H. Huber, *Das Herrenmahl im N.T.* (Leipzig, 1929), 92; W. Oehler, *Das Johannes-Evangelium, eine Missionsschrift fuer die Welt* (1936), 28 sq.; G. D. Kilpatrick in *J.T.S.* 47 (1946), 52 sq.

of secrecy. For the Hellenistic world we need only refer to the mystery religions,[1] the secret gnostic doctrines, the esoteric teachings of the philosophical sects,[2] and the world of magic.[3] It is generally recognised that all this is true of the Hellenistic world, but it is frequently overlooked that in New Testament times we find a *disciplina arcani* even in Palestine. Here we can first of all refer to the Essenes,[4] that remarkable fraternity whose members called themselves חֲשָׁאִים, "the hidden ones".[5] Only after a year of strict probation did the Essenes admit their novices to the sacred lustrations, and only after two more years were they admitted into the fraternity.[6] At his admission the new member had to take terrible oaths to keep the secret doctrines of the fraternity from non-members, to hide the—probably magical—names of the angels, and to guard the secret books of the fraternity.[7] These secret books contained, as Josephus indicates, occult teachings in medicine and alchemy,[8] and probably also the angelic names.[9] Their meals too were kept secret. Only after a novitiate of three years and subsequent admission to the fraternity was participation in them permitted;[10] no "unbeliever"

[1] P. Batiffol, *Études d'histoire et de théologie positive*, première série, 7th ed. (Paris, 1926), 1, "La discipline de l'arcane", pp. 10–15.

[2] These are mentioned, for instance, by Clem. Alex. *Strom.* 5. 10.

[3] Cf. G. Bornkamm s. v. μυστήριον in *Theol. Woerterb. zum N.T.* 4 (1942), 810 sq., with copious references to further literature.

[4] E. Schuerer, *Gesch. des jued. Volkes*, 4th ed., Vol. 2 (Leipzig, 1907), 651–80; W. Bauer, art. "Essener" in Pauly-Wissowa suppl. 4 (1924), 386–430; A. Schlatter, *Gesch. Israels von Alexander d. Gr. bis Hadrian*, 3rd ed. (Stuttgart, 1925), 173–8; W. Bousset-H. Gressmann, *Relig. d. Judentums im hellenist. Zeitalter*, 3rd ed. (Tuebingen, 1926), 456–65. The evidence for our problem comes only from the elaborate description of the Essenes in Jos., *Bell.* 2. 8. 2–13. §§119–61.

[5] Cf. Sheq. 5. 7, and A. Schlatter, op. cit. 173.

[6] Jos., *Bell.* 2. 8. 7. §§137–8.

[7] Ibid. 2. 8. 7. §§141–2.

[8] Ibid. 2. 8. 6. §136.

[9] Ibid. 2. 8. 7. §142. Whether the "prophetic sayings" which were found in "sacred writings", ibid. 2. 8. 12. §159, refer to the prophecies of the O.T. or to those of prophetically gifted members of the fraternity cannot be decided from the report of Josephus.

[10] Ibid. 2. 8. 7. §138–9.

could enter the room,[1] and at meal-times such silence was kept that "those outside the house were given the impression of an awe-inspiring mystery".[2] It has already been stated that admission to the lustrations was granted only after a whole year's novitiate. A picture similar in several respects comes from the book of the Community of the New Covenant at Damascus. Here too admission to the community is granted on oath, "the covenant-oath".[3] Here too nobody may be told before his admission about "the rules" of the community;[4] and the book of the community, especially in its polemical parts, is full of pseudonyms and allusions, intelligible only to the initiate.[5] All these features are to be found also in the newly discovered Dead Sea Scrolls.

But we need not confine ourselves to the sects in order to discover a *disciplina arcani* in Palestine in New Testament times. The orthodox religious writings exhibit similar characteristics. First we can mention the apocalyptic books which from the days of Daniel spoke in symbolic language, often enough for political reasons. All the apocalypses are secret writings.[6] Daniel receives the order "shut up the words, and seal the book, even to the time of the end" (12. 4, cf. v. 9; 8. 26); pseudo-Ezra is told to publish only twenty-four books (the canonical books of the Old Testament) of the ninety-four which he has written, and to keep back the last seventy (the apocalypses) and give them only to the wise among the people.[7] Origen testifies to the existence of Jewish

[1] Ibid. 2. 8. 5. §129. The ξένοι who, according to ibid. §132, share in the meals, should be understood therefore as visiting members of the fraternity who have come from abroad.

[2] Ibid. 2. 8. 5. §133.

[3] Ed. L. Rost (Berlin, 1933), 15. 6, 8.

[4] Ibid. 15. 10–11.

[5] The "Man of *hybris*", 1. 14, and in the plural, 20. 11; the "builder of the wall", 4. 19; 8. 12; 19. 24 sq.; the "removers of boundaries", 5. 20; 19. 16; "the decorators with whitewash", 8. 12; 19. 25; the "men of battle", 20. 14; the "man of untruth", 20. 15, and the like. The fact that political reasons were partly responsible is shown by the description of the princes of Judah as the "removers of boundaries", 19. 16, quoting Hosea 5. 10.

[6] H. Gunkel, "Das 4. Buch Esra" in E. Kautzsch, *Die Pseudepigraphen des A.T.* (1900), 394 note *k*.

[7] 14. 44–6, cf. 12. 36–8; 14. 26. It is said in 4 Ezra 14. 6 that Moses had been ordered to make public only the one part of God's words (the Torah), and to conceal the other (the apocalyptic traditions).

secret writings.[1] The fact that the post-Danielic apocalyptic literature of the Jews in its entirety, down to the third century A.D., has not been preserved in the original language,[2] but only in translations, is partly due to the concealment of apocalyptic writings. Equally important is the fact that the *disciplina arcani* occupied an important place for the Rabbis in another way.[3] I have attempted to show elsewhere[4] that the enormous influence of the scribes at the time of Jesus can be understood only if it is recognized that the respect paid to them was due to their being the bearers of a secret knowledge, an esoteric tradition.[5] Right down to the second century A.D. the entire oral tradition was treated as "the secret of God",[6] which must be kept from the heathen by the command not to commit it to writing.[7] The esoteric traditions of the Rabbis in a narrower sense contained, according to *Ḥagh.* 2. 1; *Tos. Ḥagh.* 2. 1, 7 (223 sq.), four groups of secret teaching: (1) at the interpretation of the O.T. laws about incest no more than two hearers were allowed to be present; (2) the story of the creation of the world was not to be interpreted in the presence of more than one hearer; (3) the vision of the chariot (Ezekiel 1. 10), i.e. the secrets of the Divine nature, was to be

[1] "*Ex libris secretioribus, qui apud Iudaeos feruntur*" in Matt. comment. ser. 28, ad Matt. 23. 37–9 ed. E. Klostermann (1933), p. 50, 6; "*fertur in scripturis non manifestis*", ibid. p. 50, 24, among them: "*secretum Esaiae*", ibid. p. 50, 27; "*multa secretorum*", ibid. p. 51, 9; "*secreta quae feruntur in nomine sanctorum*", ibid. p. 51, 12. A remark of Origen about 2 Thess. 2. 1 sq. (ibid. p. 124, 17 sq.) also belongs to this evidence for secret traditions amongst the Jews: "It may be—in view of the fact that there were people among the Jews who claimed to know from books either of the time of the destruction (of the universe) or about other secret things—that therefore he (Paul) wrote this (2 Thess. 2. 1 sq.), warning his followers not to believe the claims of these people."

[2] *The Third Book of Enoch*, ed. H. Odeberg (Cambridge, 1928), which is preserved in the original Hebrew, dates only from the second half of the third century A.D.

[3] The neglect with which this fact has been treated is shown e.g. in the article "Arkandisziplin" by G. Anrich in *R.G.G.*, 2nd ed., 1. 530–3, who ignores it just as much as the evidence from the writings of the Palestinian heretics and the Jewish Apocalypses.

[4] *Jerusalem zur Zeit Jesu* IIB (Leipzig, 1929), 106 sq.

[5] Cf. Jesus' rebuke of the scribes in Luke 11. 52 ἤρατε τὴν κλεῖδα τῆς γνώσεως.

[6] b. *Ḥagh.* 14b (Bar.).

[7] Pesiq. R. 5.

taught with veiled head[1] and in whispers[2] to one hearer only, who had to be a scholar and a man of discretion;[3] (4) it was altogether prohibited to give instruction about the topography of the universe, i.e. to describe the heavenly and the subterranean world, and about the eternity existing before the creation and after the destruction of the world.[4] Moreover, the esoteric traditions were by no means limited to the subjects just mentioned, which were partly kept secret for fear of gnostic influences. The most holy name of God was kept safe from profanation in this way that—as is said in one instance—it was permitted to be mentioned by the teachers to their pupils no more than once a week;[5] "the grounds of the Torah", i.e. the grounds of God's laying down the particular commandments, were not to be disclosed to the multitude;[6] it is highly probable that the doctrine of the suffering Messiah also belonged to esoteric tradition.[7] Furthermore certain passages out of the Old Testament were either not to be read at all in the worship of the Synagogue, or else to be read in Hebrew only without translation into Aramaic;[8] certain relaxations of regulations concerning purification, working on the minor feast-days, and hallowing the Sabbath, were not to be read in public;[9]

[1] Joach. Jeremias, *Jerusalem zur Zeit Jesu* IIB (1929), 110; P. Billerbeck 1. 659.

[2] b. Ḥagh. 14a: secret doctrines are passed on in a whisper, cf. F. J. Doelger, *Der Exorzismus im altchristlichen Taufritual* (1909).

[3] According to j. Ḥagh. 2. 77a. 13 sq., Rabbi '*Aqibha* laid down the second and the third rule cited above, cf. P. Benoit, Rabbi Aqiba in *Rev. Bibl.* 54 (1947), 70.

[4] W. Bousset in his book *Der Antichrist* (Goettingen, 1895), has proved that the apocalyptic ideas of later Judaism have largely come down to us only in late, and sometimes even very late, Christian writings, whereas all the earlier evidence exists only in fragments. "How is that to be explained? It seems to me that in very many cases the eschatological revelations were not written down, but handed on orally as secret traditions, to be treated with fear and trembling", op. cit. p. 18.

[5] b. Qid. 71a.

[6] b. Sanh. 21b, etc.

[7] Joach. Jeremias, op. cit. 108; id., "Erloeser und Erloesung im Spaetjudentum und im Urchristentum" in *Deutsche Theologie* 2, Bericht ueber den 2. Theologentag (Goettingen, 1929), 106–19.

[8] Megh. 4. 10; Tos. Megh. 4. 31 sq. (228. 5).

[9] Joach. Jeremias, *Jerusalem zur Zeit Jesu* IIB (Leipzig, 1929), 109.

certain teachings which had not attained validity were to be handed on only in a whisper.[1] Finally, the Rabbis refer repeatedly to secret writings.[2] Still more elaborate were the precautions taken against the heathen: Josephus mentions, for instance, that to speak of the worship in the Holy of Holies was forbidden.[3] The secrecy was partly for dogmatic reasons, partly in order to keep from the people teaching which was liable to be misused. At any rate, the aim is primarily to protect sacred knowledge from profanation.

The rôle of the esoteric in the teaching of Jesus and in the early Church is very much akin to all this. The main facts can be briefly stated.[4]

In the Synoptic preaching of Jesus the esoteric material comprises: (1) Jesus' Messiahship. After Peter's confession He reveals it to the disciples, but expressly enjoins silence upon them (Mark 8. 30; 9. 9 par.). Only once, before the Sanhedrin, did Jesus publicly proclaim Himself as the Messiah (Mark 14. 62 par.). The feature of this part of Jesus' esoteric teaching is His self-description as *υἱὸς τοῦ ἀνθρώπου*, which from Caesarea Philippi onwards invariably has an apocalyptic-messianic significance in Mark, and is without exception[5] used esoterically until the unveiling before the Sanhedrin, Mark 14. 62 par. (2) The prediction of the Passion (Mark 8. 31 sq. par.; 9. 31 sq. par.; 10. 32–34 par., etc.) which, according to Mark, also begins with Peter's confession, and is in any case confined to the circle of the disciples. (3) The eschatological prophecies: Jesus spoke (according to Mark 13. 3) only to His four most trusted disciples about the signs of the end. (4) Individual items of in-

[1] j. Beza 1. 61a. 1.

[2] E.g. b.B.M. 92a, etc.

[3] *Adv. Apion.* 2. 7. §82.

[4] Characteristic terms of esoteric speech in the N.T. are among others: *ἄρρητος*; *γάλα* (i.e. elementary instruction)—*βρῶμα*; *γάλα—στερεὰ τροφή*; *οἱ ἔξω* (Mark 4. 11); *οὐκ ἐξὸν λαλῆσαι*; *ἐπιλύειν*; *ἐπιτιμᾶν* (meaning: to exhort, scil., to keep silent); *καλύπτειν*; *κατ' ἰδίαν*; *κρυπτός*; *μυστήριον* (Rev. 15. 5, 7); *νοῦς* (*ὧδε ὁ νοῦς ὁ ἔχων σοφίαν, ὁ ἔχων νοῦν*); *οὖς* (*ὁ ἔχων ὦτα* [*ἀκούειν*], *ἀκουέτω*; *οὖς—δῶμα*); *παραλαμβάνειν* (i.e. "to take aside"); *παρρησίᾳ*; *πνευματικός—σάρκινος—ψυχικός*; *σκοτία—φῶς*; *σοφία* (*ὧδε ἡ σοφία ἐστίν*); *τέλειος—νήπιος, τελειότης*; *φανερός* (Mark 3. 12); *φανερόω* (Mark 4. 22); *χωρεῖν* (*ὁ δυνάμενος χωρεῖν χωρείτω*).

[5] In Mark 8. 34, the words *τὸν ὄχλον σύν* probably do not belong to the original tradition, cf. its parallel Matt. 16. 24.

struction were couched by Jesus in enigmatic speech, as the Saying about eunuchs (Matt. 19. 12 *ὁ δυνάμενος χωρεῖν χωρείτω*) and the Saying about the destruction and the rebuilding of the Temple (Mark 14. 58 par.). When Jesus followed the Saying in Matt. 11. 15, which declared that John the Baptist was Elias, with *ὁ ἔχων ὦτα ἀκουέτω*, that meant that there was also a hidden meaning: if the Baptist be Elias, Jesus is Messiah. (5) Finally, a secret teaching of Jesus receives mention in quite general terms without specification of content, and this teaching, according to Christ's will, is to be made public in the future, Matt. 10. 27 par.; Mark 4. 22 sq. Matt. 10. 26bc also seems to have had this meaning originally.[1] Matt. 10. 27 par. should be compared with the rabbinical custom in which the most sacred secret traditions are "whispered".[2] Even if one or the other of the passages and expressions quoted have been introduced by the Evangelists, the general picture will remain unaffected.

In the Fourth Gospel the last discourse is the main material for comparison (John 13. 31—17. 26): following His revelation to the world (2. 1–12. 50), Jesus reveals in private conversation with His disciples the meaning of His departure and of His mission. Further, we should recall John 3. 1 sq. K. Bornhaeuser[3] has rightly seen that Nicodemus did not come to Jesus by night for fear of the Jews—for nothing is said to this effect—but because he desires of the prophet in secret conversation a revelation about the mysteries of the kingdom of God (cf. 3. 3).

When we turn to the early Church, we repeatedly come across cryptic sayings and a care to keep the most sacred things from profanation.[4] Paul,[5] who calls himself and his fellow workers "stewards of the mysteries of God", 1 Cor. 4. 1, speaks in general terms in 1 Cor. 2. 6–3. 2 about the Divine *σοφία* which could be offered only to the *τέλειοι* (2. 6), i.e. the *πνευματικοί*

[1] Cf. also the warning in Matt. 7. 6 not to give what is holy to dogs, nor to cast pearls before swine.

[2] K. Bornhaeuser, *Die Bergpredigt* (Guetersloh, 1923), 7, cf. supra, p. 77 n. 2.

[3] *Das Johannes-Evangelium* (Guetersloh, 1928), 26.

[4] Of course, there is here no question of the elaborate *disciplina arcani* of the mystery religions.

[5] On Paul as a "mystagogue" cf. H. Windisch, *Paulus und Christus* (Leipzig, 1934), 215–29, who, however, gives a rather one-sided account of the subject.

(2. 13): it is *θεοῦ σοφία ἐν μυστηρίῳ* (2. 7). Paul could offer the Corinthians only milk (i.e. elementary instruction, 3. 2), not yet the solid food of the *σοφία* for the *τέλειοι* (3. 2; 2. 6). In particular we are told of the following themes which were treated —whether universally or occasionally—as esoteric traditions: (1) the deepest secrets of Christology. The clearest evidence for this is Heb. 5. 11–6. 8. In this passage elementary instruction, consisting of three parts: (*a*) repentance from dead works, (*b*) faith towards God, (*c*) the doctrine of baptism, of the laying on of hands, and of the last things (Heb. 6. 1-2), is distinguished from instruction for those mature in the faith—*τελειότης* (ibid. 6. 1) —which is expounded in the christological passages of Heb. 7. 1–10. 18. In addition there are secrets of Christology which no one ventures even to touch on: no Gospel—apart from the heretical Gospel of Peter—gives any description of how the resurrection of Jesus took place. This is probably the solution of the abrupt ending of Mark at 16. 8.[1] Although the appearances of the risen Lord formed a fixed part of the teaching of the faith, Mark felt that they were among the things which should not be disclosed to pagan readers. The same applies to Mark's account of the temptation (Mark 1. 12 sq.): Mark here used symbolic language on purpose. Jesus' victory over Satan is an event which "may be told to the faithful with holy awe, but which must not be portrayed in a book which might fall into the hands of unbelievers".[2] (2) Next, included in the esoteric material were certain eschatological doctrines which had to be kept secret partly for political reasons. Revelation affords a good deal of evidence for this, and its allegorical language is very largely cryptic.[3] The clearest example is the secret number in Rev. 13. 18, which is moreover emphasized

[1] The proof of the fact that Mark 16. 8 was always the end of the Gospel I find in the close correspondence which exists between the accounts in Matthew 28 and Luke 24 up to the point where Mark closes (Matt. 28. 8a; Luke 24. 9a), for from that point onward they have nothing in common any more.

[2] E. Meyer, *Ursprung und Anfaenge des Christentums* 1. (1921), 95. The fact that the Christ-hymn in 1 Tim. 3. 16 begins with the enigmatic *ὅς* may also be due to an intentional obscurity. This is all the more probable since reference is made to "the great *μυστήριον*". (This has been suggested to me by Hugo Duensing.)

[3] C. Clemen in *Z.N.W.* 26 (1927), 173–86.

by the two phrases ὧδε ἡ σοφία ἐστίν and ὁ ἔχων νοῦν. Only the initiate can explain the number: the interpretation of the Satanic beast as a man—"for it is the number of a man"—is intentionally veiled. When the reader finds in Rev. 13. 9 the esoteric phrase εἴ τις ἔχει οὖς, ἀκουσάτω, he is at once warned that the preceding description of the beast and the subsequent mention of persecution is purposely put in enigmatic language. A similar esoteric phrase is found in the passage describing the "great harlot" Babylon in Rev. 17. 9, where the phrase ὧδε ὁ νοῦς ὁ ἔχων σοφίαν occurs just before the number seven is enigmatically applied to the seven hills and the seven kings. The woman, Babylon, and the beast on which she is seated, are a μυστήριον (17. 5, 7): once more the reader is warned that the true meaning is hidden by enigmatic language. Similar to the veiled reference to Rome is that to Jerusalem in Rev. 11. 8. In fact, according to Rev. 10. 7, the entire book is a μυστήριον. Similar phenomena are found in other New Testament writings: Babylon is the pseudonym for Rome in 1 Pet. 5. 13. The noteworthy phrase ὁ ἀναγινώσκων νοείτω (Mark 13. 14; Matt. 24. 15) is another instance: the reader is reminded of contemporary events, in which the prophecy of the "abomination of desolation" is being fulfilled, but which for political reasons must not be more clearly indicated. (3) The material which had to be kept from profanation also contained the mysteries of the Divine nature, "the deep things of God", 1 Cor. 2. 10. A specially significant instance may be found in 2 Cor. 12. 1–10. Only under compulsion and with circumlocutory expressions does Paul mention "a man" being "caught up" into Paradise (cf. 2 Cor. 12. 2 ἄνθρωπον ἐν Χριστῷ; 12. 3 τὸν τοιοῦτον ἄνθρωπον; 12. 5 ὑπὲρ τοῦ τοιούτου). The things which he there heard he is not permitted even to hint at: they are "unspeakable words, which it is not lawful for a man to utter", 2 Cor. 12. 4. (4) Finally, from a very early time we can detect an effort to safeguard the words of institution from profanation and misrepresentation: (*a*) several scholars discern a tendency to enigmatic writing as early as in the account of the Last Supper in Mark—or more accurately in the earlier tradition which underlies both Marcan and Pauline accounts[1]: "La parole essentielle 'Ceci est mon corps' est pro-

[1] Cf. infra, p. 127-32.

prement inintelligible pour le lecteur non averti", is the opinion of M. Goguel,[1] following A. Loisy.[2] (*b*) The complicated form given by Paul to the word spoken over the wine was, as we shall see,[3] in all probability due to his attempt to combat misinterpretations of the Eucharist, or to exclude possibilities of its misinterpretation (blood-drinking, etc.). (*c*) In the Acts of the Apostles Luke goes still further. Whenever he speaks of the communal meals of the primitive Church,[4] he follows earlier traditions and uses only enigmatic terms: *ἡ κλάσις τοῦ ἄρτου* Acts 2. 42;[5] *κλᾶν ἄρτον*

[1] "La relation du dernier repas de Jésus dans 1 Cor. 11 et la tradition historique chez l'apôtre Paul. Observations sur deux théories récentes" in *Rev. d'histoire et de philosophie rel.* 10 (1930), 64.

[2] "Les origines de la Cène Eucharistique" in Congrès d'histoire du Christianisme, Jubilé A. Loisy, *Annales d'histoire du Christianisme* 1 (Paris, 1928), 78 sq.

[3] cf. infra, p. 112.

[4] Luke seems to have taken the communal meals of the Primitive Church for the celebrations of the Eucharist; whether he was correct in this does not enter into our discussion.

[5] Cf. Luke 24. 35 *καὶ αὐτοὶ ἐξηγοῦντο τὰ ἐν τῇ ὁδῷ καὶ ὡς ἐγνώσθη αὐτοῖς ἐν τῇ κλάσει τοῦ ἄρτου.* Here *ἡ κλάσις τοῦ ἄρτου* may mean: (1) The breaking of bread in its literal sense. If this version is accepted, it must be assumed that Jesus had a special manner characteristic for Him, in which He broke the bread—perhaps lifting His eyes to heaven, as in Mark 6. 41, cf. R. Hupfeld, *Die Abendmahlsfeier* (1935), 87. (2) However, the phrase "breaking of bread" has also a wider meaning, in which the whole ritual at the beginning of the meal is comprised: Grace, breaking of bread and its distribution (b. Ber. 46a, 47a, etc.). This ritual joined the guests at table into a fellowship. If the words *ἐν τῇ κλάσει τοῦ ἄρτου*, Luke 24. 35, are understood in this way it may be assumed either (*a*) that Jesus, who in the Lord's prayer gave His disciples their own prayer, had also created a special form for the daily blessing at the breaking of the bread, by which the disciples of Emmaus recognized Him, so G. Dalman, *Jesus-Jeschua* (1922), 124; or (*b*) it might be assumed that as the blessing before the meal is said by the host (b. Ber. 46), it was exceptional that Jesus, as a guest, should have taken the place of the master of the house, and the disciples might have recognized Him by this. (3) However, it is questionable whether Luke 24. 35 really meant by *ἡ κλάσις τοῦ ἄρτου* either the actual breaking of the bread (1) or the blessing before the meal (2). In view of the uses of *ἡ κλάσις τοῦ ἄρτου* by Luke in Acts 2. 42, and of *κλᾶν ἄρτον* in Acts 2. 46; 20. 7, 11, it is more likely that these words refer *a parte potiore* to the whole common meal. The risen Lord granted to His disciples at Emmaus the fellowship at His table, and "at the common meal" (*ἐν τῇ κλάσει τοῦ ἄρτου* Luke 24. 35, taking it as *ἐν temporale*, as in Matt. 21. 22 *ἐν τῇ προσευχῇ*, i.e. "during", "at", cf. W. Bauer, *Woerterb. zum N.T.*, s.v. *ἐν* II. 3)

Acts 2. 46; 20. 7, 11;[1] possibly also τροφή Acts 2. 46.[2] For the fact that in Acts 2. 42,[3] 46; 20. 7, 11, the "breaking of bread" refers to a part of the Church's cult is clear each time from the context and is supported by Ignatius, *Eph.* 20. 2; Did. 14. 1; notice should also be taken of Acts 2. 46, where τε . . . τε emphasizes the distinction between participation in the worship of the Temple on the one hand, and the breaking of bread at home on the other.[4] Now, as H. Lightfoot (died 1675) saw long ago,[5] the phrase "breaking of bread" was never used in Judaism to describe a meal,[6] but only (α) the actual breaking of the bread into pieces, or (β) the ritual at the beginning of the meal.[7] The description of

"their eyes were opened and they knew Him", Luke 24. 31. Cf. Joach. Jeremias, *Jesus als Weltvollender* (Guetersloh, 1930), 78, and infra, p. 136 n. 2, on the table fellowship between the risen Lord and His disciples.

[1] Acts 27. 35, λαβὼν ἄρτον εὐχαρίστησεν τῷ θεῷ ἐνώπιον πάντων καὶ κλάσας ἤρξατο ἐσθίειν, probably refers to an ordinary morning meal, hardly to an eucharistic meal. The general view, e.g. K. Voelker, *Mysterium und Agape* (Gotha, 1927), 28, and others, errs in any case, assuming that Paul ate alone. This is excluded by the word κλάσας: for the bread is broken to be distributed among the table companions after the blessing has been said. The addition in various MSS, sa syr-harcl 614 pc., adding ἐπιδιδοὺς καὶ ἡμῖν to ἤρξατο ἐσθίειν, is therefore substantially correct. The companions of the common meal referred to are the author of the "we-report" and Aristarchus, Acts 27. 2. The example of the Christian prisoner and his companions eating encouraged their fellow travellers to do the same, Acts 27. 36.

[2] Cf. A.Schlatter, *Die Theologie der Apostel*, 2nd ed. (Stuttgart, 1922), 520.

[3] It seems to me probable that Acts 2. 42 describes the course of an early Christian service. The sequence was (1) the instruction by the Apostles; (2) the offering, cf. Acts 6. 1; (3) the celebration of the meal; (4) the prayers.

[4] Acts 2. 46 sq. calls for the following comment: the comma should not follow καρδίας (as e.g. in the Nestle text), but τροφῆς: it is not the eating which takes place "with gladness and singleness of heart", but the praise of God. If this is the correct punctuation, great care should be taken with regard to the widespread view that the jubilation at the primitive Eucharist was in open contrast to the sombre attitude—remembering the death of Jesus—which was observed at the Eucharist in the Pauline congregations.

[5] "Horae Hebraicae et Talmudicae" in *Opera Omnia* 2 (Roterodami, 1686), 696 sq., cf. 768.

[6] The constantly repeated statement that "breaking of bread" is a term for "holding a meal" in Jewish sources seems to be an ineradicable misapprehension.

[7] Cf. supra, p. 82 n. 4.

the holy meal as "the breaking of bread" is the completely new usage of the primitive Church, which can hardly be explained otherwise than as a cryptogram: the non-Christian was not supposed to understand its meaning. (*d*) Heb. 6. 1/2 offers evidence which points in the same direction. The conspicuous absence of the Eucharist from the list of subjects taught to beginners is probably to be explained by the consideration that the doctrine of the Eucharist was among the subjects reserved for the *τέλειοι*.[1] (A similar piece of evidence for the Eucharist being treated esoterically would be found in Matt. 7. 6, if the assumption be correct that by "holy things" and "the pearls" Matthew meant the Eucharist[2]; in any event a connexion between Matt. 7. 6 and the celebration of the meal by the congregation was already established by the time Did. 9. 5 was written). (*e*) We now examine the Didache. The lively discussion which has gone on since its first publication in 1883, as to whether the prayers in chapters 9–10 are intended for an Agape[3] or for the Eucharist,[4] seems to have been settled by the investigations of Martin Dibelius, who has shown that neither of the two theories does justice to the facts, and that rather Agape with a subsequent celebration of the Eucharist is envisaged.[5] Did. 9. 1–10. 5[6] contains the opening and closing prayers of the Agape, 10. 6 is the opening liturgy of

[1] Cf. M. Goguel, *L'Eucharistie des origines à Justin Martyr* (Paris, 1910), 217; W. Goossens, *Les origines de l'Eucharistie. Sacrement et sacrifice* (Gembloux-Paris, 1931,) 222.

[2] So e.g. W. Bussmann, *Synoptische Studien* 2 (Halle, 1929), 34.

[3] P. Ladeuze, F. Kattenbusch, P. Drews, Ermoni, van Crombrugghe, E. Baumgaertner, P. Cagin, R. Knopf, T. E. J. Ferris, W. Goossens, J. Brinktrine, R. H. Connolly, G. Dix.

[4] P. Batiffol, Briscout, K. Voelker, A. Greiff, O. Casel.

[5] M. Dibelius, *Z.N.W.* 37 (1938), 32–41. The correct view had already been stated in 1884 by Theod. Zahn, *Forschungen zur Geschichte des N.T. Kanons und der altkirchl. Literatur* 3. 293 sq., who also gave the correct reasons for it. Cf. also E. v. d. Goltz, *Das Gebet in der aeltesten Christenheit* (1901), 213; E. Hennecke, *N.T. Apokryphen*, 2nd ed. (1924), 559; R. Stapper, *Kathol. Liturgik* (1931), 182; R. Hupfeld, *Die Abendmahlsfeier* (1935), 77; J. Quasten, *Monumenta Eucharistica et Liturgica vetustissima* 1 (1935), No. 9, p. 12 n. 5; A. Arnold, *Der Ursprung des christlichen Abendmahls* (1937), 26 sq.

[6] Did. 10. 5 belongs to the Grace after meat, as follows from its similarity to Did. 9. 4.

the subsequent Eucharist.[1] If that be so, it is most significant that it should be expressly required that only baptized persons should be admitted to the meal preceding the Eucharist. The unbaptized were excluded with the forceful words: *καὶ γὰρ περὶ τούτου εἴρηκεν ὁ κύριος* (Matt. 7. 6)· *μὴ δῶτε τὸ ἅγιον τοῖς κυσί*, Did. 9. 5. More significant still is the fact that the actual celebration of the Eucharist is not described, much less the words that are used: instead the text stops abruptly with the *μαρανα θά· ἀμήν*, 10. 6, from the opening liturgy.[2] Moreover, in chapter 14 the passage about the Sunday celebration is limited to emphasizing the duty of mutual reconciliation beforehand. The only thing we are told is that the Eucharist is called a *θυσία* (14. 1, 2, 3). What followed after the opening liturgy 10. 6? How did the "sacrifice" proceed?[3] Were the words of institution said? or words of administration? We are not told anything. (*f*) When Pliny mentioned in his letter to Trajan (A.D. 112/3) that the Christians examined by him declared that the food at their common meals was harmless, ordinary fare,[4] he made implicit reference to the slander that the Christians held Thyestean meals.[5] But that slander was one of the consequences of the esoteric character of the Eucharist.[6]

[1] The main arguments are as follows: (1) a celebration of the Eucharist at which the wine was administered before the bread has never at any time taken place; (2) the celebration of the Eucharist was not called *εὐχαριστία* in the Didache (9. 1, 5), but *θυσία* (14. 1, 2, 3); (3) the liturgical exclamations in 10. 6 saluting the coming Lord, and the exhortation *εἴ τις ἅγιός ἐστιν, ἐρχέσθω· εἴ τις οὐκ ἔστι, μετανοείτω*, are meaningless, unless they are spoken at the beginning of the Eucharist and not at the end of either the Eucharist or the Agape.

[2] K. G. Goetz, *Der Ursprung des kirchlichen Abendmahls* (1929), 8, assumes that the eucharistic words are omitted in the prayers in Did. 9–10 "from fear of profanation".

[3] Only one—rather vague—hint at the course which the celebration used to take may be obtained from the words in 14. 1 *κλάσατε ἄρτον καὶ εὐχαριστήσατε*; but it is equally possible that they refer to the preceding Agape.

[4] Pliny, *Ep.* 96.

[5] A similar allusion may be found already in the mention made of false accusations in 1 Pet. 2. 12; 4. 12–19.

[6] F. Blanke, Zürich, has kindly reminded me of the fact that, according to the report in Pliny's letter, baptism belonged also to the ceremonies incriminated by the heathen (on a postcard, dated the 2nd of February, 1941).

(*g*) The next item for consideration, the shorter text of Luke, will be dealt with below on p. 105. (*h*) Justin Martyr in 1 Apol. 66. 1 (about A.D. 150) confirms that only baptized Christians were admitted to the Eucharist. The fact that he speaks openly about its meaning and discloses the words of institution (66. 3) is evidently due to his desire to oppose the wild rumours to which its esoteric character had given rise. Yet even he quotes the word over the cup only in the shortened version, "this is my blood". (*i*) The inscription of Abercius (end of the second century A.D.) is couched altogether in symbolical and mysterious speech. It says about the Eucharist: "13. and everywhere she (*Pistis*) sets before me as my food a fish (Christ) from the spring, 14. great beyond measure and pure, which was caught by a pure virgin (Mary); 15. and this she offered everywhere as food for her friends: 16. excellent wine she had, which she offered as mixed wine together with bread".[1]

This evidence shows that as early as the first century in various places and increasing measure the tendency to safeguard the holy Eucharist and its words of institution from profanation was making itself felt, although we are warned by the three Synoptic Gospels and by Justin's Apology against mistaking it for a *disciplina arcani* as strict and as universally binding as was the case in the mystery religions. John's Gospel belongs to this development.[2] It proceeded from the first, earliest rudiments of enigmatic speech in the early Church to the Acts of the Apostles (with its pseudonym for the Eucharist), then to the Epistle to the Hebrews (reserving the instruction about the Eucharist to the τέλειοι), and from there to John (where the report on the Last Supper is omitted). Later on it continues to the Didache (which is silent about Eucharistic procedure), the letter of Pliny (which serves as an indirect evidence for the esoteric character of the Eucharist), the shorter text of Luke (which is limited to the word over the

[1] J. Quasten, *Monumenta Euchar. et Lit. vet.* 1 (1935), 21–5; H. Strathmann-Th. Klauser, *Reallexikon f. Antike u. Christentum* 1 (1941), 12–17.

[2] Cf. supra, p. 73 n. 5. Cf. also W. L. Knox, *Some Hellenistic Elements in Primitive Christianity* (1944), 66, who explains the omission of the words of institution in the Fourth Gospel by "the hellenistic tradition that the actual words of the mysteries should not be made public"; G. D. Kilpatrick in *J.T.S.* 47 (1946), 52 sq.

bread), and finally to the symbolical representation of the Eucharist in the inscription of Abercius.

(2) *Luke: The Shorter or the Longer Text?*

Luke's text of the words of institution has come down to us in two forms, a longer and a shorter text.[1] Both these versions read Luke 22. 15–18, but then diverge: the longer text adds verses 19–20; the shorter version only verse 19a, stopping abruptly after *τὸ σῶμά μου*. The question, therefore, arises, whether verses 19b–20 (*τὸ ὑπὲρ ὑμῶν διδόμενον· τοῦτο ποιεῖτε εἰς τὴν ἐμὴν ἀνάμνησιν*. 20. *καὶ τὸ ποτήριον ὡσαύτως μετὰ τὸ δειπνῆσαι, λέγων· τοῦτο τὸ ποτήριον ἡ καινὴ διαθήκη ἐν τῷ αἵματί μου, τὸ ὑπὲρ ὑμῶν ἐκχυννόμενον*) are original or not. This question is not just one subordinate problem of textual criticism. Anyone versed in the eucharistic research of the last fifty years will know that the discussion about the shorter and the longer text of Luke has time and again marked the point from which, according to the answer given, fundamentally different conceptions of the Eucharist have arisen.

Our first task is to determine the evidence for the two versions:

(*a*) *The textual evidence*

The longer text is supported (1) by all the Greek MSS with the exception of D; (2) by all the versions[2] with the exception of vet-syr (cf. infra) and some of the old Latin;[3] and (3) by Marcion,[4] Justin Martyr,[5] and probably Tatian.

The exact wording of the Diatessaron is unknown; it is, however, certain that Tatian chose Mark-Matthew and not Luke

[1] The most important texts are printed in A. Merx, *Die vier kanonischen Evangelien* 2. 2 (1905), 441–8.

[2] sa bo (with the exception of one MS.) vg sy-pesh (omitting vv. 17–18) arm georg aeth (cf. P. Benoit, *Rev. Bibl.* 48 (1939), 358).

[3] The longer text is found in the Itala MSS c f q r[1] r[2] aur δ; cf. about c infra, p. 88 n. 8.

[4] It follows from Tert. *adv. Marc.* 4. 40 that Marcion read Luke 22. 20, probably omitting the word *καινή*.

[5] Justin 1 *Apol.* 66. 3, has a text in which the command to repeat refers to the bread. He is following Luke—and not 1 Cor. 11. 24–5—for (1) he has only the command concerning the repetition of the bread rite; and (2) he reads with Luke *καὶ τὸ ποτήριον ὁμοίως*; and (3) he calls his source the "analects called Gospels".

as the basis of his account of the Last Supper. Nevertheless, some influence of the longer text of Luke is suggested (*a*) by the term "the new covenant" (Tat$^{\text{arab aphr1}}$) and (*b*) by the command to repeat (Tat$^{\text{ephr2 aphr arab fuld ned3}}$). Although this command—according to all the MSS (Tat$^{\text{ephr aphr arab fuld ned}}$)—follows the cup (so only in Paul), and is missing after the bread (where it appears in Luke), and although there is in Aphr and Tat^{ned} the uncommon form "thus shall you do, in remembrance of me, whenever you meet" (a free rendering of 1 Cor. 11. 25 *τοῦτο ποιεῖτε, ὁσάκις ἐὰν πίνητε, εἰς τὴν ἐμὴν ἀνάμνησιν*), the conclusion that Tatian combined Mark-Matthew with Paul in his account of the Last Supper,[4] would be premature: (1) the addition of "whenever you meet" has little weight since, as Burkitt has shown,[5] it is also found in the Nestorian liturgy of Theodore (sixth century A.D.). The wording of Aphraates is therefore probably that of the liturgy of his time and not that of the Diatessaron. (2) Tatian gives the command to repeat, not twice (like Paul), but only once (like Luke); and not immediately following the cup (like Paul), but only after the Saying about "the fruit of the vine", adding it on to the end of Mark-Matthew's account, presumably because he referred it to both actions.[6] So Tatian is nevertheless a witness for the longer text of Luke.[7]

The shorter version is to be read in D a d ff^{2} i l,[8] also in b and e (where the verse sequence is 15, 16, 19a, 17, 18).[9] It is disputed

[1] *The Homilies of Aphraates*, ed. W. Wright (1869), 221.

[2] G. Moesinger, *Evangelii conc. expositio facta a S. Ephraemo* (1876), 222, 230.

[3] D. Plooij, *A Further Study of the Liège Diatessaron* (1925), 8.

[4] Id. loc. cit., and at one time Th. Zahn, *Forschungen zur Gesch. des N.T. Kanons* 1 (1881), 205, who, however, at a later time has changed his view, cf. infra, note 7.

[5] *Evang. da-Mepharreshe* 2 (1904), 300.

[6] Brought to my attention by Ernst Haenchen.

[7] Th. Zahn, *Das Evangelium des Lukas*, 3–4th ed. (1920), 671 n. 34; P. Benoit, *Rev. Bibl.* 48 (1939), 359.

[8] The careful study of G. D. Kilpatrick, "Luke XXII 19b–20" in *J.T.S.* 47 (1946), 49–56, makes it clear that the archetype of c has to be added (c in its present state has been completed by the addition of vv. 19b–20 from vg).

[9] Placing of v. 19a earlier in b and e aims at establishing the sequence bread/wine, and at avoiding the very difficult transition from v. 19a to v. 21.

whether the old Syriac version (sy$^{cur\ sin}$) is derived from the shorter[1] or the longer text.[2] This question can be answered with certainty.

Sy^{cur} has the sequence vv. 15, 16, 19 (omitting *διδόμενον*), 17, 18; sy^{sin} has the same wording with five additions, which will be bracketed and put in spaced type in the following: "15, 16, (19) And He took the bread and recited the benediction over it and brake and gave to them and said (sy^{sin} + d^{e}): This is my body which (+ I give) for your sakes. Do this in remembrance of me. (17) And (+ after they had eaten supper) He took the cup and recited the benediction over it and said: Take this, divide it among you, (+ this is my blood, the new covenant). (18) (+ For) I say unto you that from now on I shall not drink of this {^{cur}: product of the vine / ^{sin}: fruit} until God's reign shall come."

It is thus quite certain (1) that the text of sy^{sin} is based upon that of sy^{cur}. For sy^{sin}—apart from two insignificant variations[3] —gives the exact reading of sy^{cur} with additions in five places.[4] This simplifies our problem which can now be put thus: is sy^{cur} based upon the shorter or the longer version? (2) The agreement of sy^{cur} in the unusual verse-sequence 15, 16, 19, 17, 18 with the witnesses to the shorter version b and e demonstrates that it is based on the shorter version. Moreover, sy^{cur} cannot be derived from the longer version because, in verse 19, after "this is my body, which for you" *διδόμενον* is lacking, and all the witnesses to the longer version read it without exception. Thus the words "which for you. Do this in remembrance of me" (v. 19 sy^{cur}) do not come from the longer text of Luke (22. 19), but from 1 Cor. 11. 24.

[1] F. C. Burkitt, op. cit. 2. 300–2; Sanday, *Outlines of the Life of Christ* (1911), 159; H. Lietzmann, *Messe und Herrenmahl* (1926), 217.

[2] A. Merx, op. cit. 2. 2. 416 sq., 432 sq.; P. Benoit, op. cit. 372–8, who on p. 376 regards vet-syr as a compromise between the shorter and the longer text; E. Schweizer in *Theol. Zeitschr.* 2 (1946), 85.

[3] First, sy^{cur} reads in v. 15 "until it will be accomplished in His reign", sy^{sin} on the other hand—without "in"—"until the reign will be accomplished". Secondly, in v. 18 sy^{cur} has "product of the vine", whereas sy^{sin} puts instead the more usual "fruit"—yet another proof for the earlier date of sy^{cur}.

[4] Both specific readings of the shorter text mentioned in the following note are also found in sy^{sin}.

The conclusion that sy^cur is in no way derived from the longer version receives cogent confirmation in that it shares with two witnesses to the shorter version D and e two insignificant but unusual readings.[1] This means that there cannot be any doubt about sy^cur being a representative of the shorter text in the form of b and e (15, 16, 19a, 17, 18), with an enlargement of verse 19 from 1 Cor. 11. 24. (3) There still remains the question about the origin of the five additions to the text of the Curetonianus in sy^sin (put in brackets above). Do they originate from the longer text which in the meantime must have become known in Syria? No, for on the one hand sy^sin omits the *τὸ ὑπὲρ ὑμῶν ἐκχυννόμενον* of Luke 22. 20, and on the other it reads "this is my blood, the new covenant", whereas the longer text has *τοῦτο τὸ ποτήριον ἡ καινὴ διαθήκη ἐν τῷ αἵματί μου.*[2] It follows therefore that neither sy^cur nor sy^sin shows any knowledge of the longer text; both old Syriac versions are to be regarded rather as amplified shorter texts. Only with the Syriac Peshitta (15, 16, 19, 20) can we really speak of the appearance of the longer text in Syria.

It follows that the shorter text is represented not only by D and it, but also by vet-syr, which enables us to trace the following development:

D a d ff² i l: 15–19a (original form of the shorter version);
b and e: 15, 16, 19a, 17, 18 (restoration of the bread-cup sequence);
sy^cur: 15, 16, 19a, 1 Cor. 11. 24b, 17, 18 (amplification using 1 Cor. 11. 24b);
sy^sin: the same as sy^cur with five additions.

[1] They are the following two: (1) the omission of *καί* before *διαμερίσατε* in v. 17 (missing only in D e sy^cur sin sa bo), and (2) the omission of *τῷ ἀνθρώπῳ* in v. 22 (missing only in D e sy^cur sin). I am indebted to E. Kerlen for this important observation.

[2] Where do the five enlargements in sy^sin come from? (*a*) the d^e is used to introduce the direct speech; (*b*) "I give" probably does not come either from Luke (who has "which is given" in the passive) or from John 6. 51, but has been added for stylistic reasons; (*c*) "after they had eaten supper" is taken from 1 Cor. 11. 25; (*d*) "this is my blood, the new covenant", is from Matt. 26. 28 sy^sin pal; Tat^arab; Aphraates, *Homilies* (1869), 1. 221; (*e*) "for" is found in Matt. 26. 29 sy^sin. The most important addition (*d*) comes, as is shown by Aphraates, from the Syriac liturgy of the Eucharist.

In view of the fact that the ancient Syriac versions are not independent witnesses but derive from the west, and that one western text tradition, first represented by Marcion, has the longer version, we may conclude that the shorter version is only to be found in one branch of the western tradition.

It is therefore clear that the weight of the evidence favours the longer text: be it noted that it is the reading of all the Greek MSS with the one exception of D. To regard the shorter text as original would mean accepting the greatest improbability, for it would involve assuming that an identical addition had been made to the Lucan text in *every* MS with the exception of D a b d e ff^{2} i l sy$^{cur\ sin}$. Only the most cogent reasons could warrant such an assumption.[1] At least we should have to inquire whether there were any analogous cases. In other words, Luke 22. 19 sq. must not be isolated, but we must examine every instance in which D it vet-syr have a shortened text of Luke.

(*b*) *Shortened passages of Luke in D it* (*vet-syr*).[2]

The following paragraph deals with the problem of the so-called "western non-interpolations" in Luke, of which Luke 22. 19b–20 is one. This name which itself contains a verdict in textual criticism, the validity of which is going to be examined here, was introduced by Westcott and Hort.

The question to be asked with regard to each of the following passages (as in Luke 22. 19b–20) is this: is the longer or the shorter text original? If the longer be original, then D it vet-syr has been shortened in the west; if the shorter text be original, then all the ecclesiastical provinces outside the west read an interpolated text. These two possibilities, it must be emphasized once more, are not on the same level from the point of view of textual criticism: the assumption that the archetype of the group D it vet-syr had suffered some loss is a comparatively easy one, whereas it is exceedingly difficult to visualize the historical evolution of a text where an interpolation could find its way into every

[1] The only practical hypothesis would be that the original MS. of Luke had been interpolated, after an intact copy had made its way to the west.

[2] The sign "it" will be employed in the following paragraph, even where only part of the evidence for the Old Latin is referred to. For the sake of completeness, those cases in which only D it (without vet-syr) represent the shorter text will also be noted.

Greek MS. with the exception of D only. The originality of the shorter text could be assumed, therefore, only for very cogent reasons.

Before the various passages in Luke's Gospel are examined in which D it vet-syr read a shorter text, something must be said about Marcion and Tatian, because they read in several places the same shorter text as D it (vet-syr). First Marcion. When we come on a reading attested by D it (vet-syr) Marcion, we are not seeing Marcion's influence upon the western text, but rather the text which Marcion found in Rome about A.D. 140. This has been shown by the independent and mutually confirmatory researches of A. Pott[1] and Harnack.[2] This pre-Marcionite western text is characterized in Luke by numerous assimilations to Matthew (and Mark).[3] So even before Marcion there was a tendency in Rome to harmonize the Gospels by a process of assimilation. It was not by accident that Rome was the place where Tatian thought of producing his harmony of the Gospels. With regard to Tatian, what has been said about Marcion applies equally to the combination D it (vet-syr) Tat. Textual criticism in the New Testament is in need of a reconstruction of Tatian's text, but this task has been repeatedly interrupted by the death of the scholars concerned: E. Preuschen (died 25 May 1920), A. Pott (died 24 February 1926), and D. Plooij (died 1936). However, our views have been much clarified, because to the number of witnesses already known [1. Tat^{ephr}: Ephraem's (died A.D. 373) commentary on the Diatessaron, preserved unfortunately only in the Armenian;[4] 2. Tat^{arab}: the Arabic version of the Diatessaron by '*Abdullah*

[1] In its final form in E. Preuschen-A. Pott, *Tatians Diatessaron* (1926), 13 sq.

[2] A. v. Harnack, *Marcion*, 1st ed. (1921), 222* sq.; 2nd ed. (1924), 242* sq. Harnack, op. cit., 2nd ed., 247*, enumerates eight exceptions in which a Marcionite reading may have penetrated into the western text as against 200 to 300 normal cases in which the opposite took place. Even these eight are rightly disputed by A. Pott, op. cit. 17 sq., cf. Th. Zahn, *Das Evangelium des Lukas*, 3–4th ed. (1920), 766.

[3] A. v. Harnack, op. cit., 2nd ed., 243* sq., cf. the lists which Harnack published only in the 1st ed., 223*–6*. Harnack's material is completed and his conclusions confirmed by the list of harmonizations which Marcion and Tatian have in common in A. Pott, op. cit. 18.

[4] A Latin translation by J. B. Aucher was published (1876) by G. Moesinger, *Evangelii conc. expositio facta a S. Ephraemo.*

ibn at-Tayib (died 1043), made from the Syriac with a strong leaning towards sy^{pesh};[1] 3. Tat^{fuld}: the harmony of the Gospels which is found instead of the four Gospels in the *Vulgata-Codex Fuldensis*, written A.D. 540-6 for bishop Victor of Capua, aud now preserved at the *Landesbibliothek* at Fulda, with Vulgate text][2] has been added 4. Tat^{ned}: the Liège Diatessaron[3]. This Dutch Diatessaron goes back to a Latin Diatessaron with essentially an OL text, and is therefore much closer to the original Diatessaron than Tat^{fuld} with its Vulgate text. So we have the text of the Diatessaron only in translations, Armenian, Arabic, Latin, and Dutch, whose value is diminished by their assimilation to the dominant ecclesiastical text of their time.[4] Nevertheless, since the Dutch Diatessaron was added to our textual sources, we have been able to judge Tatian's text more confidently than we could a few years ago. An examination of the text of Tat^{ned}, in so far as it has been published, shows that it frequently agrees with Marcion where it departs from the dominant or from the ancient Alexandrian text.[5]

[1] Edited by A. Ciasca, *Tatiani Evangeliorum harmoniae Arabice* (1888).

[2] Edited by E. Ranke (1868).

[3] Excellent edition: The Liège Diatessaron ed. with a textual apparatus by D. Plooij—C. A. Philipps—A. J. Barnow, *Verh. d. Kon. Akad. van Wetens. te Amsterdam, Afd. Letterk., N.R.* 31 (1929 sq.). Five fascicles have appeared (1929–38), covering the text as far as Matt. 22. 40, with a most careful apparatus.

[4] Ephraem least.

[5] Instances of identical readings in D Marc Tat^{ned}:

Luke 4. 34 omits ἔα: D 33 it sy^{sin} (^{cur}) ^{pal} sa bo Marc Tat^{ned}.
6. 5 follows 6. 10 in D Marc, omitted in Tat^{ned}.
6. 12 omits τοῦ θεοῦ: D Marc Tat^{ned}.
6. 26 omits πάντες: ℜ D sy Marc Tat$^{arab\ ned}$.
6. 26 omits γάρ: D lat Marc Tat^{ned}.
6. 37 omits καί³: A C D pl lat Marc Tat^{ned}.
10. 1 has ἀπέδειξεν instead of ἀνέδειξεν: D it sa sy Marc Tat$^{ephr\ fuld\ ned}$.
11. 38 reads ἤρξατο διακρινόμενος ἐν ἑαυτῷ λέγειν: D pc lat sy^{cur} Marc Tat^{ned}.
12. 47 omits ἑτοιμάσας ἤ: 𝔓 45 D 69 Marc Tat^{ned} Ir Or Ambr.
12. 49 has εἰς instead of ἐπί: 𝔓 45 ℜ D Δ sy lat Marc^{tert} Tat^{ned}.
16. 23 omits καί, so that the reading is ἐτάφη ἐν τῷ ᾅδῃ: ℵ lat (sy^{sin}) Marc Tat$^{fuld\ ned}$.

If we add to this the numerous similarities between Marcion and Tatian which A. Pott[1] had already listed before the publication of $\mathrm{Tat}^{\mathrm{ned}}$, we can draw a definite conclusion: both Marcion and Tatian used the western text current in Rome about the middle of the second century A.D. This result demolishes the so-called Tatian hypothesis of H. v. Soden,[2] who wanted to make Tatian responsible for almost all the divergences from the original text in the Greek

---

16. 23 adds *ἀναπαυόμενον* to *ἐν τοῖς κόλποις αὐτοῦ*: D θ it arm Marc $\mathrm{Tat}^{\mathrm{ned}}$.

16. 29 adds *αὐτῷ* after *λέγει δέ*: 𝔎 D θ pl lat Marc $\mathrm{Tat}^{\mathrm{arab\ ned}}$.

Instances of identical readings in Marc and $\mathrm{Tat}^{\mathrm{ned}}$ without D:

6. 38 adds *καί* before *ὑπερεκχυννόμενον*: A C pl it vg Marc $\mathrm{Tat}^{\mathrm{ned}}$.

7. 24 puts *εἰς τὴν ἔρημον* after *θεάσασθαι*: Marc $\mathrm{Tat}^{\mathrm{ephr\ ned}}$.

8. 25 has *ὅς* instead of *ὅτι καί*: Marc $\mathrm{Tat}^{\mathrm{ned}}$.

9. 7–8 has *ἄλλοι . . . ἄλλοι . . . ἄλλοι* (cf. Mark 6. 15) instead of *ὑπό τινων . . . ὑπό τινων . . . ἄλλων* sy $\mathrm{Marc}^{\mathrm{tert}}$ $\mathrm{Tat}^{\mathrm{ar\ ned}}$.

10. 5 omits *πρῶτον*: D^{2} 579 r Marc $\mathrm{Tat}^{\mathrm{ned}}$ Or.

10. 21 has *εὐχαριστῶ σοι* instead of *ἐξομολογοῦμαί σοι*: sy Marc $\mathrm{Tat}^{\mathrm{ephr\ ned}}$.

10. 22 has *ἀποκαλύψῃ* instead of *βούλομαι ἀποκαλύψαι*: Marc Just $\mathrm{Tat}^{\mathrm{ned}}$ Ir Tert Cl-Al Or Eus.

11. 7 omits *μου* after *παιδία*: C M it $\mathrm{sy}^{\mathrm{sin\ cur}}$ Marc $\mathrm{Tat}^{\mathrm{ned}}$ (who, however, reads "of the house" instead of *μου*).

11. 8: $\mathrm{Tat}^{\mathrm{ned}}$ reads an enlarged text: "and he who stands without continues to shout and to knock at the door". Similar: it *et ille si perseveraverit pulsans.* D. Plooij, p. 84, remarks that the text of Marcion (and Tert.) plainly also mentions "the door": Tert., *adv. Marc.* 4. 29, p. 297, *cuius ianuam norat*; *Praescr.* 12, p. 6, *etiam pulsator ille vicini ianuam tundebat.* (Possible, but not certain, for Luke 11. 7 also mentions the door: *ἤδη ἡ θύρα κέκλεισται.*)

11. 28: instead of *φυλάσσοντες*, 9 2145 (=min with Tat influence) $\mathrm{sy}^{\mathrm{pesh}}$ Arm Marc read: *ποιοῦντες*. $\mathrm{Tat}^{\mathrm{ned}}$ combines the two readings: *ē̄n dat behouden ē̄n dar na werken.*

12. 3 has "whisper" instead of *ἐλαλήσατε*: $\mathrm{Marc}^{\mathrm{tert}}$ *quae inter se mussitarent*, sy $\mathrm{Tat}^{\mathrm{ar}}$ "what you whisper", $\mathrm{Tat}^{\mathrm{ned}}$ *dat ic v rune.*

12. 47 omits *ἐκεῖνος*: sy sa Marc $\mathrm{Tat}^{\mathrm{ned}}$.

13. 15 has the sequence *ὄνον . . . βοῦν*: 69 aeth Marc $\mathrm{Tat}^{\mathrm{ned}}$.

[1] *Zeitschr. f. Kirch.-Gesch.* 42 (1923), 202 sq.; *Tatians Diatessaron* (1926), 18 n. 1–3.

[2] *Die Schriften des N.T. in ihrer aeltesten erreichbaren Textgestalt* 1 (1902–10), 2 (1913).

MSS, the versions, and the Fathers. That this hypothesis presupposed a maximum number of improbabilities had long been recognized. As a matter of fact, the influence of Tatian upon the development of the New Testament text was mainly limited to Syria: sy^{cur} as well as sy^{sin} are largely indebted to the Diatessaron.[1] For our particular question we may conclude that wherever we meet with the combination D it vet-syr Tat, we are not faced with the influence of Tatian upon the western text, but the text which Tatian found and used during his stay in Rome (about A.D. 150-72).[2]

After this preliminary survey, let us turn to individual passages in Luke. Apart from unimportant omissions and minor abbreviations (for the most part harmonizing omissions), the following major gaps occur in the text of Luke in D it vet-syr.

5. 39 is missing from D it (sy$^{\text{cur sin}}$ *deest*) Marc Eus. Here we have an adjustment of the pre-Marcionite text of Luke to the Synoptic parallels: Luke 5. 39 has no parallel in Mark or Matthew. The omission of the offending verse may have been encouraged by encratite tendencies. Its antiquity is attested by the Semitism of the positive *χρηστός* in place of a comparative. The longer text is therefore the original one.

7. 7a: *διὸ οὐδὲ ἐμαυτὸν ἠξίωσα πρὸς σὲ ἐλθεῖν* is omitted in D pc it sy^{sin} (sy^{cur} *deest*) Tat$^{\text{ar ned}}$. These words are missing in Matthew for a very good reason. According to Matt. 8. 5, the centurion came to Jesus in person; but Luke 7. 1–10 knows nothing of such a personal meeting: according to him, the centurion first sent (7. 3) some of the Jewish Elders and afterwards his friends (7. 6) to Jesus, and excused his own absence with the words quoted. Tatian has harmonized Matthew and Luke by saying that the centurion came to Jesus together with the Jewish Elders.[3] In view of what has been stated above as a

[1] This has been shown by F. C. Burkitt, *Evangelion da-Mepharreshe* 2 (1904), chap. 4, "The Diatessaron and the Old Syriac", pp. 173–212.

[2] Already shown by Burkitt, op. cit. 5, 209, 240. When Old Latin and Old Syriac agree, we are faced with "the old Greek text of Rome, which Tatian has used for his Diatessaron"; such is the correct verdict of A. Juelicher in *Journ. Bibl. Lit.* 43 (1924), 170.

[3] Thus unanimously Tat^{ar} and Ephraem's commentary on the Diatessaron, ed. Moesinger, p. 74.

general rule about the combination of D it syr Tat, it is highly probable that Tatian did not have verse 7a in the text of Luke he had before him. The omission of Luke 7. 7a was probably one of the many assimilations of Luke to Matthew in the text current in Rome about A.D. 150. The reason for the omission was in any case the contradiction to Matt. 8. 5. Once more the longer text is *certainly* the original.

7. 33 omits *ἄρτον* and *οἶνον*: φ D min it sy$^{sin\ cur}$ arm Tat^{ned}. The two words are also missing in Matt. 11. 18. A harmonizing omission.[1]

10. 41-2 omits *μεριμνᾷς καὶ θορυβάζῃ* (preserved in D) *περὶ πολλά*, 42. *ὀλίγων δέ ἐστιν χρεία ἢ ἑνός*: D it sy^{sin};[2] and omits *γάρ*: D it sy$^{sin\ cur}$ Tat^{ned}. The longer text is without doubt the original: the abbreviation is caused by the offence taken at the allusion to "material things", as the remaining variants confirm.

11. 35-6 is omitted by D it Tat$^{ephr\ fuld\ ned}$, only verse 36 by sy^{cur}. Both verses contain typically Lucan language: *σκοπεῖν* (only in Luke), *τὶς* (*τὶ*) used as an adjective (twice in Mark, once in Matthew, seven times in John, 105 times in Luke and Acts), *λύχνος* (once in Mark, twice in Matthew, six times in Luke), and are therefore original. Why then the omission? The answer is that all the witnesses quoted read instead: Matt. 6. 23b. So we have another harmonizing omission in the pre-Tatian western text, and the longer version is again the original.

12. 19 omits *κείμενα εἰς ἔτη πολλά· ἀναπαύου, φάγε, πίε*: D it. The language shows the genuineness of the longer text.[3]

12. 21 missing in D it, is probably an accidental omission.[4]

12. 39 omits *ἐγρηγόρησεν ἂν καί*: ℵ* (D) it sy$^{sin\ cur}$ sa arm Marc. Pre-Marcionite western text. (Scribe's omission, facilitated by the subsequent *ἄν*?)

[1] "The frequent assimilation to Matthew", E. Preuschen-A. Pott, op. cit. 43 n. 1.

[2] The words were originally missing also from sy^{cur}, F. C. Burkitt, op. cit. 2. 242, 292; cf. the omission of *γάρ* in sy^{cur}.

[3] *Ἔτος* is a favourite word of Luke (once in Matthew, twice in Mark, three times in John, twenty-six times in Luke and Acts).

[4] Th. Zahn, *Das Evangelium des Lukas*, 3–4th ed. (1920), 499 n. 24.

19. 25 is missing from D W it $sy^{sin\ cur}$ bo. The verse is not found in Matthew. So here is probably another harmonizing omission by the western text.

21. 30 omits *βλέποντες ἀφ' ἑαυτῶν*: D lat $sy^{sin\ cur}$ Marc Tat. The language is characteristically Lucan: *ἀφ' ἑαυτῶν* (= of your own selves) is found only in Luke (12. 57; 21. 30) among the Synoptists. As the words are missing from Mark 13. 28 and Matt. 24. 32, this is another harmonizing omission in the pre-Marcionite western text.

24. 6 omits *οὐκ ἔστιν ὧδε ἀλλὰ ἠγέρθη* ($Marc^{epiph}$ preserves *ἠγέρθη*): D it $Marc^{epiph}$. That these words are genuinely Lucan, and not a harmonizing interpolation in an original shorter text, is suggested by the independence of their form from Mark and Matthew. Only Luke 24. 6 has the antithesis.

24. 12 omits *ὁ δὲ Πέτρος ἀναστὰς ἔδραμεν ἐπὶ τὸ μνημεῖον καὶ παρακύψας βλέπει τὰ ὀθόνια κείμενα* (omitted in ℵ B al) *μόνα* (omitted in ℵ A K al) *καὶ ἀπῆλθεν πρὸς ἑαυτὸν θαυμάζων τὸ γεγονός*: D it (sy)[1] Marc $Tat^{ar\ fuld}$. Many regard this verse as a summary of John 20. 3–10, which has been interpolated here. This would mean that D it Marc Tat had indeed preserved the original text of Luke. But the reasons given are not very convincing: (1) the similarity with John 20. 4–6, 10, is remarkable but not unparalleled,[2] for Luke shows a number of other affinities with John precisely in his account of the Passion and the resurrection.[3] (2) Admittedly the words

[1] The verse was probably missing from the original of $sy^{cur\ sin}$ as well, for this is the only place in Luke where $sy^{cur\ sin}$ have Shim'on instead of Greek *Πέτρος*, and this suggests that v. 12 is a later addition.

[2] Cp. e.g. John 12. 8 with Mark 14. 7.

[3] Parallels in the Easter narrative: Luke 24. 9–11/John 20. 2, the message of the women (woman); Luke 24. 13/John 19. 25, the name Cleopas (Clopas) occurs only here in the N.T.; Luke 24. 24/John 20. 3–10, ascertaining the empty tomb; Luke 24. 25/John 20. 27, rebuke for unbelief; Luke 24. 36/John 20. 19, visitation of the Twelve on the evening of Easter Sunday; Luke 24. 39/John 20. 27, command to touch the stigmata; Luke 24. 40/John 20. 20, showing of the stigmata; Luke 24. 41/John 21. 5, "have you anything to eat?"; Luke 24. 42/John 21. 10, fish brought to Jesus; Luke 24. 49/John 20. 21, commissioning of the Apostles; Luke 24. 49/John 20. 22, (promise of) the gift of the Spirit. Cf. J. Schniewind, *Die Parallel-Perikopen bei Lukas und Johannes* (1914); F. Hauck, *Das Evangelium des Lukas* (1934), 6 sq.

ὀθόνιον, παρακύπτειν, ἀπέρχεσθαι πρὸς ἑαυτόν, are not found elsewhere in Luke, but in John too *ὀθόνιον* is found only in 19. 40; 20. 5, 6, 7, *παρακύπτειν* only in 20. 5, 11, *ἀπέρχεσθαι πρὸς ἑαυτόν* only in 20. 10. The use of the words is simply required by the subject-matter, and there can be no question of a specifically Johannine idiom. On the contrary, Luke 24. 12 shows Lucan idiom: *ἀναστάς*, used pleonastically as a Semitism without its strict meaning, is totally absent from John, is found once in Matthew and five times in Mark, but another twenty-eight times in Luke-Acts; *τὸ γεγονός* is found, apart from Mark 5. 14, only in Luke (another four times in the Gospel and three times in Acts). The verse is indeed "in good Lucan style".[1] There is only one difficulty, which so far has gone unnoticed: the present tense of *βλέπει*. On the whole Luke avoids the historic present. Mark has it 148 times, but Luke has, with one exception (8. 49), changed it in all the passages he has taken from Mark, and otherwise has used it only eight times (five of which are *λέγει* or *λέγουσιν*) in the Gospel and fourteen times in Acts. However, the difficulty is not insuperable: the historic present may indicate a change in the source that is being used.

24. 21 omits *σὺν πᾶσιν τούτοις*: it sy$^{\text{sin cur pesh}}$ Tat$^{\text{ar ned}}$. *Σύν* is a favourite word of Luke (four times in Matthew, six times in Mark, three times in John, seventy-five times in Luke and Acts). An emphatic, amplifying *σύν* to introduce a new point—Heb. עִם, apart from—is found in the New Testament only here. This Semitism has a parallel in the New Testament in *ἐν πᾶσι τούτοις* Luke 16. 26, where the meaning is the same. The words are without doubt the original text of Luke.

24. 36 omits *καὶ λέγει αὐτοῖς· εἰρήνη ὑμῖν*: D it. This half-verse is found verbatim in John 20. 19. In view of the historic present *λέγει*, which is as rare in Luke as it is frequent in John, the possibility of an interpolation has to be admitted, although the passage is found in all the MSS with the exception of D it.

24. 40 omits *καὶ τοῦτο εἰπὼν ἔδειξεν αὐτοῖς τὰς χεῖρας*

[1] A. Harnack, *Marcion*, 2nd ed. (1924), 238*, 247*.

καὶ τοὺς πόδας: D it $sy^{sin\ cur}$ Marc. An interpolation of John 20. 20 (which reads *τὴν πλευράν* instead of *τοὺς πόδας*) is less likely than a harmonizing omission in the western text to avoid a supposed contradiction of John 20. 17.

24. 50 omits *ἕως*: D lat Tat. *ἕως* with a preposition following is found in the New Testament only in Luke (Acts 17. 14; 21. 5; 26. 11). It is therefore genuine.

24. 51 omits *καὶ ἀνεφέρετο εἰς τὸν οὐρανόν*: ℵ* D it sy^{sin} (^{cur} *deest*). The shorter text omits the ascension on the evening of Easter Day for harmonizing purposes, because it appears to contradict the report in Acts 1. 1–11, where the ascension takes place forty days later (1. 3). The shorter text also makes a stylistic break: verses 50 and 52 each show two co-ordinated clauses, and the same construction is to be expected in verse 51.

24. 52 omits *προσκυνήσαντες αὐτόν*: D it sy^{sin} Tat^{ned}.

The result of all this is that in the great majority of the cases discussed Marcion or Tatian or both add their testimony to D it vet-syr; it follows that we are dealing with readings of the western text just before and about A.D. 150. In most instances the longer version seemed in all probability to be original. Disputed verses or words often revealed Lucan style. The assumption of abbreviations in the west is supported by the tendency, distinctive of the western text, to harmonize with Matthew (and Mark), by an encratite tendency, and by the desire to spiritualize. We must also be willing to admit some abbreviations as due to scribal error. In two cases only (Luke 24. 12, 36) did an historic present make it difficult though not impossible to regard the longer text as the original. One of the best authorities has concluded: "It is not reasonable to suppose that the original text was preserved in a pure form only in the West and was wholly obliterated in the East, from which it came."[1]

This result is a decisive argument in favour of the longer text of Luke's account of the Last Supper.

(*c*) *Are there objections to the genuineness of the longer text —despite the MS. evidence?*

Since the year 1881 the opinion has nevertheless gained ground

[1] F. G. Kenyon, *The Text of the Greek Bible* (1937), 220.

that the shorter text is the original text of Luke.[1] That view was taken in the first edition of this book. The reasons in favour of it are weighty enough. (1) At first sight it is plain that the shorter reading is the more difficult one. What could have caused the deletion of verses 19b–20? Their addition, on the other hand, is very easily explained, because the abrupt break after verse 19a cries out for some completion. Thus the two main rules of textual criticism, "the shorter reading is the older one" and "the more difficult reading is to be preferred", join in endorsing the superiority of the shorter text. (2) Moreover, there are weighty considerations against the Lucan origin of the longer version: (a) a comparison with the parallels shows that the longer text from *τὸ ὑπὲρ ὑμῶν διδόμενον* to *ἐν τῷ αἵματί μου* (verses 19b–20) is identical with 1 Cor. 11. 24–5, save for slight stylistic polishing[2] and

[1] First: B. F. Westcott-F. J. A. Hort, *The New Testament in the Original Greek* (Cambridge-London, 1881). These were followed, according to the list in H. J. Holtzmann-A. Juelicher-W. Bauer, *Lehrbuch der N.T. Theologie*, 2nd ed., 1 (Tuebingen, 1911), 374 n. 1, by Robinson, Gardner, Andersen, Brandt, Loisy, Nicolardot, Zahn, Wendt, Rietschel, E. Haupt, Titius, B. and J. Weiss, P. W. Schmiedel, Grafe, E. Schuerer, Pfleiderer, Barth, v. Dobschuetz, R. A. Hoffmann, Heitmueller. More recent works are: G. Dalman, *Jesus-Jeschua* (Leipzig, 1922), 141; v. Dobschuetz-Nestle, *Einfuehrung in das griech. N.T.*, 4th ed. (Goettingen, 1923), 133; W. Bauer, *Goettinger Gel. Anz.* 185 (1923), 13; H. Lietzmann, *Messe und Herrenmahl* (Bonn, 1926), 215–17; id., *An die Korinther*, 3rd ed. (Tuebingen, 1931), 57; A. Oepke in *Allgem. Evang.-Luth. Kirchenzeitung* 59 (1926), 55; in a spirited style, F. C. Burkitt, "On Luke 22. 17–20" in *J.T.S.* 28 (1927), 178–81; R. Harris, *Eucharistic Origins* (Cambridge, 1927), 11 sq.; Joh. Jeremias, *Das Evangelium nach Markus*(Chemnitz, 1928), 182; id., *Das Evangelium nach Lukas* (Chemnitz, 1930), 240; E. Klostermann, *Das Lukas-Evangelium*, 2nd ed. (Tuebingen, 1929), 207; F. Hauck, *Das Evangelium des Markus* (Leipzig, 1931), 169, who, however, takes a different view in *Das Evangelium des Lukas* (Leipzig, 1934), 262, where he finds a "smoothing" tendency in the shorter text of Luke; R. Otto, *Reich Gottes und Menschensohn* (Munich, 1934), 227–34; J. Finegan, *Die Ueberlieferung der Leidens- und Auferstehungs-Geschichte Jesu* (Giessen, 1934), 11; A. Hoffmann, *Das Gottesbild Jesu* (Hamburg, 1934), 162 sq.; R. Hupfeld, *Die Abendmahlsfeier* (1935), 60, 62; E. Lohmeyer in *Journ. of Bibl. Lit.* 56 (1937), 248; A. D. Nock, *Paulus* (1939), 152; G. D. Kilpatrick in *J.T.S.* 47 (1946), 49–56.

[2] Luke 22. 19b adds *διδόμενον*. The mere *τὸ ὑπὲρ ὑμῶν* 1 Cor. 11. 24, is linguistically very difficult. The addition of *διδόμενον* to the word over the bread in Luke also corresponds to the *ἐκχυννόμενον* in the case of the wine.

two unimportant inversions,[1] whereas verse 19a (down to *σῶμά μου*) and the closing words *τὸ ὑπὲρ ὑμῶν ἐκχυννόμενον* (which take the place of the second Pauline command to repeat the rite)[2] are in substantial agreement with Mark 14. 22, 24.[3] So Luke's longer version is evidently secondary in relation to both Paul and Mark: to Paul because of the stylistic adjustments and the attempt to make the sayings over the bread and over the wine parallel; to Mark because of traces of liturgical development. The longer version is thus a compilation from Paul and Mark. Among the words based upon the Pauline version, the most marked similarity is found in the connecting clause *ὡσαύτως καὶ τὸ ποτήριον* (Luke: *καὶ τὸ ποτήριον ὡσαύτως*) *μετὰ τὸ δειπνῆσαι*, which shows most clearly the close relation between the two texts, because connecting clauses are far more subject to change than Sayings attributed to Jesus Himself. Where else do we find in Luke such a close verbal dependence on Paul? (b) It can also be shown that Luke himself cannot possibly be the author of the longer text. First, the words *τὸ ὑπὲρ ὑμῶν ἐκχυννόμενον* are added to those taken from Paul, but they are added very clumsily and at a considerable distance from *ποτήριον* to which they belong; the unexpected nominative instead of a grammatically correct dative indicates that the words come from a passage where *αἷμα* was in the nominative,[4] like Mark 14. 24; Matt. 26. 28. The pre-

[1] Luke 22. 20: *καὶ τὸ ποτήριον ὡσαύτως* (1 Cor. 11. 24 reads *ὡσαύτως καὶ τὸ ποτήριον*); Luke 22. 20: *ἐν τῷ αἵματί μου* (1 Cor. 11. 24 reads *ἐν τῷ ἐμῷ αἵματι*). The second change has the aim of establishing a perfect parallel to Luke 22. 19: *τὸ σῶμά μου*, and therefore places the possessive pronoun in the same position in the word over the cup, which it has in that over the bread. In addition to this, the copula *ἐστίν* which is found in 1 Cor. 11. 25 is missing from Luke 22. 20b.

[2] On the omission of the command to repeat the rite of the cup, cf. supra, p. 29 n. 1.

[3] Notice, however, that Luke 22. 19a reads *εὐχαριστήσας* (instead of *εὐλογήσας* in Mark/Matthew), as in 1 Cor. 11. 24. Furthermore, Luke 22. 20 has *ὑμῶν* (instead of *πολλῶν* in Mark/Matthew), as in 1 Cor. 11. 23 and Luke 22. 19b, in accordance with liturgical style. Finally, the passive participle *ἐκχυννόμενον* is put at the end, corresponding to the position of *διδόμενον* in v. 19b. All these divergences from Mark show the traces of the liturgical development of the eucharistic formula.

[4] M. Dibelius, *Formgeschichte*, 2nd ed. (1933), 211 n. 1.

servation of the nominative makes Luke speak of the outpoured cup instead of the outpoured blood.[1] A compilation in such a clumsy style is certainly not Lucan. There are many points to establish the fact that Luke 22. 19b–20 is non-Lucan in idiom. Only in verses 19b and 20 in the whole of Luke/Acts is *ὑπέρ* used of the atoning work of Christ, and only here does the word *ἀνάμνησις* occur in Luke (it is rare anyhow, but Acts 10. 4 uses *μνημόσυνον*). Luke uses the possessive pronouns *ἐμός*, etc., predicatively and pronominally, but nowhere excepting verse 19 attributively.[2] The article before *ποτήριον* (v. 20) is unexpected after both *ποτήριον*[3] and *ἄρτος* have appeared without an article in verses 17, 19a; the use of the article is explicable from 1 Cor. 11. 25.[4] Luke 22. 20b omits the copula *ἐστίν*, although it is read in Paul;[5] elsewhere Luke is careful to insert the copula, even where Mark and Matthew fail to use it. Nine such cases can be pointed out.[6] These considerations make it highly probable that Luke 22. 19b–20 is not Luke's own work. But verses which were not Luke's own work (the conclusion appears unavoidable) cannot very well belong to the original text of Luke.

However, this conclusion falls to the ground once it is realized that Luke 22. 19–20 is a liturgical formula.[7] Luke or his source would almost involuntarily copy the familiar liturgical formula when he came to the words of institution in his Gospel; Mark did exactly the same. Therefore we cannot expect to find Lucan idiom at this point. Even the close relation of Luke 22. 19b–20 to Paul is no longer surprising in a liturgical formula. Indeed, Paul himself expressly states that he owes the words of institution to tradition (1 Cor. 11. 23). So it by no means follows that Luke must have known 1 Corinthians if he wrote verses 19b–20.

[1] The words *τὸ ὑπὲρ ὑμῶν ἐκχυννόμενον* Luke 22. 20 refer grammatically to *τὸ ποτήριον*, but according to their meaning to *ἐν τῷ αἵματί μου*, and should therefore be in the dative.

[2] G. D. Kilpatrick in *J.T.S.* 47 (1946), 51.

[3] The variant in A D W Θ al by which *τό* is added in v. 17 is probably secondary.

[4] Th. Zahn, *Das Evangelium des Lukas*, 3–4th ed. (1920), 675 sq.

[5] F. C. Burkitt, "On Luke 22. 17–20" in *J.T.S.* 28 (1927), 180.

[6] H. J. Cadbury, *The Style and Literary Method of Luke* (Cambridge, 1919), 149. Instances showing the opposite procedure are very rare.

[7] E. Lohmeyer, *Theol. Rundschau* N.F. 9 (1937), 178.

It is much nearer the truth to explain the similarity of Luke and Paul by reference to ecclesiastical usages. The Lucan formula may, because of its affinity to that in use at Corinth, originate from some field of Paul's missionary activity. Indeed, seeing that it also shows strong resemblance to the Marcan tradition, which derived from Palestine, and that the incongruence of the final participial construction suggests an origin in a bilingual area, we may with some probability suggest Luke's home Church in Syria as the place of origin, where Paul worked for some time before his missionary journeys began.[1] And, lastly, the incongruence of the participial construction *τὸ ὑπὲρ ὑμῶν ἐκχυννόμενον* is tolerable in a liturgical formula. The liturgical language of the sanctuary which was recited in worship phrase by phrase[2] and so enabled the last clause to be heard as an announcement in its own right,[3] the parallel to the corresponding participial construction in the nominative for the formula used over the bread, the familiarity with an old-established formula[4]—all this probably removed the feeling of incongruity in liturgical usage.[5] The complete absence of any stylistic emendation shows that nobody was offended by it in the early Church. This means that Luke 22. 19–20 is not a literary compilation from Mark and Paul, but a "third variation"[6] on the liturgical formula of the Eucharist, a variation showing an advance on Mark and Paul. So the un-Lucan style of the longer version constitutes no valid argument against its originality.

The only remaining difficulty is how to derive the puzzling shorter version from it. What could have occasioned the omission of verses 19b–20? How can the genesis of the shorter version be adequately explained? The shorter text of Luke 22. 15–19a is highly distinctive in its surprisingly abrupt ending with the words "this is my body". This cannot possibly be explained by the assumption that the explanatory word over the wine was unknown to Luke: such an assumption is excluded by the fact that he had

[1] Syrian origin is already suggested by A. Schlatter, *Der Evangelist Lukas* (1931), 421; J. Héring, *Le royaume de Dieu et sa venue* (1937), 227.

[2] E. Lohmeyer in a letter, dated September 17, 1937.

[3] A. Schlatter, op. cit. 422.

[4] On the age of the participial construction cf. infra, p. 114.

[5] Remember the grammatical inaccuracies in the formal language of Revelation (1. 4–5, 8; 3. 12).

[6] M. Dibelius, *Formgeschichte*, 2nd ed. (1933), 211.

Mark's Gospel before him, and in it Mark's account of the Last Supper. A *communio sub una* as the original form of the Eucharist cannot therefore be founded upon the shorter text of Luke.[1] Equally impossible is an explanation that the shorter text of Luke presupposed a Eucharist with the sequence wine-bread (Luke 22. 17–19a); for there never has been such a Eucharist. Neither would the frequently advocated removal of verse 19a[2] solve the problem: such a radical operation is inadmissible,[3] because verse 19a is found in all our authorities. Lastly, the popular view that the shorter text is due to the exception taken to the two cups, Luke 22. 17/8, 20, and a consequent elimination of the second, is no more satisfactory. For this view cannot explain why it was not the first cup—the less important theologically and liturgically—which was removed to preserve the Eucharistic sequence. Above all, it cannot explain why verse 19b was removed too, for which there was no occasion whatever. Rather, since we cannot believe that "Luke altogether avoids the concept of an atoning sacrifice"[4] in view of Acts 20. 28,[5] there is only one explanation for the abrupt ending

[1] The same result, although for different reasons, is reached by C. Clemen, *Religionsgeschichtliche Erklaerung des N.T.*, 2nd ed. (Giessen, 1924), 174–7.

[2] G. Loeschcke, *Zeitschr. fuer wiss. Theol.* 54 (1912), 196; G. Bertram, *Die Leidensgeschichte Jesu* (1922), 27; K. L. Schmidt, art. "Abendmahl" I. im N.T. in *R.G.G.*, 2nd ed., 1 (1927), 7–10; H. N. Bate, "The 'shorter text' of St. Luke XXII 15–20" in *J.T.S.* 28 (1927), 367 sq.; H. Huber, *Das Herrenmahl im N.T.*, diss. Berne (Leipzig, 1929), 68; R. Bultmann, *Gesch. der synopt. Tradition*, 2nd ed. (Göttingen, 1931), 286 n. 1.

[3] R. Otto, *Reich Gottes und Menschensohn* (Munich, 1934), 227, calls it "arbitrary" and "nonsensical".

[4] L. v. Sybel, "Das letzte Mahl Jesu" in *Theol. Stud. u. Krit.* 95 (1923–4), 123; M. Kiddle in *J.T.S.* 36 (1935), 277 sq. A similar view on Luke's theology is taken by A. Hoffmann, *Das Gottesbild Jesu* (Hamburg, 1934), 167 sq., esp. 172–3.

[5] The fact that Luke knows—and accepts—the idea of the atoning sacrifice also follows from his references to Is. 53: Luke 22. 37 = Is. 53. 12; Acts 8. 32 sq. = Is. 53. 7–8; Acts 3. 13, 26; 4. 27, 30 (παῖς); 3. 14; 7. 52; 22. 14 (ὁ δίκαιος, cf. Is. 53. 11); 2. 23; 3. 18; 13. 27, 29; 17. 3, 11; 26. 22 sq. (the suffering of the Messiah is predicted in Holy Scripture). E. Schweizer, *Theol. Zeitschr.* 2 (1946), 100 n. 94, also suggests that the expression "hanged on a tree" in Acts 10. 39 = Deut. 21. 22, is probably used with the idea expressed in Gal. 3. 13 in mind.

of the shorter version: the intention was to keep the Eucharist from profanation.[1] This means that the shorter version belongs to the authorities cited above[2], which in various ways undertook this protection of the Eucharist. In the beginning of the second century somewhere in the West a copyist, himself perhaps a theologian, shortened Luke's account of the Last Supper, omitting the words "for you" spoken over the bread and all that followed, leaving only the opening words to point towards the sacred formula by way of *aposiopesis* rather as a first line of a poem can stand for the whole.[3] Then a small group of western and Syriac

[1] This explanation I heard as a student in a lecture of Joh. Leipoldt, in the winter of 1919–20 (cf. also the allusion made by him in *Die urchristliche Taufe im Lichte der Religionsgeschichte*, Leipzig, 1928, 33 n. 5), and I have found it confirmed by observations made about keeping of secrets among the Rabbis and in the New Testament. I now see that the same explanation is given by Th. Zahn, *Das Evangelium nach Lukas*, 3–4th ed. (Leipzig, 1920), 677–8: the fact that Luke gives such an incomplete account of the words and deeds of Jesus "can hardly be explained in any other way than by his reserve towards his first reader, Theophilus, and those subsequent readers who, like him, had not yet been received into the Church". In addition to this it seems possible that already at the time when Luke's Gospel was written the Eucharist was involved in the slanderous accusations which were brought against the Christians; "and finally, apart from all this, it seemed right to limit the instruction about this supreme mystery of the Christian faith to full members of the Church" (ibid., p. 678). Cf. also A. Schlatter, *Die Theologie der Apostel*, 2nd ed. (1922), 520, "perhaps it is possible to some degree to speak of a secrecy which covered and protected the Eucharist right from the beginning of the work of the Apostles". H. N. Bate, "The 'shorter text' of St. Luke 22. 15–20" in *J.T.S.* 28 (1927), 367–8, who regards only Luke 22. 15–18, 21 as the original text of Luke, says, "I am tempted to think that we have here such a genuine trace of a *disciplina arcani* as reappears in the Fourth Gospel. One can quite readily conceive that St. Luke's narrative was published under circumstances which made it inadvisable to disclose the inner meaning of Christian worship." H. Huber, *Das Herrenmahl im Neuen Testament*, diss. Berne (Leipzig, 1929), 26, 68: for Luke the Lord's Supper is an "*arcanum*".

[2] Cf. supra, pp. 81-7.

[3] In a comprehensive article in *J.T.S.* 47 (1946), 49–56, G. D. Kilpatrick states that in Luke 22. 19a we are confronted with a cue, "which the faithful would know how to supplement, but which would tell the uninitiated little. This explains the abrupt ending of the account at τοῦτό ἐστιν τὸ σῶμά μου. The abruptness of the ending is deliberate in order to preserve the *arcanum* of the rite" (p. 53). For the technique

MSS adopted this shortened text (there is no question of a universal development over the whole area in which Luke's Gospel circulated, but only of an offshoot of the textual tradition confined to Syria and the West). If this explanation be correct, there are no decisive objections against the originality of the longer text, which is demanded by the principles of textual criticism.[1]

(3) *The Oldest Form of the Words of Institution*

Our next task is to compare the four texts of the words of institution (1 Cor. 11. 23–5; Mark 14. 22–5/Matt. 26. 26–9; Luke 22. 15–20), in order to determine their earliest form.

(*a*) *The Word of Interpretation over the bread.*

The expression "word of interpretation" (*Deutewort*) is used, because it is familiar in Germany. It should be remembered, however, that we do not intend to convey that the meaning of Jesus' words is exhausted in calling them words of interpretation.

The introductory words (1 Cor. 11. 23–4a; Mark 14. 22a par.) describe the common rite of Grace at table; at the Passover, Grace was said at the beginning of the main meal which followed the preliminary dish and the first part of the Passover liturgy. The Paterfamilias rose from his recumbent position, took as he sat[2] a cake of unleavened bread (*ἔλαβεν ἄρτον* Paul; *λαβὼν ἄρτον* Mark/Matthew/Luke), and recited the blessing over it "for all"

---

of obscuration by allusions cf. Apuleius, *Metam.* 11. 23, ed. R. Helm (1913), 285, on the Isis mystery: "5. You, kind reader, will now probably be curious and ask, what was said and what was done. I would gladly tell you, if I were allowed to; you would certainly be informed, if you were allowed to hear it. However, the ears and the tongue would have to pay the penalty for any such foolhardy curiosity. Nevertheless, I shall not torment such devout curiosity as you may possess for too long. Listen, therefore, but also believe, for this is true: 'I approached the boundary of death, crossed the threshold of Proserpina, passed through all the elements and returned. I saw the sun at midnight shining with a bright light, the subterranean as well as the celestial deities I saw face to face, and I worshipped them from the closest proximity.'—See, I have told it you; but have you understood it? By no means."

[1] In favour of the longer text are: A. Merx; P. Batiffol; M. Goguel; M. J. Lagrange; P. Feine; P. W. Schmiedel; H. J. Vogels; G. H. C. Macgregor; W. Goossens; M. Dibelius; F. Hauck; H. Windisch; K. G. Goetz; K. H. Rengstorf; K. Grobel; E. Lohmeyer; P. Benoit; F. C. Cirlot; E. Gaugler; E. Schweizer; B. H. Throckmorton; Th. Preiss.

[2] b. Ber. 51b.

(i.e. in the name of all).[1] The blessing runs, "praised be thou, O Lord our God, king of the world, who causest bread to come forth from the earth"[2] (*εὐλογήσας* Mark/Matthew, *εὐχαριστήσας* Paul/Luke).[3] But it is very likely that Jesus gave this daily blessing a form of His own.[4] The table companions identified themselves with the blessing by saying "amen". Only after the amen had been said[5] did the Paterfamilias break for each person present a piece at least the size of an olive[6] from the bread (*ἔκλασεν* Paul/Mark/Matthew/Luke) and gave it to him (*ἔδωκεν αὐτοῖς* Mark/Luke, *δοὺς τοῖς μαθηταῖς* Matthew), though it had to be passed from hand to hand to reach the more distant guests; lastly he broke a piece for himself and ate it, and thus gave the company the sign to eat theirs too.[7] During the distribution, which normally took place in silence,[8] Jesus spoke the words of institution.[9]

In Paul[10] the introductory words have a ceremonial sound: *ὁ κύριος Ἰησοῦς ἐν τῇ νυκτὶ ᾗ παρεδίδοτο ἔλαβεν ἄρτον καὶ εὐχαριστήσας ἔκλασεν καὶ εἶπεν* 1 Cor. 11. 23–4. The very first words, *ὁ κύριος Ἰησοῦς*, are ceremonial. This is not narrative style (the term is missing in all the four Gospels[11]); it is originally a liturgical confession of faith (1 Cor. 12. 3; Rom. 10. 9), which in its position at the beginning almost has the character of proclamation. Ceremonial too is what follows: *ἐν τῇ νυκτὶ ᾗ παρεδίδοτο* is not a mere chronological statement, for *παραδίδοσθαι* refers to an action of God, when it is used absolutely. The passive is, as in Rom. 4. 25, a periphrasis for the Divine name (translate: "in the night in which God delivered Him up"), and one cannot fail to hear the echo of Is. 53. Lastly, the detailed description of the rite used for the prayer

[1] Ber. 6. 6.

[2] Ber. 6. 1. It seems that a special word of praise over the unleavened bread was added at the Passover.

[3] On *εὐχαριστήσας* cf. infra, pp. 108, 119, 121.

[4] This conclusion is suggested as much by the Lord's Prayer as by the early Christian Graces at meat Did. chap. 9–10.

[5] b. Ber. 47a.

[6] j. Ber. 6. 10a. 51; b. Ber. 37b.

[7] b. Ber. 47a; j. Ber. 6 10a, 58.

[8] G. Dalman, *Jesus-Jeschua* (1922), 127.

[9] That is shown most clearly by the word *λάβετε* Mark 14. 22.

[10] Cf. E. Lohmeyer in *Theol. Rundschau* N.F. 9 (1937), 184 sq., for the subsequent remarks on Paul.

[11] It only occurs as a variant in Ps.-Mark 16. 19.

at table with its three verbs (ἔλαβεν ἄρτον καὶ εὐχαριστήσας ἔκλασεν) has contemporary analogies in ritual texts, and may indeed be regarded as a liturgical rubric. In the verb εὐχαριστεῖν (instead of εὐλογεῖν, which is normal for the Grace before meat) we find the earliest testimony in the New Testament[1] for that Graecising which caused the Lord's Supper to be known as the Eucharist. So from the form of the introduction, the absence of any historical detail not liturgically necessary, and the un-Pauline style, it follows that Paul was passing on an established liturgical formula (1 Cor. 11. 23 παρέλαβον).

In Mark the passage begins with a genitive absolute (καὶ ἐσθιόντων αὐτῶν Mark 14. 22) which resumes Mark 14. 18. This resumptive insertion, which reveals a joint in the text, is probably put in instead of a preface which did not suit the Marcan context, and which we must imagine as similar to 1 Cor. 11. 23a.[2] Afterwards, when Jesus' action is described by Mark in the same three verbs as by Paul (only Mark reads the earlier εὐλογήσας), we can detect an earlier common tradition. A fourth verb, καὶ ἔδωκεν αὐτοῖς, is added, strengthening the impression that this is a liturgical rubric. As we have already seen (p. 68 sq.), there is nothing in Mark which goes beyond what is liturgically necessary.

The Matthaean account keeps closely to Mark—as it does in what follows. However, by the addition of ὁ Ἰησοῦς and τοῖς μαθηταῖς in Matt. 26. 26, the introduction reads like a new beginning,[3] and the liturgical tone becomes even more emphatic. In connecting λαβών and εὐλογήσας by καί and in substituting δούς for ἔδωκεν, the whole emphasis is laid upon the breaking of the bread: the κλάσις τοῦ ἄρτου has become the essential feature of the first act.

Mark's account is also the basis of Luke; though Luke—like Paul—has εὐχαριστήσας for εὐλογήσας. This shows the influence of liturgical language, in which the Graecising first found in Paul was rapidly adopted.

The variations in the four introductions, therefore, are not

[1] Paul is followed by Mark 8. 6; Matt. 15. 36; Luke 22. 19; Acts 27. 35; John 6. 11, 23.

[2] H. Lietzmann, *Messe und Herrenmahl* (1926), 219; P. Benoit in *Rev. Bibl.* 48 (1939), 384.

[3] E. Lohmeyer in *Theol. Rundschau* N.F. 9 (1937), 177.

literary corrections, but the reflection of liturgical development.

We now come to the word over the bread.

Paul: τοῦτό μού ἐστιν τὸ σῶμα τὸ ὑπὲρ ὑμῶν· τοῦτο ποιεῖτε εἰς τὴν ἐμὴν ἀνάμνησιν.

Mark/Matthew: λάβετε (Matthew adds, φάγετε) τοῦτό ἐστιν τὸ σῶμά μου.

Luke: τοῦτό ἐστιν τὸ σῶμά μου τὸ ὑπὲρ ὑμῶν διδόμενον· τοῦτο ποιεῖτε εἰς τὴν ἐμὴν ἀνάμνησιν.

What is common has been underlined. Each authority has the words: τοῦτό ἐστιν τὸ σῶμά μου (in Paul the possessive has been put in front of the noun). The remainder consists of (1) the invitation to take (Mark/Matthew) and eat (Matthew). The expansion in Matthew, as compared with Mark, might easily suggest that the λάβετε as well as the φάγετε are additions arising quite naturally in the liturgical use of the words of institution. This is correct for φάγετε (Matthew),[1] but hardly for λάβετε (Mark/Matthew); for this λάβετε is not really omitted by Luke: he has only just used it (22. 17). Apart from this, it appears from the inscription on the famous Jewish golden beaker in the Vatican Library,[2] *ΛΑΒΕ ΕΥΛΟΓΙΑ*, that such formulae of invitation[3] were used when the bread and the cup of blessing were handed round. (2) τὸ ὑπὲρ ὑμῶν (Paul). The secondary character of these three words is shown by the fact that they cannot be translated back into Aramaic.[4] It is likely that this clause—of great linguistic

[1] The addition of φάγετε is connected with the corresponding imperative πίετε ἐξ αὐτοῦ πάντες Matt. 26. 27, the secondary character of which will be discussed infra, p. 113.

[2] Published lately by H. Lietzmann and K. H. Rengstorf in *Z.N.W.* 31 (1932), plate after p. 32; W. G. Kuemmel in *Judaica* 2 (1946), 16, plate 4.

[3] The explanation of K. H. Rengstorf, op. cit. 57 sq., regarding the words as a wish for blessing (approx.: may you receive the blessing—εὐλογία[ν]—for keeping the commandments) is unconvincing. It seems more likely that εὐλογία is an abbreviation for [ποτήριον τῆς] εὐλογία[ς], i.e. (*kōs shel*) *berākhā*, cf. J. B. Frey, *Corp. Inscr. Jud.* 1 (1936), 377–8, nr. 515; I. Zolli, *Il Nazareno* (1938), 211. In Cyril of Jerusalem, at any rate, and elsewhere, the consecrated cup is called εὐλογία, cf. H. W. Beyer, *Theol. Woerterb. z. N.T.* 2. 758 n. 25. The meaning is therefore: "take, (it is the) blessed cup".

[4] G. Dalman, *Jesus-Jeschua* (Leipzig, 1922), 132; but J. Schniewind has pointed out to me that a re-translation into Hebrew would be possible.

difficulty even in Greek[1]—has found its way across to the bread from the wine[2] (omitting the participle ἐκχυννόμενον which was not applicable), because the liturgical usage required some parallelism between words spoken over the wine and those spoken over the bread. (The need for a theological explanation of the bread analogous to that over the wine became even more urgent when the celebration was *sub una*.) This conclusion is supported by Luke 22. 19b, for here the tendency towards parallelism has led to a further addition (τὸ ὑπὲρ ὑμῶν διδόμενον) making the participial construction for the bread precisely parallel to that for the wine (τὸ ὑπὲρ ὑμῶν ἐκχυννόμενον). (3) The command to repeat the rite (the words of institution proper) in Paul and Luke. This command also is not likely to be part of the original formula,[3] because its insertion is more easily explained than its omission.

So the original text was: λάβετε· τοῦτό ἐστιν τὸ σῶμά μου.

(*b*) *The Word of Interpretation over the wine.*

The introductory words (1 Cor. 11. 25a; Mark 14. 23; Matt. 26. 27a; Luke 22. 20a) describe the rite of thanksgiving after the meal (μετὰ τὸ δειπνῆσαι Paul/Luke) as it took place when

[1] There were early attempts to remove this difficulty by adding a participle: κλώμενον F G 𝔎 pl it sy, θρυπτόμενον D, or διδόμενον sa bo arm (Luke 22. 19).

[2] So already W. Wrede, *Z.N.W.* 1 (1900), 69–74.

[3] This has long been known. Schleiermacher already was doubtful, cf. *Der Christliche Glaube* II, §139. 3. H. J. Holtzmann-A. Juelicher-W. Bauer, *Lehrbuch der N.T. Theologie*, 2nd ed. (Tuebingen, 1911), 1, 377 n. 4, mention as representatives of this view: Paulus, Kaiser, Rueckert, Br. Bauer, D. F. Strauss, Wittichen, Immer, Pfleiderer, W. Brandt, Wellhausen, Grafe, Mensinga, Gardner, Titius, B. Weiss, Juelicher, Spitta, A. Réville, A. Neumann, Joh. Hoffmann, Stage, P. W. Schmiedel, Hollmann, P. W. Schmidt, Goetz, Bousset. Cf. also A. Schweitzer, *Das Abendmahlsproblem* 1 (1901=1929), 52; G. Beer, *Pesachim* (Giessen, 1912), 102; K. L. Schmidt in *R.G.G.*, 2nd ed., 1 (1927), 6–11; A. Loisy, "Les origines de la Cène Eucharistique" in *Congrès d'histoire du Christianisme* 1 (Paris-Amsterdam, 1928), 77 sq.; W. Michaelis, *Täufer, Jesus, Urgemeinde* (1928), 110; A. Schweitzer, *Die Mystik des Apostels Paulus* (Tuebingen, 1930), 237–8, 258; J. Schniewind, *N.T.D.* 1. 1 (1933), 175; R. Otto, *Reich Gottes und Menschensohn* (Munich, 1934), 275–6; H. Strathmann, *Theologie der Gegenwart* 30 (1936), 152; J. Behm, *Theol. Woerterb. z. N.T.* 3 (1937), 731; E. Lohmeyer, *Das Evang. d. Markus* (1937), 309; K. H. Rengstorf, *N.T.D.* 1. 2 (1937), 225, and many others, esp. those authors mentioned on p. 160, n. 1.

wine had been drunk. The Paterfamilias rose again from his recumbent position, sat up[1] and said the exhortation: "Speak praises to our God, to whom belongs what we have consumed", and the company replied "Praised be our God for the food we have eaten."[2] Then he took the "cup of benediction" (1 Cor. 10. 16) in his right hand,[3] lifted it up a span above the table (λαβών),[4] and with his eyes on the cup[4] said the Grace "for all",[5] which in the days of Jesus probably had the following wording:

(1) Praised be Thou, O Lord our God, King of the universe, Thou who feedest the whole world with goodness, grace, and mercy.
(2) We give thanks to Thee, O Lord our God, that Thou hast caused us to take possession of a good and large land.
(3) Have mercy, O Lord our God, on Israel, Thy people,
and on Jerusalem, Thy city,
and upon Zion, the dwelling-place of Thy glory,
and upon Thy altar and upon Thy temple.
Praise be to Thee, O Lord, who buildest Jerusalem.[6]

The company joined in the prayer with the "amen".[7] After this, Jesus—apparently not Himself drinking,[8] contrary to custom—passed the cup round and spoke the words of institution as He did so.

[1] b. Ber. 51b. [2] Ber. 7. 3; b. Ber. 50a.

[3] According to b. Ber. 51a, the cup is first lifted with both hands. It contains red wine mixed with water.

[4] j. Ber. 7. 11c, 63 sq.; b. Ber. 51a–b, cf. V. Kurrein, "Die Genuss-Symbolik in den rituellen Braeuchen" in *Monatsschrift f. Gesch. u. Wiss. d. Judentums* 67 (1923), 263.

[5] Ber. 6. 6.

[6] L. Finkelstein, "The *Birkat ha-mazon*" in *Jew. Quart. Rev.* n.s. 19 (1928–9), 211–62, has collected the widely scattered evidence for the various forms of the Grace after meat and has reconstructed by way of a careful analysis the text quoted as presumably the earliest. At about 120 B.C., the triad of benedictions was firmly established, cf. the triad of benedictions after the meal of Abraham in Jub. 22. 6–9. (The fourth benediction was only decided upon at Jabne after A.D. 100, cf. L. Finkelstein, op. cit. 217–18, 222; C. Albeck, "Die vierte Eulogie", *Monatsschrift f. Gesch. u. Wiss. d. Judentums* 78 (1934), 430–7.) [7] Ber. 8. 8.

[8] Infra, p. 165. The same is suggested by the otherwise superfluous words καὶ ἔπιον ἐξ αὐτοῦ πάντες Mark 14. 23, with the emphasis upon πάντες because of its position at the end of the sentence.

Once more the introductory words betray liturgical usage, though in different ways: in Paul/Luke by the concise *ὡσαύτως καί*, which reads like a short liturgical rubric, and by the article in front of *ποτήριον*, which points to the ritual "cup of blessing" (1 Cor. 10. 16); in Mark/Matthew by the detailed description in language reminiscent of ritual practice and by the parallelism with the introduction to the word over the bread, which may result from an assimilation to it.

Paul: *τοῦτο τὸ ποτήριον ἡ καινὴ διαθήκη ἐστὶν ἐν τῷ ἐμῷ αἵματι.*[1] *τοῦτο ποιεῖτε, ὁσάκις ἐὰν πίνητε, εἰς τὴν ἐμὴν ἀνάμνησιν.*

Mark/Matthew: (Matthew adds *πίετε ἐξ αὐτοῦ πάντες·*) *τοῦτό* (Matthew adds *γάρ*) *ἐστιν τὸ αἷμά μου τῆς διαθήκης τὸ ἐκχυννόμενον ὑπὲρ πολλῶν* (Matthew: *τὸ περὶ πολλῶν ἐκχυννόμενον εἰς ἄφεσιν ἁμαρτιῶν*).

Luke: *τοῦτο τὸ ποτήριον ἡ καινὴ διαθήκη ἐν τῷ αἵματί μου, τὸ ὑπὲρ ὑμῶν ἐκχυννόμενον.*

The great disparity in the common words is only superficial. When Paul and Luke say, "this cup is the new covenant in my blood", while Mark and Matthew have, "this is my blood of the covenant", the meaning of the two forms is the same. That appears from the separate comparison of the subjects and predicates of both. The subject in Mark and Matthew is the red wine in the cup, and the same is true of Paul and Luke—their words *τοῦτο τὸ ποτήριον* do not mean the cup, but its contents. The predicate too is identical in both forms: Mark/Matthew—the wine "is my blood of the covenant"; Paul/Luke—the wine "is the new covenant by (causal *ἐν*)[2] my blood", both compare the wine with the blood, the outpouring of which is the basis for the establishment of the new covenant. The unusually complicated form found in Paul is probably due to his intention to avoid the misapprehension that real blood was consumed at the Eucharist.[3] The common text is therefore: "this (wine) is my blood (outpoured for the conclusion) of the covenant".

[1] 𝔓[46] A C *ἐν τῷ αἵματί μου*, as in Luke.

[2] A. Schlatter, *Das Evangelium des Lukas* (Stuttgart, 1931), 422.

[3] Cf. G. Dalman, *Jesus-Jeschua* (Leipzig, 1922), 147; T. H. W. Maxfield, *The Words of Institution* (Cambridge, 1933), 20; P. Benoit, *Rev. Bibl.* 48 (1939), 363.

The remainder consists of (1) the command to drink (Matthew). This is secondary, as appears from a comparison with Mark (Mark 14. 23: *καὶ ἔπιον ἐξ αὐτοῦ πάντες*). Matthew likes to change Mark's narrative style into direct speech.[1] In this case a change from the indicative to the imperative resulted in *πίετε ἐξ αὐτοῦ πάντες* (Matthew), a formula of administration which has its parallel in the formula of invitation in the case of the bread. But we have already repeatedly seen that the influence of ritual practice and the tendency to make the words over the bread and the wine parallel are signs of secondary elements in the words of institution. The secondary character of the command to drink (Matthew) is supported by the consideration that the words *ἐξ αὐτοῦ πάντες* in Matthew are superfluous (cf. the mere *φάγετε* Matt. 26. 26): they are nothing more than "Marcan remnants".[2] (2) Secondary is also the *γάρ* (Matthew), which is made necessary by the command *πίετε ἐξ αὐτοῦ πάντες*. It produces a fundamental change of emphasis, because it treats the subsequent words of interpretation as though they were no more than the reason given for the command to drink upon which the whole stress is laid.[3] This change of emphasis to the words of administration is plainly due to liturgical requirements. (3) The further specification of *τοῦτο* by *τὸ ποτήριον* (Paul/Luke) is explanatory. (4) Explanatory too is the addition of *καινή* to *διαθήκη* (Paul/Luke)—a reference to Jer. 31. 31–34. (5) The command to repeat the rite (Paul) does not belong to the original formula (cf. supra, p. 110); its repetition with the cup (Paul only, not Luke) is another instance of the tendency to parallelism.[4] (6) The further specification of *αἷμα* by *τὸ ἐκχυννόμενον ὑπὲρ* (Matthew: *περὶ*) *πολλῶν* (Luke:

[1] Matt. 3. 2; 10. 9; 12. 10; 13. 10; 15. 15; 17. 9; 18. 1; 21. 33; 26. 1–2, 15, 66. Instances of the opposite tendency are rare, Matt. 8. 18; 20. 20, 32.

[2] J. Finegan, *Die Ueberlieferung der Leidens- und Auferstehungsgeschichte Jesu* (Giessen, 1934), 10.

[3] E. Lohmeyer, *Theol. Rundschau* 9 (1937), 177.

[4] Cf. also Schlatter's hypothesis, mentioned supra, p. 29 n. 1, that the *ὁσάκις ἐὰν πίνητε* in 1 Cor. 11. 25, at the second command to repeat the rite, is explained by the fact that wine was only rarely available at the celebrations of the congregation. Assuming that Schlatter's suggestion is correct, we can see how the situation of the congregations is reflected in the form taken by the command to repeat the rite.

ὑμῶν) is omitted by Paul—but only apparently! For he has simply removed it to the word over the bread; and it is therefore in all our authorities (Paul, Mark, Matthew, Luke). The only question is: what was its original wording? Paul gives it as *τὸ ὑπὲρ ὑμῶν*; Mark: *τὸ ἐκχυννόμενον ὑπὲρ πολλῶν*; Matthew: *τὸ περὶ πολλῶν ἐκχυννόμενον εἰς ἄφεσιν ἁμαρτιῶν*; Luke: *τὸ ὑπὲρ ὑμῶν ἐκχυννόμενον*. (*a*) As we have seen, the short form in Paul is impossible in Aramaic and extraordinarily hard in Greek. This hardness is explained by the inevitable omission of *ἐκχυννόμενον* when the participial construction was transferred from the wine to the bread, and the participle was no longer suitable. *Ἐκχυννόμενον* is therefore original, a contention the more confidently made because it will shortly be proved to be a Semitism. (*b*) *πολλῶν* or *ὑμῶν*? The former has to be regarded as the earlier because it is also a Semitism (cf. infra, p. 123 sq.). *Ὑμῶν* is primarily neither a removal of a Semitism nor a limitation of the atoning work of Jesus to the Church in consequence of theological considerations, but is a reflection of liturgical usage. In liturgical practice statement gives place to address: each communicant should feel himself personally addressed by the Lord.[1] The word of interpretation became a word of administration. (The same development of a formula of administration here noted in Paul/Luke has already been noted under (1) in Matthew.) (*c*) *ὑπέρ* (Mark, Paul, Luke) and *περί* (Matthew) are only differences in translation.[2] (*d*) *εἰς ἄφεσιν ἁμαρτιῶν* is probably an addition—correct in substance—by Matthew. (*e*) The order of words in Mark, *τὸ ἐκχυννόμενον ὑπὲρ πολλῶν*, must be reckoned as earlier than that in Matthew/Luke *τὸ περὶ πολλῶν* (Luke: *ὑπὲρ ὑμῶν*) *ἐκχυννόμενον*, because Matthew/Luke avoid Mark's hiatus.

Thus the earliest text of the words of institution which can be established is:

[1] Cf. E. Lohmeyer, *Journ. of Bibl. Lit.* 56 (1937), 243; J. Leipoldt, *Der Gottesdienst der aeltesten Kirche* (1937), 39.

[2] In favour of the greater antiquity of *ὑπέρ* it has to be noticed, however, that in N.T. Greek *ὑπέρ* with the genitive "is strongly controlled by the use of *περί*", Blass-Debrunner, *Grammatik des neutestamentlichen Griechisch*, 7th ed. (Goettingen, 1943), §231. Whilst *περί* sometimes replaces *ὑπέρ* (§229. 1), the opposite change from *περί* to *ὑπέρ* is rare (§231. 1).

(1) *Λάβετε· τοῦτό ἐστιν τὸ σῶμά μου.*

(2) *Τοῦτό ἐστιν τὸ αἷμά μου τῆς διαθήκης τὸ ἐκχυννόμενον ὑπὲρ πολλῶν.*

This means—and this result has surprised me very much—that the earliest text of the words of interpretation which can be established by comparison of the texts is identical with the text of Mark.[1]

(*c*) *The looking forward to the Eschatological Meal.*

The so-called eschatological looking forward (*Ausblick*) is found in all the authorities, for Mark 14. 25; Matt. 26. 29; Luke 22. 15–18 have in Paul an analogy in the last three words of 1 Cor. 11. 26, *ὁσάκις γὰρ ἐὰν ἐσθίητε τὸν ἄρτον τοῦτον καὶ τὸ ποτήριον πίνητε, τὸν θάνατον τοῦ κυρίου καταγγέλλετε* (indicative, as appears from the initial *γάρ*) *ἄχρι οὗ ἔλθῃ*. Luke differs from Mark and Matthew in two respects: first, in his order, for Luke puts the eschatological looking forward at the beginning of the passover meal, whereas Mark and Matthew place it at the end of the Grace after meat, towards the end of the celebration; second, by his duplication of the looking forward, Luke 22. 16, 18. Recently many scholars have inclined to the view that both these differences

[1] The early age of Mark's text also follows from the fact that it is the shortest. Liturgical texts tend to grow and to branch out. The supremacy of the Marcan version of the words of institution is also maintained by, amongst others, C. v. Weizsaecker, *Das Apostolische Zeitalter*, 2nd ed. (Freiburg i. Br., 1892), 576; A. Juelicher, "Zur Geschichte der Abendmahlsfeier in der aeltesten Kirche" in *Weizsaecker Festschr.* (Freiburg i. Br., 1892), 237–8; P. W. Schmiedel, "Die neuesten Ansichten ueber den Ursprung des Abendmahls" in *Protestant. Monatshefte* 3 (1899), 135 n. 1; A. Schweitzer, *Das Abendmahlsproblem* 1 (Tuebingen, 1901), 56 sq.; J. Wellhausen, *Das Evangelium Marci*, 2nd ed. (Berlin, 1909), 113; M. Werner, *Der Einfluss paulinischer Theologie im Markusevangelium* (Giessen, 1923) 70, 139 sq.; A. Oepke in *Allg. Ev.-Luth. Kirchenzeitung* 59 (1926), 56; H. Weinel, *Biblische Theologie des N.T.*, 4th ed. (Tuebingen, 1928), 67, "the wording of Paul may be explained by that of Mark, but not vice versa"; M. Goguel, "La relation du dernier repas de Jésus dans 1 Cor. 11 et la tradition historique chez l'Apôtre Paul" in *Rev. d'histoire et de philos. relig.* 10 (1930), 69, "le texte donné par Marc représente un état de l'évolution de la tradition moins avancé que celui que nous avons dans l'épître aux Corinthiens"; A. Schweitzer, *Die Mystik des Apostels Paulus* (Tuebingen, 1930), 258–9; T. H. W. Maxfield, *The Words of Institution* (Cambridge, 1933) 20–1; E. Lohmeyer, *Das Evang. d. Markus* (1937), 306; V. Taylor, *Jesus and His Sacrifice* (1937=1943), 115; R. Bultmann in *Theolog. Blaetter* 20 (1941), 271.

are the result of the Evangelist's editing.[1] Luke, who supposedly also "transposes" other pieces of the Passion story, is said to have put the eschatological looking forward of Mark 14. 25 at the beginning of his account of the Last Supper, and to have enlarged it by the free invention of a parallel Saying in 22. 16, in order to give greater prominence to its eschatological character.[2] This view can be conclusively disproved. It has already been seen[3] that Luke dislikes transpositions. So much follows clearly from his treatment of Mark's material. Differences in the order of Luke's Gospel as compared with Mark are therefore invariably signs that Luke followed his own special source. This is confirmed here by the parallelism of verse 16 with verse 18: it is quite unbelievable that Luke could have invented it, since Luke tends rather the opposite way and eradicates parallelisms where they are found in his source.[4] We therefore have the so-called eschatological looking forward in a twofold tradition: a shorter form in Mark/Matthew, and a valuable[5] longer one in Luke.[6]

[1] H. Lietzmann, *Messe und Herrenmahl* (Bonn, 1926), 215–16; E. Klostermann, *Das Lukasevangelium*, 2nd ed. (Tuebingen, 1929), 208; H. v. Soden, *Sakrament und Ethik bei Paulus* (1931), 29 n. 2; M. Dibelius, *Die Formgeschichte des Evangeliums*, 2nd ed. (1933), 180 n. 1; F. Hauck, *Das Evangelium des Lukas* (Leipzig, 1934), 262; J. Finegan, *Die Ueberlieferung der Leidens- und Auferstehungsgeschichte Jesu* (Giessen, 1934), 11 sq.; W. G. Kuemmel, *Verheissung und Erfuellung* 2nd ed. (Zürich, 1953), 25; E. Schweizer in *Theol. Zeitschr.* 2 (1946), 98.

[2] P. Benoit, *Rev. Bibl.* 48 (1939), 378–93, has founded this view upon three expressions which he deems to be characteristic for Lucan style: (1) ἐπιθυμίᾳ ἐπεθύμησα 22. 15, cf. Acts 5. 28; 23. 14 (4. 17 in a variant) for this construction; (2) παθεῖν 22. 15, cf. Luke 24. 46; Acts 1. 3; 3. 18; 17. 3; (3) διαμερίζειν 22. 17, which, apart from Mark 15. 24, is found in Luke only, cf. 11. 17, 18; 12. 52, 53; Acts 2. 3, 45. However, πάσχειν used absolutely is found as well in Heb. 2. 18; 9. 26; 1 Pet. 2. 23, and διαμερίζειν has the meaning "to distribute" only in Acts 2. 45, but in no other of the passages quoted. Above all, Lucan style must not mislead us to assume a Lucan invention.

[3] Cf. supra, p. 69.

[4] P. Wendland, *Hellenist.-Roem. Kultur*, 2nd ed. (Tuebingen, 1912), 285; E. Norden, *Agnostos Theos* (Berlin-Leipzig, 1913), 357 sq.; W. Larfeld, *Die neutestl. Evangelien* (Guetersloh, 1925), 322; F. Hauck, *Das Evangelium des Lukas* (Leipzig, 1934), 9, and others.

[5] In Luke, verse 18 has that organic connexion which is lacking in Mark, cf. infra, p. 133.

[6] The same view is held by W. Bussmann, *Synoptische Studien* I (Halle, 1925), 191–2; H. N. Bate in *J.T.S.* 28 (1927), 362–8; A. Schlatter,

Both forms are derived from a Semitic original. On the Semitisms in Mark 14. 25 cf. infra, p. 125 sq. In Luke 22. 15–18, the following Semitisms occur: the parallelism between verse 16 and verse 18; verse 15 τὸ πάσχα φαγεῖν, i.e. אֱכַל פִּסְחָא, i.e. to eat the paschal lamb;[1] verse 17 δεξάμενος ποτήριον εὐχαριστήσας, a reference to Jewish table rites, where δεξάμενος signifies the taking of the cup from the hand of the person who waits at table;[2] verse 18, the simple "not" (οὐ μή) instead of an expected "no more" is typically Semitic;[3] also the circumlocution γένημα τῆς ἀμπέλου for wine and the saying that the kingdom of God "shall come".[4] However, there has been a much more thorough linguistic editing in Luke than in Mark. The Hebraism in Luke 22. 15 ἐπιθυμίᾳ ἐπεθύμησα[5] is unexpected on the lips of Jesus. Several Graecisms also strike us: verse 15, παθεῖν used absolutely can hardly be retranslated into Aramaic,[6] but it was in popular use in the early Church; verse 16, τοῦ θεοῦ takes the place of an expected periphrasis for the Divine name; verse 17, εὐχαριστήσας is a Graecism;[7] verse 18, τοῦ θεοῦ (cf. ad verse 16). But above all the comparison between Mark 14. 25 and Luke 22. 18 shows that several un-Greek turns of phrase in Mark are not found in Luke: ἀμήν has been omitted and replaced by γάρ;[8] the barbarian οὐκέτι οὐ μή does

---

Das Evangelium des Lukas (Stuttgart, 1931), 137, 420–1; W. Goossens, *Les origines de l'Eucharistie* (Gembloux-Paris, 1931), 105–6, 194–5; R. Bultmann, *Gesch. d. synopt. Tradition*, 2nd ed. (1931), 286; E. Lohmeyer in *Theol. Rundschau* 9 (1937), 178, 194; C. H. Dodd, *The Parables of the Kingdom*, 4th ed. (1938), 56 n. 1; J. Behm in *Theol. Woerterb. z. N.T.* 3. 731; K. H. Rengstorf, *N.T.D.* 1. 2 ad h. l.

[1] Cf. e.g. Targ. 2 Chron. 30. 18 אֲכָלוּ יַת פִּסְחָא.

[2] Cf. Siphre, Deut. 11. 10 §38 (ed. princ. Venice, 1545) 34c, 32: קִיבְּלוֹ, i.e. "he accepted it" (the cup).

[3] P. Joüon, "L'Évangile de Notre-Seigneur Jésus-Christ", *Verbum Salutis* 5 (Paris, 1940), 102, commenting on Matt. 15. 32. The same observation applies to v. 16, where the variant οὐκέτι should be regarded as secondary.

[4] G. Dalman, *Die Worte Jesu*, 2nd ed. (Leipzig, 1930), 88.

[5] G. Dalman, *Jesus-Jeschua* (Leipzig, 1922), 116–17.

[6] Ibid. 117–18.

[7] The literal translation of בָּרֵיךְ would be εὐλογεῖν, cf. infra, p. 119.

[8] Luke also avoids the original ἀμήν in other passages: he says instead ἀληθῶς (9. 27; 12. 44; 21. 3); γάρ (10. 24; 22. 18); δέ (10. 12); ναί (11. 51); πλὴν ἰδού (22. 21); or he omits it altogether. Only six times does he use ἀμήν, and of these three come from his special source (4. 24; 12. 37; 23. 43).

not make its appearance in Luke, who reads instead *οὐ μή . . . ἀπὸ τοῦ νῦν*; the phrase *πίνειν ἐκ*, which is impossible in Greek when it is followed by the mention of the beverage, is softened to *πίνειν ἀπό* (alternative translation!); and *ἕως τῆς ἡμέρας ἐκείνης*, an expression typical of Mark, is not found in Luke.

Thus we have in Luke (22. 15–18) the original duplication of the eschatological looking forward. Nevertheless, in so far as the two are comparable, Mark's wording is earlier than Luke's.[1]

(4) *The Authenticity of the Marcan Tradition*

(*a*) *The Semitisms of the Marcan Text.*

The very early date of Mark's text is decisively confirmed by the large number of Semitisms and of Palestinian idioms which it contains.

(1) 14. 22 *καὶ ἐσθιόντων*. Conjoining with *καί* is common in the vernacular speech of all times, but the consistency with which in Mark the finite verbs are connected with *καί* is nevertheless a Semitic usage:[2] 14. 22 *καὶ . . . ἔκλασεν καὶ ἔδωκεν . . . καὶ εἶπεν . . .* 23. *καὶ . . . ἔδωκεν . . . καὶ ἔπιον . . .* 24. *καὶ εἶπεν*. Instead of these six "ands" (*καί*), Matthew, Luke, and Paul each have only two "ands" (*καί*) connecting finite verbs.

(2) 14. 22 *καὶ ἐσθιόντων*; Matt. 26. 26 *ἐσθιόντων δέ*. The un-Semitic[3] particles *δέ* and *γάρ* are missing in Mark 14. 22–5 (cf. infra, No. 11a and 15).

(3) 14. 22 *λαβὼν ἄρτον εὐλογήσας* is a regular expression for the action of the Paterfamilias at Grace before meat, cf. Mark 6. 41 par.; 8. 6 par.; Luke 24. 30; John 6. 11. "Take (the bread) and say the Grace."[4] "He takes the bread and pronounces the bless-

[1] The question whether the eschatological looking forward has been given its correct place in Luke (at the beginning of the meal) or in Mark (at the end of the meal), can only be answered when the passage is analysed, cf. infra, p. 167 n. 6.

[2] Cf. Blass-Debrunner, *Grammatik des N.T. Griechisch,* 7th ed. (Goettingen, 1943), §458.

[3] J. Wellhausen, *Einleitung in die drei ersten Evangelien,* 2nd ed. (Berlin, 1911), 10.

[4] j. Ber. 8. 12a. 45; 6. 10a. 63: סב בריך.

ing over it".[1] The elevation[2] of the bread introduces the Grace before meat.[3]

Typically Semitic is the circumstantiality of the expression. *Λαμβάνειν* is one of those verbs which in Semitic speech describe, in a way which we find superfluous and formal, a movement (or posture) preparatory to the action which is emphasized. This applies as much to the Hebrew לָקַח, נָטַל as to the Aramaic נְסַב. E.g. Matt. 13. 31 (*ὃν λαβὼν ἄνθρωπος ἔσπειρεν*); 13. 33 (*ἣν λαβοῦσα γυνὴ ἐνέκρυψεν*); 14. 19; 15. 36; 17. 27; 21. 35; 21. 39; 25. 1; 26. 26, 27; 27. 24, 48, 59; Mark 6. 41; 8. 6; 9. 36; 12. 3, 8; Luke 6. 4; 9. 16; 13. 19, 21; 24. 30, 43; John 6. 11; 13. 4, 26; 19. 1, 6, 23, 40; 21. 13; Acts 9. 25; 16. 3; 27. 35; 1 Cor. 11. 23; Rev. 8. 5. The following can be used analogously to *λαβών*: *ἀναστάς, ἀπαγαγών, ἀπελθών, ἀπερχόμενος, ἀφείς, ἐγερθείς, εἰσελθών, ἐλθών, ἐρχόμενος, ἑστώς, καθίσας, καταλιπών, πορευθείς, σταθείς.*[4]

(4) 14. 22 *εὐλογήσας*. In secular Greek *εὐλογεῖν* means predominantly "to praise or glorify someone", and is used with a personal or impersonal object. The meaning "to bless", as well as the technical meaning "to say Grace" (i.e. Heb. בֵּרֵךְ; Aram. בָּרֵיךְ) is a Semitism, as is also the omission of the object. How strange such an absolute use of *εὐλογεῖν* appeared to a non-Palestinian is shown by Mark 8. 7 and Luke 9. 16, where it is said of the loaves and fishes *εὐλογήσας αὐτά* or *εὐλόγησεν αὐτούς*, so that by the addition of an object the Grace becomes a consecration. This linguistic misunderstanding of the Semitic use of *εὐλογεῖν* among the Greeks has had far-reaching consequences in the history of the Eucharist. The substitution of *εὐχαριστήσας* for *εὐλογήσας* in the parallel texts of 1 Cor. 11. 24, Luke 24. 19a, is a Graecising of the Semitism.[5]

[1] j. Ber. 6. 10a. 49; cf. "he took an olive and pronounced the blessing", j. Ber. 6. 10a. 9; "he took a lupin and pronounced the blessing over it", ibid. 10a. 45.

[2] Only the lifting of the bread is meant. A "consecrating elevation or waving", (so K. G. Goetz, *Die heutige Abendmahlsfrage in ihrer geschichtl. Entwicklung*, 2nd ed. [Leipzig, 1907], 190–1, on 1 Cor. 11. 23) is out of the question.

[3] This is the obvious meaning of John 21. 13.

[4] Cf. esp. G. Dalman, *Die Worte Jesu*, 2nd ed. (Leipzig, 1930), 16–19.

[5] Paul is as it happens the earliest witness for the designation of the Grace by *εὐχαριστεῖν*, in Hellenistic Judaism.

(5) 14. 22 ἔκλασεν. κλᾶν (i.e. Heb. בָּצַע, less frequently פָּרַס, Aram. קְצָא) is a technical term[1] for the Jewish custom of breaking the bread[2] before a meal;[3] it took place only after the company had responded to the Grace with their "Amen".[4] The expression κλᾶν ἄρτον is foreign to classical Greek.[5] The absolute use of κλᾶν is also a Semitism.[6]

[1] E.g. j. Ber. 8. 12a, 45, "he gave him bread that he might break it. He said: Take and say Grace".

[2] The translation of κλᾶν by "sacrifice with blessing, consecrate" in K. G. Goetz, *Die heutige Abendmahlsfrage in ihrer geschichtlichen Entwicklung*, 2nd ed. (Leipzig, 1907), 186–8, is impossible—linguistically as much as materially—cf. my article "Das paulinische Abendmahl—eine Opferdarbringung?" in *Theol. Stud. u. Krit.* 108 (1937), 124–41.

[3] פָּרַס לֶחֶם is already used in Jer. 16. 7 (read: instead of יִפְרְסוּ לָהֶם—in accordance with LXX κλασθῇ ἄρτος, לֶחֶם) with the meaning of breaking the bread at a (funeral) meal. Talmudic sources illustrating the rite of breaking the bread may be found in P. Billerbeck 1. 687; 2. 619 sq.; 4. 621 sq.; G. Dalman, *Jesus-Jeschua* (Leipzig, 1922), 125 sq., also in b. R. H. 29b; b. Ber. 46a.

[4] b. Ber. 47a. Following Fr. Spitta, *Beitraege zur Geschichte und Literatur des Urchristentums* 1 (1893), 238, b. Pes. 115b–116a, is repeatedly quoted for proof that—different from ordinary custom—the bread was broken at the passover meal before prayer was said, cf. only lately A. Greiff, *Das aelteste Pascha-Rituale der Kirche, Did.* 1–10, *und das Johannes-Evangelium* (Paderborn, 1929), 149 n. 2. On the erroneousness of this assertion cf. supra, p. 43 sq.

[5] Th. Schermann, "Das 'Brotbrechen' im Urchristentum" in *Biblische Zeitschrift* 8 (1910), 33–52, 162–83, states on p. 39–40, "in classical literature the terms used instead of κλάω seem to have been σχίζω or ψωμίζω (the latter mainly in the meaning "to feed"), also μερίζω and διαμερίζω. However, I have found only one passage which mentions the dividing of something baked, in an inscription connected with one of the cults of Samothrace: here the priest offers the sacrificial cake (τὸ πέμμα) after he has divided it (σχίξας) and pours forth the drink for the *mystae* (καὶ ἐκχέει τὸ ποτὸν τοῖς μύσταις)." Cf. on this inscription A. Dieterich, *Eine Mithras-Liturgie* (Leipzig, 1903), 105. *Κλᾶν ἄρτον* is therefore foreign to classical Greek. There is, however, a passage in the great Parisian magical papyrus, καταλιπὼν ἀπὸ τοῦ ἄρτου, οὗ ἐσθίεις, ὀλίγον καὶ κλάσας ποίησον εἰς ἑπτὰ ψωμούς, K. Preisendanz, *Papyri Graecae Magicae* (1928 sq.), 1. 118 No. IV. 1392 sq., but J. Behm, in *Theol. Woerterb. z. N. T.* 3. 727 n. 2, has rightly said that this is of little weight, because this magical papyrus shows traces of Jewish-Hellenistic and Christian influences.

[6] An established usage: Tos. Sukka 4. 23 (200. 9); j. Ber. 6. 10a. 62; b. Ber. 46a (lines 6, 9, 11, 12 twice), 47a.

(6) 14. 22 ἔκλασεν καὶ ἔδωκεν. The bread was broken for the purpose of distribution. "He broke and gave" is therefore the conventional phrase. "*Rabh* (died A.D. 247) was accustomed after he had broken (the bread) to eat (his piece immediately) with his left hand and (simultaneously) to distribute the rest with his right hand."[1] Cf. Mark 6. 41 par.; 8. 6 par.; Luke 24. 30.[2]

(7) 14. 22 τὸ σῶμά μου (Paul: μού ἐστιν τὸ σῶμα). The position of the possessive pronoun in Mark corresponds to the Semitic suffix; to give the pronoun first place, as in Paul, is possible in the Greek only.[3]

(8) 14. 22 σῶμα/αἷμα. This twin concept constitutes a Semitism.[4]

(9) 14. 23 λαβὼν ποτήριον εὐχαριστήσας, a conventional phrase, cf. Luke 22. 17: δεξάμενος[5] ποτήριον εὐχαριστήσας. "Take (the cup) and pronounce the blessing".[6] "He took the cup and said: Let us praise God".[7] Λαβών indicates the elevation of the cup a hand's breadth above the table,[8] an action which introduces the Grace.

On λαβών as a Semitism, cf. supra, No. (3).

Εὐχαριστήσας: in Aramaic there is only one word for saying Grace before and after meat, בָּרֵיךְ, Gr. εὐλογεῖν. The use of εὐχαριστήσας for the thanksgiving after meat is tolerable.[9] But it is otherwise with εὐχαριστήσας in 1 Cor. 11. 24; Luke 22. 19a (Grace before meat), cf. supra No. (4).

(10) 14. 23 καὶ ἔπιον ἐξ αὐτοῦ. It follows from the analogous πίνειν ἐκ τοῦ γενήματος τῆς ἀμπέλου in 14. 25 that ἐξ αὐτοῦ does not refer to the vessel ("they all drank out of Jesus' cup")

[1] j. Ber. 6. 10a. 62. This was an act of courtesy: the host himself opened the meal by beginning to eat, and *Rabh* wanted to avoid keeping his guests waiting until he had finished the distribution. Cf. on the passage P. Billerbeck 4. 622 n.o.

[2] Cf. also John 21. 13 καὶ λαμβάνει τὸν ἄρτον καὶ δίδωσιν αὐτοῖς. Here, too, δίδωσιν means the distribution of the broken bread.

[3] E. Lohmeyer, *Das Evangelium des Markus* (1937), 305.

[4] Cf. infra, p. 140 sq. and p. 143 sq. P. Fiebig in *Neues Saechsisches Kirchenblatt* 42 (1935), 374.

[5] On δεξάμενος cf. supra, p. 117 n. 2.

[6] j. Ber. 7. 11c. 5; Lev. R. 9 (ad Lev. 7. 11) 22a. 24, סב בריך.

[7] j. Ber. 7. 11b. 62.

[8] j. Ber. 7. 11c. 63 sq.; b. Ber. 51a–b, cf. Ps. 116. 13.

[9] Cf. the wording of the second benediction of the Grace after meat: "we thank thee . . .", supra, p. 111.

but to the liquid contained in the vessel ("they all drank from the wine in Jesus' cup"). This is not a Greek construction: this is a Semitism, ἐκ=מִן, cf. infra, No. (17) p. 125 sq.

(11a) 14. 24 *τοῦτο*, Matt. 26. 28 *τοῦτο γάρ*, cf. supra No. (2).

(11b) 14. 24 *τὸ αἷμά μου* (Paul: *ἐν τῷ ἐμῷ αἵματι*), cf. supra, No. (7/8).

(12) 14. 24 *ἐκχυννόμενον*. The striking present tense is explained by the fact that in Hebrew and Aramaic the present participle is used, not only for the actual present, but also for the immediate future.[1] Further examples are Mark 10. 30; Matt. 3. 11; 11. 3 par.; 26. 25; Luke 1. 35; 22. 21; (John 1. 29; 12. 25; 13. 11; 16. 13; 17. 20; 18. 4; 21. 20).[2] The correct translation is therefore "which will (soon) be shed." Failure to observe these facts has led to serious misunderstandings, in particular that Jesus referred to an outpouring of His blood at the Last Supper—and not on the Cross![3]

(13) 14. 24 *ἐκχυννόμενον*. We possess a series of linguistic pointers to the *ipsissima vox* of Jesus, as for instance the emphasizing of His own sayings by the use of *ἀμήν*, which is unparalleled in the whole of contemporary literature. Another of these pointers is the frequent use of the passive to speak of God in devout periphrasis,

[1] C. F. Burney, *The Aramaic Origin of the Fourth Gospel* (Oxford, 1922), 94–5; P. Joüon, "L'Évangile de Notre-Seigneur Jésus-Christ", *Verbum Salutis* 5 (Paris, 1930), 69; W. B. Stevenson, *Grammar of Palestinian Jewish Aramaic* (Oxford, 1924), §21, 9; H. Odeberg, "The Aramaic Portions of Bereshit Rabba 2. A Short Grammar of Galilean Aramaic", *Lunds Univ. Årsskrift N.F.*, Avd. 1, vol. 36, No. 4 (1939), §439, p. 101. With particular reference to the passive participle as denoting an expected event, cf. for Hebrew: W. Gesenius-G. Bergstraesser, *Hebr. Grammatik*, 29th ed. (Leipzig, 1926), 2 §13d[c] and h[a], and for Aramaic may be mentioned as examples Dan. 2. 13 (*mithqaṭṭ[e]līn*); G. Dalman, *Aram. Dialektproben*, 2nd ed. (Leipzig, 1927), 15. 9 (*mithb[e]nē*); M. L. Margolis, *Lehrbuch der aram. Sprache des babylon. Talmuds* (Munich, 1910), 80. 10 (*mithb[e]'ēnā*).

[2] On the related future use of the present participle in various passages of Acts, cf. Blass-Debrunner, *Grammatik des N.T. Griechisch*, 7th ed. (Goettingen, 1943), §339, 2a-c.

[3] Roman Catholic authors especially have been misled (cf. e.g. H. Lamiroy, *De Essentia SS. Missae Sacrificii*, Diss. Louvain (1919), 206–13; F. Ruffenach, "Hoc est Corpus Meum, Hic est Sanguis Meus" in *Verbum Domini* 4 (1924), 266, "sacrificium praesens sit oportet"), where considerations of doctrine may have been determinative.

for instance in Matt. 5. 4 *παρακληθήσονται*, God shall comfort them; 5. 6 *χορτασθήσονται*, God shall fill them; 5. 7 *ἐλεηθήσονται*, God (on the Last Day) shall have mercy on them. In the same way, the subject of the outpouring in *ἐκχυννόμενον* remains hidden, because it is God's action, God's providence, which is behind this being poured out.

(14) 14. 24 *πολλῶν*. Whereas "many" in Greek (as in English) is in opposition to "all", and so has an exclusive connotation ("many, but not all"), the Hebrew רַבִּים can have an inclusive connotation ("the whole, comprising many individuals"). This linguistic usage comes about, because Hebrew and Aramaic have no word for "all" in the plural.[1]

Firstly, this is true for the use with an article. הָרַבִּים is in the entire Talmudic literature the constant expression for "the whole", for instance *Pirqē 'Abh.* 5. 18: Moses זִכָּה אֶת־הָרַבִּים, Jeroboam הֶחֱטִי אֶת־הָרַבִּים ; R.H. 1. 6; 3. 8; 4. 9; Tos. Sanh. 13. 5 (434. 23); Siphre Deut. 27 ad Deut. 3. 24; and often elsewhere. The same usage occurs in the writing of the "community of the new covenant in Damascus", ed. L. Rost (1933), 13. 7; 14. 12; 15. 8. This usage also passed over into Jewish Greek as Josephus shows.[2] In the New Testament the clearest example for this use of *οἱ πολλοί* is found in Rom. 5. 15 *εἰ γὰρ τῷ τοῦ ἑνὸς παραπτώματι οἱ πολλοὶ ἀπέθανον, πολλῷ μᾶλλον ἡ χάρις τοῦ θεοῦ καὶ ἡ δωρεὰ ἐν χάριτι τῇ τοῦ ἑνὸς ἀνθρώπου Ἰησοῦ Χριστοῦ εἰς τοὺς πολλοὺς ἐπερίσσευσεν*. Here the meaning "all men" for *οἱ πολλοί* is determined not only by the double contrast to *ὁ εἷς*, but also by the sense. "The many died" must mean "all men died" (*οἱ πολλοί* 5. 15a =*πάντες ἄνθρωποι* 5. 12). The same is true of Rom. 5. 19 (twice *ὁ εἷς*, meaning Adam-Christ, is contrasted with *οἱ πολλοί*, meaning mankind). Cf. also Mark 6. 2 *οἱ πολλοὶ ἀκούοντες ἐξεπλήσσοντο*, where the parallel, Luke 4. 22, has *πάντες*; Mark 9. 26 *τοὺς πολλούς*, meaning "all present"; Rom. 12. 5 *οἱ πολλοὶ ἓν σῶμά ἐσμεν ἐν Χριστῷ*, "we are all one body in

[1] In the Greek the use of *οἱ πολλοί* in the meaning of "the multitude, the masses, the people" (2 Macc. 1. 36), "the audience" (ibid. 2. 27), often with a derogatory connotation: "the lower orders, the (all too) many, the plebs" (e.g. *τῶν πολλῶν εἷς*), is very near this Hebrew usage.

[2] Evidence in A. Schlatter, *Der Evangelist Matthaeus* (1929), 701.

Christ"; similarly 1 Cor. 10. 17 *ἓν σῶμα οἱ πολλοί ἐσμεν*; 1 Cor. 10. 33 *μὴ ζητῶν τὸ ἐμαυτοῦ σύμφορον, ἀλλὰ τὸ τῶν πολλῶν* ("of all"), *ἵνα σωθῶσιν*; Heb. 12. 15 *καὶ διὰ ταύτης μιανθῶσιν οἱ πολλοί* (i.e. "the whole community").[1] As an adjective it is used in Luke 7. 47 *ἀφέωνται αἱ ἁμαρτίαι αὐτῆς αἱ πολλαί*, meaning that God (supra, No. 13) has forgiven her her sins, howeverall many they are.

Moreover, even the form without an article may have the same inclusive meaning. Targ. Is. 52. 14 paraphrases the indefinite רַבִּים by בֵּית יִשְׂרָאֵל. In the New Testament we can compare Mark 1. 34 *καὶ ἐθεράπευσεν πολλούς*, where it is unlikely that the author meant that Jesus healed only a proportion of the sick, cf. the parallels Matt. 8. 16 *πάντας*, Luke 4. 40 *ἑνὶ ἑκάστῳ*; also cf. Mark 10. 48 *πολλοί* par. Matt. 20. 31 *ὁ ὄχλος*. When 4 Esra 8. 3 says *multi quidem creati sunt, pauci autem salvabuntur*, the first clause "many have been created" obviously includes all men.[2] Similarly in the almost exactly parallel sentence *πολλοὶ γάρ εἰσιν κλητοί, ὀλίγοι δὲ ἐκλεκτοί* Matt. 22. 14, the indefinite *πολλοί* is to be understood inclusively (*πολλοί* meaning "all"). So may this *crux interpretum*[3] be solved. Even the adjectival use of *πολλοί* may have this sense: when we find Abraham called *πατὴρ πολλῶν ἐθνῶν*, Rom. 4. 17–18 (quoting Gen. 17. 5), the rabbinical exegesis of Gen. 17. 5 shows that the meaning is that Abraham is the father of all nations.[4] The adjectival and then the substantival use of an indefinite *πολλοί* are found in the one verse 2 Cor. 1. 11:[5] *ἵνα ἐκ πολλῶν προσώπων* ("by many persons", i.e. "out of

[1] Cf. A. Seeberg, *Der Brief an die Hebraeer* (Leipzig, 1912), 136, 140.

[2] The same in 4 Esra 4. 34, "you press (for the coming of the end) for your own sake; but the Most Highest (hesitates) because of many (Lat.: *pro multis*; Arab. ed. Gildemeister: because of the whole number)". The word "many" means all mankind. In the (lost) Greek original the term used was certainly *πολλοί*, probably without an article.

[3] K. L. Schmidt in *Theol. Woerterb. z. N.T.* 3. 496.

[4] P. Billerbeck 3. 211; H. Lietzmann, *An die Roemer*, 4 ed. (Tuebingen, 1933), 55. The inclusive meaning is probably also found in the adjective *πολλοί* in Heb. 2. 10, where it is said of God *πολλοὺς υἱοὺς εἰς δόξαν ἀγαγόντα* i.e. that He intends to lead many sons (all His many sons) to glory.

[5] This passage has been referred to by E. Lohmeyer in *Theol. Rundschau* 9 (1937), 191.

everybody's mouth") *τὸ εἰς ἡμᾶς χάρισμα διὰ πολλῶν* by many", i.e. "by the whole Church") *εὐχαριστηθῇ ὑπὲρ ἡμῶν*. Of particular importance for our passage is Mark 10. 45 par.: *λύτρον ἀντὶ πολλῶν*.[1] That *πολλοί* possesses an inclusive connotation (meaning "all") in this phrase is shown by the reference in Mark 10. 45 to Is. 53. 10–12,[2] and the parallel in 1 Tim. 2. 6 *ἀντίλυτρον ὑπὲρ πάντων*. Our passage is just as much to be interpreted in this inclusive sense as Mark 10. 45: *πολλῶν* is thus a Semitism.

(15) 14. 25, *ἀμήν*, i.e. אָמֵן. Matt. 26. 29 Graecises by using *δέ*; Luke does the same, 22. 18, by *γάρ*. Here is one pointer to the *ipsissima vox* (cf. supra, No. 13). Mark 14. 25 is the twelfth of the thirteen Marcan *ἀμήν* Sayings.

(16) 14. 25 *οὐκέτι οὐ μή*. This accumulation of negatives, "forme de Grec barbare" (eleven times in the LXX for לֹא עוֹד or לֹא or אַיִן,[3] in the New Testament also in Rev. 18. 14; Luke 22. 16 variant) is caused by the translator's clumsiness. One who translates into an acquired tongue is likely to choose too strong expressions.[4]

(17) 14. 25 *οὐ μὴ πίω ἐκ τοῦ γενήματος τῆς ἀμπέλου*, meaning: "I shall no more drink wine", is not Greek. In Greek *ἐκ* with *πίνειν* refers to the vessel from which somebody drinks; the liquid itself is put either in the accusative or in the partitive genitive. The fact that this is not a Greek construction is borne

[1] Joach. Jeremias, "Das Loesegeld fuer Viele" in *Judaica* 3 (1948), 249–64.

[2] The omission of the article before *πολλῶν* is explained by the fact that the LXX has in Is. 53. 11 and 12b *πολλοί* without article (Targ. in both cases: סַגִּיאִין, also without article).

[3] P. Benoit, *Rev. Bibl.* 48 (1939), 379.

[4] Instead of *οὐκέτι οὐ μὴ πίω* D a d f arm read *οὐ μὴ προσθῶ πεῖν*, *Θ*: *οὐ μὴ προσθῶμεν πιεῖν*. This substitution of a verb for "any more" or "further" is also a Semitism (D= אוֹסֵיף לְמִשְׁתֵּי; Θ= נוֹסֵיף לְמִשְׁתֵּי). The use of the first person plural for "I" (*Θ*) is common in Galilean Aramaic. However, these Semitisms are not to be added to our list, since they are not of those "Semitisms which have survived in the Cantabrigiensis" (cf. J. Wellhausen, *Einleitung in die drei ersten Evangelien*, 2nd ed. [Berlin, 1911], 9), which are supposed to have been expurgated from the text one after the other (?)—the feeble support they have excludes their claim to be the original—but are rather an attempt in D and *Θ* to avoid the accumulation of negatives *οὐκέτι οὐ μή*.

out by Luke 22. 18, where the *πίνειν ἐκ* is toned down to *πίνειν ἀπὸ τοῦ γενήματος τῆς ἀμπέλου*.

On the other hand Aramaic commonly refers to the liquid drunk with מִן. Cf. Qoh. R. 3. 2 (ed. Stettin, 1864), 81a, 9 שתון מן הדין חמרא "drink this wine", etc.;[1] LXX Gen. 9. 21 *καὶ ἔπιεν ἐκ τοῦ οἴνου*. Comparable texts in the New Testament are: John 4. 13–14 *ὁ πίνων ἐκ τοῦ ὕδατος τούτου*; Rev. 14. 10 *πίεται ἐκ τοῦ οἴνου*; 18. 3 *ἐκ τοῦ οἴνου . . . πέπωκαν*.

(18) 14. 25 *τὸ γένημα τῆς ἀμπέλου* for "wine" is a fixed liturgical formula at the blessing of the cup. Before the drinking of the wine God is praised as בּוֹרֵא פְּרִי הַגֶּפֶן, Ber. 6. 1; Tos. Ber 4. 3. (8. 24); b. Pes. 103a, 106a, etc.

(19) 14. 25 *τὸ γένημα τῆς ἀμπέλου*, cf. for the use of the article Dan. 5. 1 חַמְרָא שָׁתֵה "drinking the wine".

(20) 14. 25 *ἕως τῆς ἡμέρας ἐκείνης*. *'Εκεῖνος* is not used in an emphatic sense here. Its existence is in all probability due to a pleonastic use[2] of the demonstrative pronoun in the Aramaic.[3] A further example of this use of *ἐκεῖνος* is found in Mark 14. 21 par. The reproduction of this entirely unemphasized correlative of the relative pronoun by Greek *ἐκεῖνος* can only be called a mistranslation.

Of the twenty Semitisms in Mark's text which have been enumerated, the last six are found in verse 25, which Paul does not reproduce *in extenso*. Of the first fourteen Semitisms only four reappear in Paul (Nos. 2, 3, 5 and 8). The remaining ten are either graecised (1 Cor. 11. 24 reads *εὐχαριστήσας* instead of

[1] More Rabbinic evidence is given by A. Schlatter, *Der Evangelist Johannes* (Stuttgart, 1930), 120, ad John 4. 13.

[2] Instances in F. Schulthess-E. Littmann, *Grammatik des christl.-palaestin. Aramaeisch* (Tuebingen, 1924), §190, 2b; G. Dalman, *Grammatik des jued.-palaestin. Aramaeisch*, 2nd ed. (Leipzig, 1905), §17. 9; id., *Jesus-Jeschua* (Leipzig, 1922), 58, 164; H. Odeberg, *Short Grammar of Galilean Aramaic* (1939), §340; A. Ungnad, *Syrische Grammatik* (Munich, 1913), §15c; M. L. Margolis, *Lehrb. d. aramaeischen Sprache d. babyl. Talmuds* (Munich, 1910), §51b; Th. Noeldeke, *Mandaeische Grammatik* (Halle, 1875), 344 and note 2.

[3] P. Joüon, "Quelques Aramaïsmes sous-jacents au Grec des Évangiles" in *Recherches de science religieuse* 17 (1927), 213–14; id., *L'Évangile de Notre-Seigneur Jésus-Christ* (Paris, 1930), 162, 263.

εὐλογήσας, which might have been misunderstood by Greek readers, and ὑμῶν, which interprets the Semitism πολλῶν) or avoided altogether. When we add that the word over the bread takes in Paul a form which, as we have seen, cannot be retranslated into Aramaic, that is yet another proof that Mark's account of the Last Supper is the earlier.[1] Paul's account is not only materially (vide p. 107-14) but also linguistically a remoulding of the tradition, for the sake of the Greek-speaking reader—or rather, churches, for in Paul too we are faced with a fixed liturgical formula.

This result is of far-reaching importance for determining the age of Mark's text.

(*b*) *The age of the Marcan tradition.*

(1) The Marcan text (14. 22–5) and the Pauline (1 Cor. 11. 23–6) are independent of each other; nor do they derive from a common Greek source. The divergences are too great for that. On the other hand, we have seen that in their main features the contents of the two texts are materially the same.[2] They therefore depend upon a common eucharistic tradition underlying both textual forms: we have "two mutually independent forms of the same tradition in front of us".[3] This original tradition was, as the linguistic analysis of Mark has shown, Aramaic.

(2) In Paul[4] we find a development and enlargement of the

[1] The linguistic evidence goes a fair way to demolish the thesis of G. Loeschcke in *Zeitschr. f. wiss. Theol.* 54 N.F. 19 (1912), 197, "the report in Mark is a conflation of the ancient Synoptic text, as preserved in Luke [viz. 22. 15–18] and the (Pauline) words of institution, which were customarily used in the cult of the Pauline churches."

[2] H. Lietzmann, *Messe und Herrenmahl* (Bonn, 1926), 227, "as a result of our research we can state that Paul was familiar with the same tradition about the Last Supper as that which is found in Mark." M. Dibelius, *Die Formgeschichte des Evangeliums*, 2nd ed. (1933), 207, 212; J. Finegan, *Die Ueberlieferung der Leidens- und Auferstehungsgeschichte Jesu* (Giessen, 1934), 66–7, and others.

[3] H. Lietzmann, op. cit. 218; W. Goossens, *Les Origines de l'Eucharistie—sacrement et sacrifice* (Gembloux-Paris, 1931), 345–52.

[4] A. Loisy, "Les origines de la Cène Eucharistique" in *Congrès d'histoire du Christianisme* 1 = *Annales d'histoire du Christianisme* 1 (Paris-Amsterdam, 1928), 83–4, has—with some reserve—advanced the hypothesis, and attempted to prove, that the report on the Last

earliest tradition, both linguistically and materially, which, among other things, had Greek-speaking congregations in mind.

This process of development and enlargement which produced the Pauline text arose from the interplay of different and sometimes overlapping motives, which are worth enumerating: (1) In liturgical usage the tendency soon appeared to make the words over the bread and over the wine parallel. For this reason *τὸ ὑπὲρ ὑμῶν* has been added to the word over the bread, and the command to repeat the rite has been given twice. The celebration *sub una* may well have been an additional reason for the reinforcing of the word over the bread and the restriction of the second command to repeat the rite (*ὁσάκις ἐὰν πίνητε*). The stress laid upon "my" by putting it before the noun (in the case of the bread as well as of the wine), as well as the change from *πολλῶν* to *ὑμῶν*, reflects the use of the words of interpretation as an administration formula. (2) A tendency to clarification is also discernible. The Semitisms *εὐλογήσας* and *πολλῶν* were misleading to the Gentile Christians, and were therefore replaced. The second *τοῦτο* was clarified by *τὸ ποτήριον* and *διαθήκη* by adding *καινή*, where (3) the reference to Jer. 31. 31–4, shows the beginning of theological reflection. (4) Lastly, the complicated construction of the cup-formula in Paul may well be traced to an apologetic motive.

All these changes can hardly be the work of Paul himself; his account of the Last Supper is "long since finished, long since a piece of strictly formulated ritual tradition".[1] That is made

Supper in 1 Corinthians, together with its context, is an interpolation, originating from about the time of the Didache (op. cit. 85). His reasons are amazingly slight. First, Loisy doubts that such an "unheard-of disorder" could develop at the celebrations in the Corinthian Church such a short time after the departure of the Apostle, as is described in 1 Cor. 11. 17 sq. (p. 84); secondly, he doubts whether already in A.D. 55–6 Paul and the Christians of his time could have had such a "gnosis of salvation" as is presupposed in the account of the Last Supper in 1 Cor. 11. 23–5 (p. 85). Loisy is sufficiently consistent to admit that whoever shares this second doubt will have to regard many more passages in the Pauline corpus as interpolations, as they exhibit the same "gnosis of salvation". How the rise of Christianity could ever be understood or explained if the Cross were omitted from the earliest kerygma has, however, remained Loisy's secret.

[1] R. Otto, *Reich Gottes und Menschensohn* (Munich, 1934), 277, cf. supra, p. 107 sq.

clear by the preface: *ἐγὼ γὰρ παρέλαβον ἀπὸ τοῦ κυρίου, ὃ καὶ παρέδωκα ὑμῖν* 1 Cor. 11. 23; there should never have been any doubt that *παραλαμβάνειν* and *παραδιδόναι* were the equivalents of two rabbinical technical terms, קִבֵּל מִן and מָסַר לְ (P. Abh. 1. 1 sq., etc.),[1] so that 1 Cor. 11. 23 says nothing other than that the chain of tradition goes back unbroken to the words of Jesus Himself.[2] 1 Cor. 15. 1 sq. provides immediate proof of this, where Paul in like manner reminds the Corinthians of an old-established tradition, the kerygma, and uses the same technical terms *παραδιδόναι* and *παραλαμβάνειν* (*παρέδωκα γὰρ ὑμῖν ἐν πρώτοις, ὃ καὶ παρέλαβον* 1 Cor. 15. 3). For it can be proved linguistically that the kerygma (which includes verses 3b from *Χριστός* to 5 *δώδεκα*, as shown e.g. by the syntactic break at the beginning of verse 6)[3] was not formulated by Paul. The following are un-Pauline: (*a*) the phrase *ὑπὲρ τῶν ἁμαρτιῶν ἡμῶν* 1 Cor. 15. 3. In Paul's Epistles *ἁμαρτία* is found sixty-four times;[4] three of these are in the Pastorals[5] and five are quotations from the Old Testament.[6] In the remaining fifty-six cases *ἁμαρτία* is used absolutely[7] and in the singular no less than fifty times, a fact which arises from Paul's idea that sin is a personified power.[8] In Paul a particular sin is *ἁμάρτημα* or *παράπτωμα*. The six passages where *ἁμαρτία* is used in the plural or with

[1] Cf. G. Kittel, "Die Probleme des palaestinischen Spaet-Judentums und das Urchristentum", *Beitraege zur Wissenschaft vom Alten und Neuen Testament* 3. 1 (Stuttgart, 1926), 63–4; M. Dibelius, *Die Formgeschichte des Evangeliums*, 2nd ed. (Tuebingen, 1933), 20, 207 n. 1; A. Schlatter, *Paulus, der Bote Jesu* (Stuttgart, 1934), 320.

[2] A. Schlatter, op. cit.; R. Hupfeld, *Die Abendmahlsfeier* (1935), 67; E. Stauffer, *Die Theologie des N.T.* (1941), 282 n. 552.

[3] Up to v. 5 there are *ὅτι*-clauses; from v. 6 onwards main clauses, cf. A. v. Harnack, "Die Verklaerungsgeschichte Jesu, der Bericht des Paulus (1 Cor. 15. 3 sq.) und die beiden Christus-Visionen des Petrus" in *S.B. Berlin Akad. d. Wissenschaften ph.-hist. Klasse* (1922), 62–80.

[4] Furthermore in variants of Col. 2. 11 and 2 Thess. 2. 3.

[5] 1 Tim. 5. 22, 24; 2 Tim. 3. 6.

[6] Rom. 4. 7, from LXX Ps. 31. 1; Rom. 4. 8, from LXX Ps. 31. 2; Rom. 8. 3 *περὶ ἁμαρτίας*, i.e. sin-offering, cf. LXX Lev. 5. 6 etc.; Rom. 11. 27, from LXX Is. 27. 9; 1 Thess. 2. 16, from LXX Gen. 15. 16.

[7] "I.e. without a genitive or an expression which serves as a substitute for a genitive, indicating the person who commits or bears the sin", E. Lohmeyer, "Probleme paulinischer Theologie 3. Suende, Fleisch und Tod" in *Z.N.W.* 29 (1930), 2.

[8] E. Lohmeyer, op. cit. 2 sq.

the genitive or with a personal pronoun all show the influence of a general early Christian usage (1 Cor. 15. 3, the kerygma; ibid. 15. 17, influenced by of the kerygma; Gal. 1. 4, Christological formula; Rom. 7. 5; Col. 1. 14; Eph. 2. 1) and are not specifically Pauline. (*b*) The phrase *κατὰ τὰς γραφάς* 1 Cor. 15. 3/4, for it is found nowhere else in Paul, who says: *καθὼς γέγραπται* etc. (*c*) *ὤφθη* which occurs only in 1 Cor. 15. 5–8, and in the credal formula in 1 Tim. 3. 16; (*d*) *ἐγήγερται* which occurs only in 1 Cor. 15. 4, and—clearly under the influence of this passage—in verses 12–14, 16–17, 20, and in the credal formula in 2 Tim. 2. 8; and (*e*) the expression *οἱ δώδεκα* 1 Cor. 15. 5. But more can be said. There are, if not strict proofs, at any rate signs indicating that the kerygma is translated from a Semitic original. This is indicated by (*a*) the avoidance of the name of Jesus;[1] (*b*) the use of the passive as a periphrasis for the Divine name (*ἐγήγερται*); (*c*) the word *ὤφθη* (instead of *ἐφάνη*!), which is explained by the fact that Hebrew נִרְאָה and Aramaic איתחמי have the double meaning of "He was seen" and "He appeared"; and (*d*) the introduction of the logical subject in the dative after a passive verb (instead of the expected *ὑπό* with the genitive).[2] Lastly, the double reference to the Old Testament suggests that the formulation of the kerygma took place in a Jewish-Christian milieu,[3] as does the closing assertion of 1 Cor. 15. 11, that Paul's kerygma was identical with that of the first Apostles.[4] From all this it certainly follows that the kerygma was not formulated by Paul. Since Paul, as we have seen,

[1] Cf. 3 John 7; Acts 5. 41 (*ὄνομα*), and the circumlocution *Βαρσοῦμα* (i.e. son of the name) for *Βαριησοῦς* in Acts 13. 6 sy[pesh] Ephr.

[2] Notice also the Aramaic form of the name *Κηφᾶς*. However, the use of this form proves little because Paul, although he sometimes puts *Πέτρος* (Gal. 2. 7, 8), prefers *Κηφᾶς* (Gal. 1. 18; 2. 9; 2. 11, 14; 1 Cor. 1. 12; 3. 22; 9. 5 as well as in our passage, 15. 5).

[3] Cf. A. Schlatter, *Paulus, der Bote Jesu* (Stuttgart, 1934), 395. The plural *αἱ γραφαί*, arising from כְּתוּבַיָּא, need not be a translation, since the expression is of old standing in Jewish Greek, cf. G. Schrenk in *Theol. Woerterb. z. N.T.* 1. 751–2.

[4] Cf. also F. Buechsel in *Theol. Lit.-Blatt* 55 (1934), 98, "1 Cor. 15. 3, where Cephas and James, the authorities of the Primitive Church, are specially mentioned as witnesses of the resurrection, belongs as to its contents undoubtedly to Jerusalem and probably does so also with regard to its wording."

speaks in 1 Cor. 11. 23 as well as in 15. 3 of *παραλαμβάνειν* and *παραδιδόναι* we may conclude that he owes the formulation of the account of the Last Supper, as he owes that of the kerygma, to tradition. It can be shown, in fact, that in the account of the Last Supper there are idioms foreign to Paul.

Only in 1 Cor. 11. 23–25 can there be found in Paul: *παραδίδοσθαι* used absolutely; *κλᾶν* without an object; *ἐμός* used attributively; *ἀνάμνησις* (twice); *μετά* with infinitive used as a noun; *δειπνεῖν*; *ὁσάκις* (only in 1 Cor. 11. 25–26).[1] Still more significant is the consideration that elsewhere Paul uses the central words of the account of the Last Supper *τὸ σῶμα τοῦ Χριστοῦ* with a different meaning. For elsewhere in Paul the words *τὸ σῶμα τοῦ Χριστοῦ* do not mean the body of the man Jesus[2] but the Church. (Even Rom. 7. 4 has this meaning, for *διὰ τοῦ σώματος τοῦ Χριστοῦ* means here: by—your incorporation through Holy Baptism into—the body of Christ.) Indeed, Paul connected the idea of the Church as the body of Christ even with the words of Institution, as is shown by 1 Cor. 10. 16–17. This makes it all the more clear that 1 Cor. 11. 24 is in an idiom foreign to him.[3] Here we really have to differentiate in Paul between "*Mishnā*" and "*Gemārā*".[4] In the "*Gemārā*" *σῶμα* means the Church. Therefore the "*Mishnā*" is pre-Pauline.

When did Paul receive the formula of the words of institution which he handed on (1 Cor. 11. 23 *ὃ καὶ παρέδωκα ὑμῖν*) to the Corinthians in his apostolic teaching in A.D. 49/50? At his conversion? Hardly. The fact that the wording of the tradition which he used arose in Hellenistic surroundings (p. 126-7), as well as the similarities between Luke and Paul (p. 100-1), support the view that in 1 Cor. 11. 23–25 Paul was handing on that formula of the words of institution which was in use at Antioch where he had settled about A.D. 40 (Acts 11. 26).[5]

[1] Cf. E. Lohmeyer in *Theol. Rundschau* 9 (1937), 184.

[2] For this he uses other expressions, such as *τὸ σῶμα τῆς σαρκὸς αὐτοῦ* Col. 1. 22.

[3] R. Hupfeld, *Die Abendmahlsfeier* (1935), 78.

[4] This striking metaphor comes from J. Héring, *Le Royaume de Dieu et sa venue* (1937), 223–4.

[5] Cf. supra, p. 103; A. Schlatter, *Das Evangelium des Lukas* (Stuttgart, 1931), 421; R. Otto, *Reich Gottes und Menschensohn* (Munich, 1934), 277; J. Héring, *Le Royaume de Dieu et sa venue* (1937), 227.

(3) Of the traditions which have come down to us, Mark's is the nearest to the primitive Aramaic account of the Last Supper. He exhibits, as we have seen, a tradition which is materially and linguistically nearer to the original formulation than that of Paul. His wording is therefore earlier than the development and enlargement of the Aramaic original of the account of the Last Supper, which took place long before A.D. 49/50, the results of which are to be found in Paul.

That in the remaining space of at most a decade[1] after the death of Jesus the Eucharistic rite should have been freely created, and the account of the Lord's Supper invented as an ætiological legend, is as much incapable of proof as it is improbable. It is even improbable that in the first decade after the death of Jesus the tradition should be in any essentials obscured; against that we have to set the complete unanimity in content of the mutually independent reports of Mark and Paul which came from different sections of the Church. Since the tradition of Mark, besides its material indications of a very early age, possesses a further guarantee of trustworthiness in its Palestinian origin (Semitisms), we have every reason to conclude that it gives us absolutely authentic information.

(5) *Was There a Pre-Marcan Form?*

Even this, however, is not the end of the matter. Although we now enter the field of conjecture, the question has to be asked whether the text of Mark sanctions any conclusion with regard to a pre-Marcan form of the tradition. The answer is in the affirmative. But we have to distinguish between observations on the setting of the words of institution and those on the Eucharistic Words themselves.

With regard to the framework of Mark, we have already seen (1) that the first, introductory genitive absolute *ἐσθιόντων αὐτῶν* in verse 22, may have been substituted for a more substantial introduction, and (2) that the words leading up to the bread and the wine seem to have been assimilated under the influence of a

[1] If it is correct to say that Paul reproduces the words of institution in the form used by the Church at Antioch (cf. p. 131), the time must have been shorter still.

tendency towards parallelism, a process in which (as Paul shows the introduction to the word over the bread was the first to be fixed. (3) Moreover, the connexion between verses 24 and 25 is not "organic".[1] An introduction like Luke 22. 17 could hardly be avoided, especially if verse 25 be a vow of abstinence. When verse 25 was added (which, as is shown by Paul/Luke, does not belong to the ancient liturgical formula), such an introduction may well have been omitted in view of verse 23. (4) Weightier is the observation that when Mark 14. 22–25 is read as a whole, we get the impression that the word over the wine immediately followed that over the bread; but on the other hand *μετὰ τὸ δειπνῆσαι* (Paul/Luke) makes it clear that the whole meal lay between them. The question therefore arises whether Mark reflects a change of liturgical custom. The placing together of the administration of bread and wine is certainly found in Justin Martyr in the second century A.D.,[2] and very probably already in the Didache (where the celebration of the Eucharist follows that of the Agape), and may quite well belong to the first century. The first indication of this process is found already in 1 Cor., where Paul considers the abuses which had arisen at the Lord's Supper in Corinth, and advises the individual if necessary to satisfy his hunger beforehand by a meal at home, 11. 34. The text of Mark is probably the earliest witness for the separation of such a meal from the Eucharist and the placing together of the administration of both elements at the end of the meal. This change, therefore, seems to date back to the time before A.D. 70.[3]

With regard to the words of Jesus themselves, the question arises at one point whether an earlier wording has been enlarged: *τὸ αἷμά μου τῆς διαθήκης* is an expression—difficult enough in Greek—which is impossible in Aramaic: there a noun with a pronominal suffix cannot govern a genitive.[4] This linguistic

[1] G. Loeschcke in *Zeitschr. fuer wiss. Theologie* 54 N.F. 19 (1912), 197.

[2] 1 Apol. 61, 65–7.

[3] G. Dix, *The Shape of the Liturgy* (1944), 101, also puts the separation of the Eucharist from the actual meal at a time earlier than A.D. 70. Luke 22. 20 makes it probable that in various districts the change took place only at a later date.

[4] Cf. J. Wellhausen, *Das Evangelium Marci*, 2nd ed. (Berlin, 1909), 114; G. Dalman, *Jesus-Jeschua* (Leipzig, 1922), 146. The earlier Syriac

difficulty is coupled with the material one that in late Judaism "the blood of the covenant" (*dam berīth*) is the recognized term for "the blood of circumcision".[1] Thus *τὸ αἷμά μου τῆς διαθήκης* can hardly in its present form be Palestinian.[2] So the question arises whether *τῆς διαθήκης* is not an early exegetical gloss,[3] which (with the help of Exod. 24. 8 and Jer. 31. 31–34) explains Jesus' atoning death as the covenant sacrifice[4] to inaugurate the

translations find it therefore very difficult to give an adequate version of the expression. They overcome this difficulty—unless they slavishly translate word for word—by regarding τῆς διαθήκης as an apposition: "this is my blood, the new covenant", so Matt. 26. 28 in sy[sin pal] (cur. *deest*); Luke 22. 17 in sy[sin]; Luke 22, 20 in Tat[ar] and Aphraates 1. 221 (cf. supra, p. 90 n. 2.).

[1] Instances in P. Billerbeck 1. 991–2; 4. 32, 34, 38 sub (*d*) and 40 sub (*g*); G. Dalman, op. cit. 151.

[2] The idea of the covenant plays no part at all in the ancient liturgy of the Passover.

[3] W. Wrede in *Z.N.W.* 1 (1900), 69 sq.; G. Hollmann, ibid. 135 sq.; W. Heitmueller in *R.G.G.*, 1st ed. 1 (1909), 20 sq.; G. Dalman, *Jesus-Jeschua* (1922), 147, "it is possible"; C. Clemen, *Relig.-gesch. Erkl. d. N.T.*, 2nd ed. (1924), 177–8; K. Voelker, *Mysterium und Agape* (1927), 27, 39 sq., 42; H. Windisch in *Deutsche Lit.-Zeitg.* (1935), 979–80; R. Bultmann in *Theol. Blaetter* 20 (1941), 272. Bultmann would like to see in τὸ ἐκχυννόμενον ὑπὲρ πολλῶν another still older exegetical gloss, but there are no linguistic and material difficulties here such as there are with τῆς διαθήκης.

[4] Notice from the linguistic point of view that in τὸ αἷμά μου τῆς διαθήκης (*a*) the possessive pronoun belongs to αἷμα (in analogy to the preceding τὸ σῶμά μου, cf. 1 Cor. 11. 25 ἐν τῷ ἐμῷ αἵματι), and not to διαθήκης; the blood of Jesus is referred to, not His διαθήκη. The covenant is of God. (*b*) The genitive construction is biblical Greek (twice in the LXX: Exod. 24. 8; Zech. 9. 11); διαθήκη therefore does not mean—as in Greek—"a will", but—as in biblical Greek—"covenant, disposition, order of salvation". With regard to the meaning of this expression, it has to be said that it intends to explain typologically the blood of the covenant poured out at Mount Sinai (Exod. 24. 8, cf. Zech. 9. 11), which (according to Targ. Onk. and Jerusch. I ad Exod. 24. 8) had atoning power. As this blood established the covenant of Moses, so the blood of Jesus established the New Covenant (Jer. 31. 31–4), which had as its content the perfect fellowship with God (Jer. 31. 33–34a), founded upon God's forgiveness (v. 34b), in His kingdom. Cf. pp. 77–82 of the first (German) edition of this book. All ideas of a blood-brotherhood of the members, brotherhood meal, etc., are alien to the concept and are the results of modern thought.

eschatological order of redemption. But, since *διαθήκη* is found already in Paul, it must have been added in the first decade after the death of Jesus.[1]

If this conjecture be correct, it would not destroy our confidence in the reliability of the Marcan text. The tradition was a living thing, not a dead formula. The possibility of one single addition even in the earliest times has to be taken into account, but not the obscuration of the substance of the tradition.

[1] The possibility that the word "covenant" nevertheless represents Jesus' own idea is not denied here. On the contrary, it is highly probable that Jesus declared that the time for the New Covenant had come, particularly because the promise of Jer. 31. 31 sq. was highly popular in his days, as is seen from the writing of the community of the new covenant at Damascus, cf. supra, p. 75.

CHAPTER IV

The Meaning of the Eucharistic Words of Jesus

(1) *The Meal*

"And when it was evening He cometh with the Twelve", Mark 14. 17. This meal of Jesus must not be isolated, but should rather be seen as one of a series of daily meals they had shared together. Every table fellowship is a fellowship of life;[1] table fellowship with Jesus is more. This is evident from that table fellowship which Jesus gave to sinners and outcasts. Orientals, to whom symbolic actions mean more than to us, immediately understood that the admission of the outcasts to table fellowship with Jesus meant an offer of salvation to the guilty sinners, and the assurance of forgiveness.[2] Hence the passionate objections of the Pharisees ("this man receiveth sinners and eateth with them", Luke 15. 2, cf. Mark 2. 15–17), who assumed that the pious could have table fellowship only with the righteous. In this way they revealed an understanding of our Lord's intention to accord to sinners worth before God,[3] and they objected to the placing of the sinners on the same level as the righteous.

After the confession of Peter at Caesarea Philippi, the customary daily table fellowship with Jesus was bound to assume an entirely new meaning for the disciples. From that time onward every meal with Jesus was a symbol, a pre-presentation, indeed an actual

[1] G. Dalman, *Arbeit und Sitte in Palaestina* 7 (1942), 220.

[2] Cf. Jos., *Ant.* 19. 7. 1. §321: King Agrippa I had Silas, who had fallen into disgrace, brought to his table to signify that he had forgiven him. The fact that the risen Lord ate with His disciples who had forsaken Him, Luke 24. 30, 35, 43 (where the word *ἐνώπιον* originally, as in 13. 15, signifies the table fellowship); Acts 1. 4; 10. 41; John 21. 13, means the readmission of the disciples into the old fellowship, and is a visible sign of His forgiveness; it was only secondarily that this feature was used to counter the Docetics: Luke 24. 41–3, cf. in particular the variants of verses 42–3 (the restitution of the remainder of the honeycomb is obviously meant to convince the disciples of the impress made by His teeth).

[3] This intention is most clearly discernible in Luke 19. 1–10.

anticipation of the eschatological meal.[1] The request of the sons of Zebedee to be allowed to keep the places of honour at the Eschatological Meal, which they had at times[2] occupied on earth, is clear evidence of this (Mark 10. 35 sq.), and the continuation of the daily table fellowship after the death of Jesus as a sacred rite can be understood only in this context. The self-humiliation of Jesus, too, when He ministered to His disciples like a slave (John 13. 1 sq.; Luke 22. 27) can be seen in its full depth only when it is realized that the Messiah serves at the Messiah's table. The admission of outcasts and renegades to table fellowship means more after Peter's confession than before: in them is now represented the eternal and perfected "Communion of Saints".[3] Since Peter's confession every act of eating and drinking with the Master is a table fellowship of the redeemed community with the redeemer, is the marriage feast where fasting is abolished, is the pledge of their share in the final Eschatological Meal. The meal on Maundy Thursday shares in all that significance.

This meal on Maundy Thursday is however a special one among all the other Messianic meals. It is the passover meal, the high point of the year. Already the solemn setting, the reclining on couches, the festal wine, the paschal lamb, the liturgy of the feast, mark it as a meal of rejoicing.[4] The Passover at the time of Jesus looked both backwards and forwards. God's people remember at the feast the merciful immunity afforded the houses sprinkled with the blood of the paschal lambs and their deliverance from servitude in Egypt. But that is only one side. At the same time the Passover is a looking forward to the coming deliverance of which the deliverance out of Egypt is the type.[5] This typology is a concept which "most

[1] Cf. R. Hupfeld, *Die Abendmahlsfeier* (1935), 57.

[2] Cf. John 13. 23.

[3] Cf. E. Lohmeyer, *Kultus und Evangelium* (1942), 37; id., *Journ. of Bibl. Lit.* 56 (1937), 218–26.

[4] "This night is a time of exultation for the whole of Israel", Exod. R. 18. This is justly emphasized by M. Barth, *Das Abendmahl* (1945), 7 sq.

[5] Supra, p. 35; P. Billerbeck 2. 256; G. F. Moore, *Judaism* 2. 42; G. Dalman, *Ergaenzungen und Verbesserungen zu Jesus-Jeschua* (1929), 9 sq.; A. Schlatter, *Der Evangelist Matthaeus* (1929), 732; I. Zolli, *Il Nazareno* (1938), 212 sq.; H. Riesenfeld, *Jésus transfiguré* (1947), 29 sq.

comprehensively determined already in early times, as no other concept did, the form that the doctrine of final salvation took".[1] The Messiah comes on this night! "On this night they were saved, and on this night they will be saved", is an old saying.[2] "The Messiah who is called First (Is. 41. 27) will come in the first month (Nīsān)."[3] *Traditio Judaeorum est Christum media nocte venturum in similitudinem Aegyptii temporis, quando pascha celebratum est*, says Jerome.[4] Then will the night turn to day, because the true light shines.[5] Thus the night of the Passover is even called "the sign" by which God guarantees the coming of the Messiah.[6]

The Passover liturgy reflects the vividness of this Messianic expectation[7] just as clearly as the rebellions against Roman occupation, which repeatedly took place at the Passover.[8] Jesus

[1] P. Billerbeck 1. 85, cf. L. Goppelt, *Typos* (1939).

[2] Mekh. Exod. 12. 42 (R. *Jehōshūa' b. Ḥananyā*, about A.D. 90), cf. Targ. Jer. I ad Exod. 12. 42.

[3] Exod. R. 15. 2 ad 12. 2. The context is, "God will come who is called 'the First' (Is. 44. 6) and will build His Temple which is called 'First' (Jer. 17. 22) and shall require the debt of Esau who is called 'First' (Gen. 25. 25) and the Messiah will come who is called 'First' (Is. 41. 27) —in the first month (Nīsān), cf. Exod. 12. 2".

[4] . . . *unde reor et traditionem apostolicam permansisse, ut in die vigiliarum paschae ante noctis dimidium populos dimittere non liceat, expectantes adventum Christi*, Comm. in Matt. 25. 6 (M.P.L. 26, 184 sq.).

[5] Exod. R. 18.

[6] Ibid., "this sign be in your hand: on the day on which I have prepared salvation for you—in the same night you shall know that I shall save you". All these expectations are based upon Exod. 12. 42, where the Passover night is called "the night to be observed".

[7] The interpretation of the four passover cups in terms of the four cups of punishment and the four cups of comfort in the last days has been mentioned previously, supra p. 34 sq. On the eschatological interpretation of the *Hallēl* (Ps. 113–18) cf. infra, p. 174 n. 1. Cf. also G. Dalman, *Jesus-Jeschua* (Leipzig, 1922), 166; *Ergaenzungen und Verbesserungen zu Jesus-Jeschua* (Leipzig, 1929), 9 sq.; I. Zolli, *Il Nazareno* (1938), 212 sq.

[8] Josephus passim. In the New Testament cf. Luke 13. 1–3 (that this took place at the Passover follows from the fact that lay people were sacrificing: it was only at the passover sacrifice that laymen were permitted to take an active part), and Mark 15. 7; Luke 23. 19 (the Barabbas riot appears to have taken place within the last few days, as is suggested by the vivid interest taken by the people); John 6. 15, Luke 22. 38 also show Passover atmosphere.

underlines the Messianic significance of this particular Passover on Maundy Thursday by limiting the circle of His table companions to the Twelve. The absence of the women mentioned in Mark 15. 40, 47; 16. 1, is striking.[1] There seems to be only one explanation for this—namely, that Jesus gathered the Twelve around Him as His *Passa-Ḥabhūrā*, His family. It had been recognized by the prophets since Isaiah that the true Israel consisted in the faithful remnant of a disloyal nation.[2] Thus Jesus sees in the Twelve the representatives of the new people of God.[3] By taking them apart with Himself for the passover meal, Jesus makes it clear that they are the core of the new Messianic community.

In sharp contrast with the elation of this Passover feast, which the Twelve are permitted to celebrate with the Son of Man, is the gravity of the hour. This is the last, the farewell meal. Jesus' deeds and words at the Last Supper have to be understood in the light of this contrast. In the course of this evening Jesus said more than has been preserved for us. Yet two things impressed themselves especially upon the disciples, partly because in them Jesus, to their surprise, deviated from established custom: the words of interpretation and the vow of abstinence.

(2) *The Words of Interpretation*

The passover meal began with the Kiddūsh, the blessing of the cup, and the preliminary dish. After this the paschal lamb was served and the second cup mixed. But before the meal proper began, Jesus, as the Paterfamilias, took the Passover devotions, the climax of which was the interpretation of the elements of the meal by the events of the exodus from Egypt: the unleavened bread was explained as a symbol of past misery, the bitter herbs as a symbol of slavery, the fruit-purée which had the consistency and colour of clay as a symbol of slave-labour, and the paschal lamb as a reminder of God's merciful "passing over" Israel. The wording of Jesus' devotions is not preserved. Yet it is essential to remember that the words of interpretation were not isolated for the disciples

[1] Supra, p. 19. On the absence of the women cf. "The Apostolic Church Order" ed. Hilgenfeld, *Novum Testamentum extra Canonem*, 2nd ed. (1884), 4. 118.

[2] C. H. Dodd, *History and the Gospel* (1938), 136.

[3] Matt. 19. 28; Luke 22. 29 sq.

—as they are for us—but were prepared for by the way He had interpreted the elements in His devotions.

The Passover meal, begun and ended by the two "Graces", followed immediately on the Passover devotions. Most surprisingly Jesus adds a word of explanation to each of these Graces before and after the main meal. This was contrary to custom,[1] for the explanation of the elements belonged to the Passover devotion and not to the Grace. It is even more surprising that Jesus does not partake of the bread and the cup of benediction, although He blesses them. At any rate, that is most likely in the case of the cup, as we shall see, and for that reason can be assumed in the case of the bread, and may even be hinted at in the invitation *λάβετε* (Mark 14. 22).[2] The unusual nature of Jesus' action certainly helped to impress it on the disciples more deeply than other details of the evening.

The words of interpretation are *τοῦτό ἐστιν τὸ σῶμά μου* and *τοῦτό ἐστιν τὸ αἷμά μου. Τοῦτό ἐστιν* is Aramaic *dēn* (the Greek copula *ἐστίν* has here no equivalent in Aramaic);[3] and *τὸ αἷμά μου* is Aramaic *'idhmī*. The Aramaic equivalent of *σῶμα*, however, is more difficult to find. The question is of great importance. We must start from the fact that *σῶμα* and *αἷμα* on the lips of Jesus constitute a twin concept. For this reason *gūph*[4] cannot be regarded as the equivalent to *σῶμα*, because it is nowhere coupled with blood. The twin concepts with *gūph* are rather *gūphā-naphshā*[5] or *gūph-neshāmā*[6] (body and soul), *haggūph-*

[1] Several mistakes have been committed by A. Merx, *Die vier kanonischen Evangelien* 2. 2 (1905), 416 sq., who is followed by M. Barth, *Das Abendmahl* (1945), 19.

[2] So G. Dalman, *Jesus-Jeschua* (Leipzig, 1922), 128; P. Fiebig in *Neues Saechs. Kirchenblatt* 42 (1935), 376.

[3] Because there was no reason to distinguish the bread which Jesus handed round from any other bread. It is only in later Aramaic that *hū* is put in without special emphasis (Jerus. Targums; Palest. Talmud). So G. Dalman, op. cit. 129, rightly. The reason why he nevertheless in re-translating the words of interpretation into Aramaic put *hū* for *ἐστίν* seems to be that he was subconsciously under the influence of dogmatic considerations, as in the similar case infra p. 167 n. 4.

[4] Suggested by G. Dalman, op. cit. 130 sq.

[5] Lev. R. 18 ad Lev. 15. 1; ibid. 21. 7 ad 16. 3; 34. 3 ad 25. 35; b. Sanh. 91a; Siphre Deut. 306.

[6] Mekh. Exod. 15. 1.

hārōsh (torso and head)[1] and *gūph-māmōn* (body and money).[2] If we look for twin ideas with blood, we find the following: *debher-dām* (plague and blood),[3] *mayim-dām* (water and blood),[4] *ḥēlebh-dām* (fat and blood)[5], *dām-'abhārīm* (blood and sacrificial meat)[6] and—by far the most frequent—*bāsār-dām* (flesh and blood).[7] Only this last pair can be considered appropriate to Jesus' words of interpretation. There are Aramaic examples as well: בִּשְׂרָא וּדְמָא.[8] The Greek equivalents are: *σὰρξ καὶ αἷμα*,[9] *κρέας καὶ αἷμα*[10], *αἷμα—σῶμα*.[11] Linguistically there can be no objection to the view that the Aramaic *bisrā* underlies *σῶμα* in Jesus' words of interpretation, and there is a good deal to confirm it: the LXX which in most (143) cases translates *bāsār* by *σάρξ*, renders it no less than 23 times by *σῶμα*, indeed *σῶμα*, excepting the cases in which it has the meaning of corpse, is in the LXX most frequently a rendering of *bāsār*. Paul can substitute *σῶμα* directly for *σάρξ* (Rom. 8. 13); *σῶμα* and *σάρξ* are found as variants in the tradition;[12] sy[pesh] renders *σῶμα* in Heb. 13. 11 by *bisrā*, and above all, we find in John 6. 51c–56;[13] Ignat. Rom. 7. 3; Philad. 4; Trall. 8. 1; Smyrn. 7. 1, one branch of the tradition of the words of institution which calls the elements *σὰρξ καὶ αἷμα*. That is to say, the authentic words of Jesus were probably: דֵּן בִּשְׂרִי and דֵּן אִדְמִי. What is their meaning?

[1] Zebh. 6. 6. [2] b. Ber. 61b.

[3] Ezek. 5. 17; 28. 23; 38. 22 (LXX: *θάνατος καὶ αἷμα*).

[4] Exod. 4. 9, etc.; John 19. 34; 1 John 5. 6; Rev. 11. 6.

[5] Ezekiel 44. 7, 15; 1 Sam. 1. 22, etc. [6] Joma 3. 5.

[7] Ezekiel 39. 17, cf. the evidence from the Mishna, infra, p. 143 n. 5. 144 n. 1

[8] b. Tam. 32b; Targ. Esth. 2. 1, 4. (G. Dalman's assertion, op. cit. 130 n. 2, "hardly ever in Aramaic", is mistaken.)

[9] Cf. infra, p. 143 n. 5, also in the LXX Ezek. 44. 7 *σάρκας καὶ αἷμα*; John 6. 53–6.

[10] Ezek. 39. 17, in the LXX.

[11] Heb. 13. 11; LXX Job 6. 4; Philo, *Spec Leg.* 1 §62; §231 sq.

[12] Compare the "Gospel according to the Hebrews" frg. 22 (ed. E. Klostermann, *Apocrypha* 2, 3rd ed. [1929], 11, with Luke 24. 39; cf. A. Resch, *Agrapha*, 2nd ed. (1906), 97–8.

[13] Notice that John 6. 51c gives the Johannine tradition of the word of interpretation over the bread, cf. N. Johansson, *Det Urkristna Nattvardsfirandet* (Lund, 1944).

(*a*) *Jesus the Paschal Lamb.*

In the two sentences *dēn bisrī* and *dēn 'idhmī*, *dēn* is the subject, and is not the predicative:[1] such is the usual arrangement in a Semitic nominal clause.[2] The same is the case in the ancient Aramaic Passover formula in explanation of the unleavened bread: *hā laḥmā 'anyā*;[3] above all the Primitive Church from its earliest beginnings has understood the words of explanation thus without exception.[4]

We first consider the subject (*τοῦτο, dēn*). Many scholars have taken the view that by *τοῦτο* Jesus means the action of breaking the bread and of pouring out the wine. This view, which in any case is inconsistent with *τοῦτό ἐστιν*, would only be tenable if the action had coincided with the words of interpretation. This, however, is not the case. As regards the word over the bread, its starting with *λάβετε* proves that Jesus said it at the distribution and not at the breaking of the bread. It is even more plain that the word over the wine had nothing to do

[1] The opposite view that *τὸ σῶμά μου* and *τὸ αἷμά μου* are the subjects is taken by K. G. Goetz, *Das Abendmahl, eine Diatheke Jesu oder sein letztes Gleichnis?* (1920), 64 sq.; "Der Einfluss des kirchlichen Brauchs auf die Abendmahlstexte des Neuen Testaments" in *Vischer Festschr.* (1935), 21 sq., 32; "Zur Loesung der Abendmahlsfrage" in *Theol. Stud. u. Krit.* 108 (1937), 81 sq., 108, 120. He interprets as follows: "eating and drinking is my flesh and blood, i.e. my person means for you what eating and drinking [means] for ordinary people", namely "the means of gaining strength and refreshment" (*Das Abendmahl, eine Diatheke* 84). Also E. Lohmeyer, *Das Evangelium des Markus* (1937), 306–7, understanding it as follows: "just as my body has been the centre and core of the fellowship of disciples, so is now the common eating of the bread", p. 307. Also M. Dibelius, *Jesus* (1939), 114, claiming that *τοῦτό ἐστιν* has the same sense as *ἴδε* John 19. 26–7, viz. "this shall be from now onwards."

[2] Cf. the numerous examples in G. Dalman, *Jesus-Jeschua* (1922), 129; *dēn, dā, denā* is always the subject.

[3] Cf. supra, p. 36. Obviously *hā* is the subject.

[4] The earliest evidence for this is 1 Cor. 11. 24 *τοῦτό μού ἐστιν τὸ σῶμα τὸ ὑπὲρ ὑμῶν*: the putting of *ἐστίν* between *μου* and *τὸ σῶμα* shows that *τοῦτο* is the subject, and all that follows the predicate. Equally unambiguous is 1 Cor. 11. 25 *τοῦτο τὸ ποτήριον ἡ καινὴ διαθήκη ἐστὶν ἐν τῷ ἐμῷ αἵματι*: the putting of *ἐστίν* between *ἡ καινὴ διαθήκη* and *ἐν τῷ ἐμῷ αἵματι* shows once more that *τοῦτο τὸ ποτήριον* is the subject and all the rest the predicate.

with its being poured out. For between the pouring of the wine from the mixing bowl[1] into the "cup of benediction" and the speaking of the word of interpretation by Jesus, came the Grace after meat, which consisted of the elevation of the cup (Mark 14. 23), an invitation to the table companions to join in the prayer, the several blessings[2] constituting the "Grace" proper, the response —amen—of the table companions. By way of comparison it may be remembered that, as has been shown on p. 58, the whole *Passa-Haggādhā* separates the outpouring of the second cup at the passover meal from its consumption—to wit, an estimated time of between fifteen and thirty minutes.[3] Therefore Jesus was not interpreting the actions of breaking bread and pouring out wine, but was clearly explaining the bread and the wine themselves. This view is supported by two observations: first, that in the Jewish Passover rite the explanation of the elements, which was the precedent for Jesus' words of interpretation, is not concerned with any actions but with the elements themselves; and secondly, that the entire early Church, right from its beginning, has seen in *τοῦτο* a reference to the elements themselves (cf. 1 Cor. 11. 25 *τοῦτο*=*τοῦτο τὸ ποτήριον*=this wine). Although an explanation of the unleavened bread—and probably also of the wine—had already taken place during the Passover devotions, Jesus now, in saying Grace, explained both elements again, and in reference to His own person. For this purpose He used the twin concept *bisrā ūdhemā*. This expression has a twofold meaning: on the one hand it signifies—for the first time in Ecclesiasticus[4]—man as a transient being, in contrast to God or to supernatural powers,[5] and on the other hand it also signifies—and this is found

[1] On the mixing of the wine cf. G. Dalman, *Jesus-Jeschua* (1922), 136–7; P. Billerbeck 4. 58.

[2] The probable wording of the Grace has been given supra, p. 111.

[3] Cf. supra, p. 57 n. 3: the little children have to be watched lest they fall asleep during the *Haggādhā*.

[4] Ecclus. 14. 18; 17. 31.

[5] Matt. 16. 17; 1 Cor. 15. 50; Gal. 1. 16 (in the reverse order: Eph. 6. 12; Heb. 2. 14). Three times in the Mishna: Nazir 9. 5 (twice), the fear of flesh and blood (as opposed to the fear of God); Soṭa 8. 1, the victorious power of flesh and blood (as opposed to that of God). Frequently in rabbinical texts, especially in parables: for evidence see e.g. P. Billerbeck, 1. 141, 725, 726, 730–1, etc.; A. Schlatter, *Der Evangelist Matthaeus* (Stuttgart, 1929), 108, 230, 505.

already in ancient Hebrew—the two component parts of the body, especially of a sacrificial victim, which are separated when it is killed.[1] Only the second, the cultic meaning, is of importance for us. A New Testament instance of the same cultic meaning of the twin concept *σῶμα—αἷμα*, is found in Heb. 13. 11, cf. Philo, *Spec. Leg.* 1 §231 sq. Therefore when Jesus speaks of "His flesh" and "His blood", He is applying to Himself terms from the language of sacrifice. *Bisrī* and *'idhmī* presuppose each in itself a slaying that has separated flesh and blood.[2] In other words: Jesus speaks of Himself as a sacrifice.

It can be assumed with great probability that Jesus in the Passover devotions had prepared the way for this comparison of Himself with the sacrifice. It is certain that the interpretation of the paschal lamb belonged to the *Passa-Haggādhā*. How did Jesus interpret the paschal lamb? The fact that the words of interpretation refer the bread and wine to Jesus Himself, suggests strongly that He also referred the paschal lamb to Himself.[3] This arises not only out of the close relation between the terms *bisrī* and *'idhmī* and the language of sacrifice, but above all the words about the "outpouring of the blood" (Mark 14. 24) taken, as they are, from the language of sacrifice, hardly allow of any other explanation.[4] It has to be remembered that the Pauline *Passa-Haggādhā* which has come down to us in 1 Cor. 5. 7–8 does not introduce the description of Jesus as the paschal lamb as anything new, but assumes as self-evident that the Church at Corinth was familiar with this comparison so popular in primitive Christian literature.

[1] Gen. 9. 4; Lev. 17. 11, 14; Deut. 12. 23; Ezek. 39. 17–18; Heb. 13. 11 (the bull of the sin-offering and the scapegoat); Pes. 7. 5 (the paschal lamb; the sacrificial victim); Zebh. 4. 4 (three times: the burnt offering; the sin offering of a fowl); ibid. 13. 1 (the sin offering); Ker. 6. 1, three times, 2 (the guilt offering); Me'ila 1. 2, three times (holiness offering and sin offering); ibid. 4. 3 (the reptile); Makhsh. 6. 5 (the same); Para 4. 3 (the red cow).

[2] P. Fiebig, *Neues Saechs. Kirchenblatt* 42 (1935), 374, 475–6, 517–18. I withdraw my objections to this part of Fiebig's contentions.

[3] A. Schweitzer, *Die Mystik des Apostels Paulus* (Tuebingen, 1930), 245; M. Barth, *Das Abendmahl* (1945); F. J. Leenhardt, *Le Sacrement de la Sainte Cène* (1948), 31, 37.

[4] *'Εκχεῖν αἷμα* is used in the LXX—apart from those cases where it speaks of murder or the domestic killing of cattle—only when speaking of sacrifice.

It is most probable, therefore, that in the words *dēn bisrī*, "this is my flesh (which is sacrificed)", and *dēn 'idhmī*, "this is my blood (which is sacrificed)", Jesus speaks of Himself as the paschal lamb. This sets out a comparison between Jesus and the paschal lamb, but does not identify them. When at the beginning of the Passover devotions the Paterfamilias elevates the unleavened bread with the words *hā laḥmā 'anyā*, when he interprets it as signifying the bread of the Messianic age, when he explains the clay-coloured fruit purée as the clay of which the Israelites in Egypt had to make bricks, when he relates the cups to the cups of comfort or chastisement in the last days, it always implies a comparison and not an identification. There is yet another consideration which indicates that the disciples too could only understand "my flesh" and "my blood" in this way. The consumption of blood was such a sinister, animistic horror[1] for the born Jew that it would have been quite impossible for the disciples to have understood the words in that way. The *tertium comparationis* in the case of the bread is the fact that it is broken,[2] and in the case of the wine that it is red: we know from j. Pes. 10. 37c. 27 (par. j. Shab. 8. 11a. 34; j. Sheq. 3. 47b. 64); b. Pes. 108b; b. Men. 87a, that the use of red wine at the Passover was usual. This rule was derived from Prov. 23. 31, which speaks of the "red shimmering" wine. The comparison between red wine and blood had frequently been made in the Old Testament: Gen. 49. 11; Deut. 32. 14; Is. 63. 3, 6; Ecclus. 39. 26; 50. 15; 1 Macc. 6. 34, cf. also Rev. 14. 20; b. Sanh. 70a, etc.

We therefore have a twofold parable by Jesus here,[3] which has its formal analogy in the way in which the prophets of the Old Testament used to announce future events parabolically (cf. Ezekiel 4. 1–17; 5. 1 sq.; Jer. 19. 10 sq.). Its meaning is quite simple. Each one of the disciples could understand it. Jesus made

[1] Gen. 9. 4; Lev. 3. 17; 7. 26–7; 17. 10–14; 19. 26; Deut. 12. 16, 23, 24; 15. 23, cf. 1 Sam. 14. 32–4; Acts 15. 20, 29; Jos., *Ant.* 3. 11. 2. §260. Rabbinical evidence may be consulted in P. Billerbeck 2. 737.

[2] So expressly the ancient variant κλώμενον of 1 Cor. 11. 24 cf. supra, p. 110 n. 1.

[3] This has been justly stressed by A. Juelicher, "Zur Geschichte der Abendmahlsfeier in der aeltesten Kirche" in *Weizsaecker-Festschrift* (Freiburg i. Br., 1892), 243. Everyone from H. Lietzmann to G. Dalman is agreed on this.

the broken bread a parable of the fate of His body, the blood of the grapes a parable of His outpoured blood. "I must die a victim's death", is the meaning of the last parable of Jesus. The fact that Jesus expresses the one thought in a twofold parable accords with His predilection for pairing parables: for instance, the twin parables of the mustard seed and the leaven (Matt. 13. 31–33)—two parables which in no sense contrast the external and the internal growth of God's kingdom, but have the identical aim of illustrating how the new world is being created out of nothing by the miraculous action of God[1]—or of the lost sheep and the lost coin (Luke 15. 1–10); the hidden treasure and the pearl of great price (Matt. 13. 44–46); the wheat and the tares and the net cast into the sea (Matt. 13. 24–30, 47–50), etc. In our case the synonymous parallelism has been occasioned by the twin ideas: flesh and blood.

Jesus' parable only announces that His vicarious death will happen, not the details of how; we may conclude from the parable and from the word ἐκχυννόμενον[2] no more than that Jesus foresaw a violent death. Mark 14. 25 par. makes it clear, however, that Jesus was certain that God would vindicate His death by His resurrection.

The words *dēn bisrī, dēn 'idhmī* involve:

(*b*) *A statement about the meaning of Jesus' death.*

By comparing Himself with the paschal lamb, Jesus describes His death as redemptive. Certainly the Passover of later times was not regarded as expiatory[3] but as an ordinary sacrifice, and its blood worked no expiation. But this is not true of the paschal lambs which were killed at the exodus from Egypt. Their blood had a redemptive effect,[4] and made God's covenant with Abraham opera-

[1] Joach. Jeremias, *Die Gleichnisse Jesu*, 3rd ed. (Göttingen, 1954), 91 sq.

[2] Cf. Jos., *Ant.* 19. 1. 13. §94 αἷμα . . . περὶ τὸν σταυρωθέντα ἐκκεχυμένον.

[3] Cf. A. Wuensche, *Neue Beitraege zur Erlaeuterung der Evangelien aus Talmud und Midrasch* (Goettingen, 1878), 333; G. Dalman, *Jesus-Jeschua* (Leipzig, 1922), 114–15, 152.

[4] *Pirqē R. 'Eli'ezer* 29 (14d): "for the merit of the blood of the covenant of the circumcision and the Passover blood, I have redeemed you out of Egypt, and for their merit you will be redeemed at the end of the fourth (Roman) universal empire (i.e. in the days of the Messiah)", P. Billerbeck 4. 40.

tive.[1] As a reward for the Israelites' obedience to the injunction to "strike the lintel and the two side posts with blood", God manifested Himself and "passed over" their houses and spared them;[2] because of the Passover blood God revoked the death sentence passed on Israel;[3] He said: "I see the Passover blood, and I make reconciliation for you".[4] In the same way will the

[1] Targ. Zech. 9. 11 (Wilna, 1893): "you too, for whom a covenant was decided upon over blood, have I redeemed from the servitude in Egypt". Cf. G. Dalman, *Jesus-Jeschua* (Leipzig, 1922), 151: "this must refer to the blood of the paschal lambs by which the Divine covenant regarding the deliverance out of Egypt was made valid". Mekh. Exod. 12. 6 Par. בא sect. 5, 2nd ed. (Venice, 1545), 3c, 11 sq.: " 'and you shall keep it', Exod. 12. 6. Why should the taking of the paschal lamb (Exod. 12. 3) be done four days before its killing? *Rabbī Matteyā bhen Ḥeres* (about A.D. 125) has said, 'now when I passed by thee and looked upon thee, behold thy time was the time of love', Ezek. 16. 8. [As happens so often, the decisive words of the context have not been quoted: 'and I spread my skirt over thee and covered thy nakedness; yea I sware unto thee and entered into a covenant with thee'.] The oath had come to pass which God had sworn unto Abraham, that He would redeem his children (Gen. 15. 14); but they had no (obligatory) commandments on their hands, upon which they might act, so that they might be saved (by the keeping of the commandments), as it is written: 'thy breasts are fashioned and thine hair is grown, but thou wast naked and bare', Ezek. 16. 7, bare—that is from (the keeping of) the commandments; so God gave them two commandments, the blood of the paschal lamb and the blood of the circumcision, that they might observe them, so that they should be saved, as it is written: 'I passed by thee and saw thee flutter in thy two kinds of blood' is (דָּמָיִךְ treated as a dual by the Midrash, the blood of the Passover and of the circumcision), Ezek. 16. 6. It is also written: 'as for thee also by the blood of thy covenant I have sent forth thy prisoners out of the pit wherein is no water', Zech. 9. 11." The blood of the Passover and the blood of the circumcision are both the "blood of the covenant" for the sake of which the deliverance out of Egypt was granted.

[2] Mekh. Exod. 12. 13 Par. בא sect. 7 (Venice, 1545), 4c, 20, par. 12. 23 sect. 11 (6a, 4).

[3] Exod. R. 15. 13 ad Exod. 12. 10 (Stettin, 1864), 36a, 11, "like a king who said to his sons: Know ye not that I am about to judge crimes worthy of death and to pronounce judgment. Therefore bring me a present, so that I may suppress the accusation against you when you appear before my judgment seat. In the same way God said to Israel: I am concerned with death sentences; yet I proclaim to you, how I will spare you in my mercy for the sake of the blood of the Passover and of the circumcision, and will atone for you" (מכפר על נפשותיכם).

[4] Exod. R. 15. 13 ad Exod. 12. 2 (Stettin, 1864), 35b, 26.

people of God of the last days be redeemed by the merits of the Passover blood.[1] Jesus, therefore, describes His death as this eschatological Passover sacrifice: His vicarious (ὑπέρ) death brings the final deliverance into operation.

The addition to the word over the wine,[2] *τὸ ἐκχυννόμενον ὑπὲρ πολλῶν*,[3] ("which will be shed for many", an expression where the passive reverently veils God's action in this death) continues the comparison with the sacrifice: *ἐκχυννόμενον* is taken from the language of the cult. It makes clear to whom the atoning and redeeming power of Jesus' death is directed. And indeed it links up with an Old Testament passage, Is. 53. 12: "because he poured out his soul unto death, and was numbered with the transgressors: yet he bare the sin of many, and made intercession for the transgressors". This connexion is supported by Mark 10. 45 par.: the Saying about the Son of Man who came "to minister, and to give His life a ransom *ἀντὶ πολλῶν*", is another allusion to Is. 53. 10–12.[4]

So if we wish to discover whom Jesus meant by the "many" for whom His blood would be shed, we have to ask first, how the word רַבִּים (LXX: *πολλοί*) in Is. 52. 14; 53. 11, 12a, 12b, was understood in His day. It is difficult to understand why nobody seems to have asked this question yet. In answering it we shall have to distinguish between the views of the pre-Christian and of the post-Christian writings of later Judaism. With regard to the latter, the first source to be discussed is the paraphrase of Is.

[1] Cf. supra, p. 146 n. 4.

[2] On *τῆς διαθήκης* cf. supra, p. 134.

[3] דְּמִשְׁתְּפֵיךְ עַל סַגִּיאִין.

[4] The fact that Jesus during the course of the Last Supper had Is. 53 in mind is also presupposed in Luke 22. 37, where He applies Is. 53. 12 to Himself. With regard to the question whether it is credible that Jesus foresaw His death and resurrection and regarded His death—in connection with Is. 53—as an atoning death, I may refer to my article *παῖς θεοῦ* in *Theolog. Woerterb. z. N.T.*, 5. 676-713. Cf. also my essay "Erloeser und Erloesung im Spaet-Judentum und im Urchristentum" in *Bericht des 2. deutschen Theologentages* (Goettingen, 1929) 106–19; W. Staerck, *Soter* 1 (Guetersloh, 1933); R. Otto, *Reich Gottes und Menschensohn* (Munich, 1934); N. Johansson, *Parakletoi* (1940); Joach. Jeremias, "Das Loesegeld fuer Viele" in *Judaica* 3 (1948), 249–64. Cf. also infra, p. 152.

52. 13–53. 12 in the Targum on the Prophets.[1] Here the "many" are understood as "the house of Israel" (Targ. Is. 52. 14); "many [sinners]" (53. 11); "many nations" (53. 12a); "many [faithless]" (53. 12b).[2] If, therefore, the "many" are understood here in part to be Jews and in part to be Gentiles, it is the more significant that in those passages which deal with the salvation wrought by the Servant for the "many" (Is. 53. 11, 12b), Israel alone seems to be understood. The same is true with regard to the other Talmudic interpretations of the "many" in Is. 53. 11, 12b: almost without exception these passages are applied to Israel alone. Sedh. Elij. R. 14, "the many" (Is. 53. 11) are interpreted as the rich and poor in Israel without distinction;[3] ibid. 25 as the contemporaries (each particular generation of Israel). The "many" in Is. 53. 12b are interpreted in Siphre Num. 25. 13 §131 (23b, 5) as the "children of Israel"; in b. Soṭa 14b as the ones who are guilty of the sin of the golden calf, i.e. the people of Israel as a whole; Siphre Deut. 33. 21 §355 (62c, 30) again as the whole people of Israel. An exception is the late collection of homilies *Pesiqtha Rabbathi*, where—alongside the narrower interpretation—the view is taken in chapter 36 that all who are called into life by the will of God are those thought of as the recipients of salvation in Is. 53.[4]

[1] A critical edition of our passage, based upon the ancient MSS and the edition (Venice, 1517), by G. Dalman in his *Aramaeische Dialektproben*, 2nd ed. (Leipzig, 1927), 10–11.

[2]

Is. 52. 14 רַבִּים	LXX πολλοί	Targ. בֵּית יִשְׂרָאֵל
53. 11 הָרַבִּים	LXX πολλοί	Targ. סַגִּיאִין
53. 12a הָרַבִּים	LXX πολλοί	Targ. עַמְמִין סַגִּיאִין
53. 12b רַבִּים	LXX πολλοί	Targ. סַגִּיאִין

In Targ. Is. 53. 12b, read, with G. Dalman, *Jesus-Jeschua* (Leipzig, 1922), 156 n. 3, *ḥōbhē saggī'īn* instead of *ḥōbhīn saggī'īn*.

[3] The passage "my righteous servant shall justify many", Is. 53. 11, is interpreted as meaning a faithful teacher who "teaches Israel publicly" and who makes his teaching accessible to everybody, irrespective of social differences.

[4] The passage has been printed e.g. by G. Dalman, "Der leidende und sterbende Messias der Synagoge", *Schriften des Institutum Judaicum* 4 (Berlin, 1888), 61. In this passage which describes how the Messiah, before the creation of the world, agrees to undergo vicarious suffering for the salvation of the world, Is. 53 is not explicitly mentioned. It is, however, beyond doubt that this description is based upon Is. 53.

However, all these post-Christian explanations of the "many" in Is. 53 are of small worth for our immediate purpose. No other passage in the Old Testament was so important for the Church as Is. 53, and therefore no other passage of the Old Testament has suffered more from Jewish polemics than Is. 53: one gleans from the Targum on the Prophets[1] what subtlety was used to explain away the Messiah's suffering. So the pre-Christian interpretations of the "many" in Is. 53 become the more important. The Ethiopic book of Enoch interprets the "many" of Is. 52. 14–15 as the kings, the mighty, the strong, and the sinners (1 Enoch 46. 4–5), as "the kings of the earth and the strong men who possessed the land" (48. 8), and similarly in 55. 4; 62. 1, 3, 6, 9; 63. 1–11. Here therefore it is certain that by the "many" the Gentiles are meant. The Wisdom of Solomon 5. 1–23, cf. 2. 19–20, interprets the "many" (Is. 52. 14–15) as the sinners who have afflicted the righteous (5. 1) and had him in derision (5. 3–4), as the presumptuous and the insolent (5. 8), as those who live an evil life (5. 13), and as the godless (5. 14; 2. 19 sq.); and since no distinction is made between Jews and Gentiles in this passage, it is probable that it refers to the godless among Jews and Gentiles alike,[2] but in the first instance—according to Wisd. 1. 1 sq. and Is. 52. 15—to the latter. These pre-Christian interpretations are of special weight because of their agreement with the meaning of the original text.

However, one reservation must be made: the "many" envisaged in the Ethiopic book of Enoch and in the Wisdom of Solomon are the "many" of Is. 52. 14–5, i.e. the Gentiles who are silenced into repentance and shame in the presence of the Servant, and not the "many" of Is. 53. 11, 12b, whose sins the Servant bore.[3] Yet the original text makes no difference between the two. The "many" who are seized by astonishment and terror (52. 14–5) are the very ones who confess that they have failed to recognize the Servant because "he hath no form nor comeliness", the same whose eyes are opened to see that he bore *their* griefs, carried

[1] German translation in P. Billerbeck 1. 482–3.

[2] F. Feldmann, *Das Buch der Weisheit* (Bonn, 1926), 41.

[3] If Dan. 12. 3 should refer to Is. 53. 11b, then we have a pre-Christian interpretation of this verse too. Dan. 12. 3 regards the "many" (*hārabbīm*) as those members of the people of Israel who are led to righteousness.

their sorrows, and was wounded for *their* transgressions (53. 2 sq.). It is they who acknowledge: "the chastisement of our peace was upon him" (53. 5). It is most unlikely that Jesus would interpret Is. 53 differently. For He saw Himself as the Servant of whom it is said in Is. 49. 6, that He should not only "restore the preserved of Israel", but be given "also for a light to the Gentiles that thou mayest be my salvation unto the end of the earth". Therefore ὑπὲρ πολλῶν in the words of institution has not, as we already have seen, an exclusive meaning (many, but not all) but, as is common in Semitic speech, an inclusive meaning (the sum total, consisting of many). Accordingly the translation of τὸ ἐκχυννόμενον ὑπὲρ πολλῶν has to be: "which is going to be shed for the whole world".

This is indeed an idea unheard of in rabbinical thought. Late Judaism was much concerned with the conception of atonement.[1] Tos. Joma 5. 6 sq. (190. 15 sq.) gives the following scale:

(*a*) Penitence—which atones for the breaking of a commandment.
(*b*) Penitence and the day of atonement—which atone for the violation of a prohibition.
(*c*) Penitence, the day of atonement and suffering—which atone for crimes worthy of death.
(*d*) Penitence, the day of atonement, suffering and death—which atone for profanation of the name of God.

In reality, however, the means of atonement were far more numerous. In addition to the above four, there are: fasting;[2] indemnification;[3] private and public sacrifice;[4] the High Priestly robes;[5] the merits of the fathers;[6] the vicarious suffering of the righteous;[7] the death of innocent children,[8] of the High Priest,[9] of the martyrs,[10] etc. There are recognized means of atonement for all sins and for all sinners. There is however just one exception,

[1] A. Buechler, *Studies in Sin and Atonement in the Rabbinic Literature of the First Century* (Oxford-London, 1928).

[2] Ps. Sol. 3. 9, etc.

[3] b. R. H. 17b Bar., etc.

[4] A. Buechler, op. cit. 375–461.

[5] b. Zebh. 88b, etc.

[6] P. Billerbeck 1. 117 sq.

[7] Ibid. 2. 274 sq.

[8] Ibid. 2. 281; 4. 564, 595, 768, 1109.

[9] Mak. 2. 6, 8, cf. Joach. Jeremias, *Jerusalem zur Zeit Jesu* IIB (Leipzig, 1929), 4.

[10] 4 Macc. 6. 29.

expressly stated in Mekh. Exod. 21. 30 (2nd ed. Venice, 1545) 32a, 9 sq.: "for the nations there is no ransom (in the sight of God); for the Scripture teacheth, Ps. 49. 8–9, 'none of them can by any means redeem his brother, nor give to God a ransom for him; for the redemption of their soul is costly'." Why is there no ransom for the Gentiles? The quotation from the *Mekhiltha* continues: "beloved are the Israelites: for in their stead the Holy One gives the nations of the world as an atonement for their life. For so it is written, Is. 43. 3: 'I have given Egypt for thy ransom'."[1] So there is no ransom for the nations—but Jesus says that there is a means of atonement even for the Gentile world: His vicarious (ὑπέρ) death.

The often repeated assertion that it is unthinkable that Jesus should have ascribed atoning power to His death, and that such statements belong much rather to the dogmatizing of the Primitive Church or of the Apostle Paul, will astonish anyone who knows the Palestinian sources. Speculations about the atoning effect of death play a large part in the thought of Jesus' contemporaries. Every death has an atoning power (cf. for instance supra p. 151 under *d*)—even that of the criminal if he die repentant. An innocent death offered to God has power to atone vicariously for others (cf. p. 151n. 8–10). The sources compel the conclusion that it is unthinkable for Jesus not to have thought about the atoning effect of His death.[2]

This was in the mind of Jesus when explaining at the Last Supper the meaning of His death: His death is the vicarious death of the Servant, which atones for the sins of the *πολλοί*, the whole world, and ushers in the beginnings of final salvation.

(*c*) *The gift.*

However, the words of Jesus are not only parable and instruction. They are probably more than that: for they are said by Him over the unleavened bread and the wine at the very time[3] when He

[1] Cf. S. Deut. 333 ad 32. 43; Exod. R. 11 ad 8, 19, and Joach. Jeremias, "Das Loesegeld fuer Viele" in *Judaica* 3 (1948), 256–7.

[2] Joach. Jeremias, op. cit. 249–64.

[3] Cf. Mark 14. 22 *λάβετε*. When Mark (14. 23) writes *καὶ ἔπιον ἐξ αὐτοῦ πάντες* before he gives the word of interpretation, that is an anticipation, cf. the correction in Matt. 26. 27 *πίετε ἐξ αὐτοῦ*

offers them both, bread and wine, to be taken by the disciples. Is it no more than just coincidence that when Jesus says the words over the bread and over the wine, He makes them follow Grace each time (Mark 14. 22 εὐλογήσας; 14. 23 εὐχαριστήσας) and so associates them with the distribution of the bread and wine? We cannot make that assumption because the appointed and proper time for Jesus' words of interpretation was in the *Passa-Haggādhā*, in which the interpretation of the elements was prescribed.[1] When Jesus, contrary to all expectation, did not associate His words of interpretation with the *Passa-Haggādhā*, but with the distribution of bread and wine, He must have had good reason for doing so.[2] Can we discover his purpose? It is, of course, impossible after 1,900 years to state with absolute certainty in every individual instance what purpose Jesus associated with an action, and what understanding the disciples brought to it. Nevertheless, it is by no means hopeless to try to see whether we can feel our way to the purpose which Jesus had in mind when He associated the words of interpretation with the distribution. We have to start by re-stating the ideas which His contemporaries associated with the breaking of bread and the blessing of the cup.

It is an ancient oriental idea that a common meal binds the table companions into a table fellowship. This table fellowship is religious, and therein rest its obligations: its violation is a particularly heinous crime (Ps. 41. 10), and hence the deep grief felt by Jesus, Mark 14. 20 par. Above all, the table fellowship at the Passover is religious; this is seen most clearly in the fact that the membership of every *ḥabhūrā* had to be determined before the lamb was killed and its blood sprinkled on the altar of burnt offerings. At every common meal the constitution of the table fellowship is accomplished by the rite of the breaking of

---

πάντες. This view can be proposed with all the greater confidence because: "cette phrase (i.e. Mark 14. 23 καὶ ἔπιον ἐξ αὐτοῦ πάντες) d'un grec hébraïsant peut signifier aussi bien la simultanéité que la succession des actes", J. Rivière, "Le Dogme de la Rédemption. Essai d'étude historique", 2nd ed., in *Etudes d'histoire des dogmes et d'ancienne littérature ecclésiastique* (Paris, 1905), 82.

[1] Supra, p. 31 sq.

[2] It must not be forgotten that Jesus at His Last Supper said more than has come down to us in the very concise accounts of it, which after all are cultic texts (supra, p. 42).

bread.[1] The breaking of the bread is "*l'atto di comunione*".[2] When at the daily meal the Paterfamilias recites the blessing over the bread —which the members of the household make their own by the "Amen"—and breaks it and hands a piece to each member to eat, the meaning of the action is that each of the members is made a recipient of the blessing by this eating; the common eating of the bread of benediction unites the members into a table fellowship. The same is true of the "cup of benediction", which is the cup of wine over which Grace has been spoken, when it is in circulation among the members:[3] drinking from it mediates a share in the blessing. This, it must be remembered, is true of every meal and was therefore a familiar and self-evident idea to the disciples from their earliest childhood: the eating of the broken bread and the drinking of the wine from the "cup of benediction" gives— be it said once more: at every common meal—a share in the blessing which was spoken over the bread or the wine before the distribution.

Jesus, however, not only pronounced the blessing over the bread and wine, but also added the words which connected the broken bread and the red wine with His atoning death for "many". When immediately afterwards He gives this same bread and wine to His disciples to eat and drink, the meaning is that by eating and drinking He gives them a share in the atoning power of His death.

We can state this all the more confidently when we remember that to Orientals the idea that divine gifts are communicated by eating and drinking is very familiar.[4] Reference may be made to the symbolic language of eschatology. In apocalyptic and Tal-

[1] G. Dalman, *Jesus-Jeschua* (Leipzig, 1922), 126; I. Zolli, *Il Nazareno* (1938), 236. Therefore not by taking one's place at the common meal, as P. Fiebig, *Neues Saechsisches Kirchenblatt* 42 (1935), 375, assumes, who erroneously adduces Tos. Ber.—probably referring to 4. 8 (p. 9).

[2] I. Zolli, op. cit. 236. He rightly stresses, pp. 216–24, that the sacramental character of the Last Supper consists in the table fellowship.

[3] This was probably the earlier rite, common at the time of Jesus, cf. supra, p. 44 sq.

[4] Cf. Joach. Jeremias, *Jesus als Weltvollender* (Guetersloh, 1930), 46 sq., 74 sq., and id., *Golgotha* (Leipzig-Goettingen, 1926), 60 sq., 80 sq.

mudic literature[1] as well as in the New Testament there are innumerable variations on the theme of the bread of life which satisfies all hunger;[2] the tree of life, the fruit of which cures the sick;[3] the heavenly Manna, which will be the food of the redeemed in the world to come;[4] the water of life—"for he that hath mercy on them shall lead them, even by the springs of water shall he guide them", Is. 49. 10, cf. Rev. 7. 17—which is given freely and quenches all thirst for ever;[5] the wine of the world to come which is kept for the children of the kingdom;[6] the feast of salvation in the last days, which imparts salvation and life.[7] "Those who serve God unto death, will eat of the bread of the world to come in plenty."[8] "Blessed is he that shall eat bread in the kingdom of God", Luke 14. 15. "Blessed are they which are called unto the marriage-supper of the Lamb", Rev. 19. 9. It is well known that in the New Testament the idea of the feast of salvation which imparts

[1] P. Billerbeck 4. 1146–7, 1154 sq.

[2] Joach. Jeremias, *Jesus als Weltvollender* (Guetersloh, 1930), 74 sq. As evidence, e.g. Matt. 5. 6 (χορτασθήσονται; the passive is circumscription for the Divine name, "blessed are they which hunger and thirst after righteousness: *for God shall fill them*", par. Luke 6. 21); John 6. 35, 50.

[3] Ezek. 47. 12; Enoch aeth. 24. 4–25. 7; Test. Levi 18; Rev. 22. 2, 14, 19.

[4] Syr. Bar. 29. 8; Sib. 7. 149; b. Ḥagh. 12b; Midhr. Qoh. R. 1. 9 §28 (ed. Stettin, 1864), 71b. 8; Ruth R. ad 2. 14 §6 (ed. Stettin, 1864), 15a. 26. In the New Testament this concept also plays a large part. Jesus is expected to repeat the miracle of the Manna: Matt. 4. 3 par.; John 6. 30–1. The "hidden Manna" will be the food of the redeemed: Rev. 2. 17. The fourth petition of the Lord's Prayer has also to be understood from this point of view: as the prayer for the Manna of the day to come, cf. Exod. 16. 22–3, 29, the bread of the universal Sabbath, cf. R. Eisler, *Z.N.W.* 24 (1925), 191; A. Schweitzer, *Die Mystik des Apostels Paulus* (Tuebingen, 1930), 233–5.

[5] John 4. 13–14; 6. 35; 7. 37 sq.; Rev. 21. 6; 22. 1, 17. The expectation that the miracle of Mount Horeb will be repeated in the Messianic age is found e.g. in Midhr. Gen. R. 48. 10 (ed. Stettin, 1864), 100b; see further P. Billerbeck, 2. 433–5, 492; Joach. Jeremias, *Golgotha* (Leipzig, 1926), 63, 82–3; *Jesus als Weltvollender* (Guetersloh, 1930), 49 sq.

[6] A. Schlatter, *Der Evangelist Matthaeus* (Stuttgart, 1929), 745; P. Billerbeck 1. 992; Mark 14. 25 par.; b. Pes. 119b, etc.

[7] Is. 25. 6–7; 65. 13–14; Enoch aeth. 62. 14–15; Syr. Bar. 29. 3–8. Many sources in P. Billerbeck 1. 603, 684, 992; 2. 551, 720; 3. 22, 33, 823; 4. 840, 1146–7, 1154 sq.

[8] Gen. R. 82 §9 ad Gen. 35. 17 (175b. 28).

the gifts of redemption, is very common. Matt. 5. 6; 8. 11 par.; 22. 1 sq. (par. Luke 14. 15–24); 25. 10, 21, 23 (*χαρά* means "meal of joy");[1] Luke 22. 15–18 (par. Mark 14. 25); 22. 29–30; Rev. 3. 20; 19. 7, 9 may be mentioned here.[2] I am indebted to my colleague Rudolf Hermann for pointing out to me that even the story of the Canaanite woman (Mark 7. 24–30 par.) becomes fully understandable only in this connexion: Jesus' Saying about the bread which is meant for the children and not for the dogs refers to the bread of life, and the great faith of the woman consists in this that, by her word about the crumbs which are eaten by the dogs, she acknowledges Jesus as the giver of the bread of life.[3] The passages in the Fourth Gospel where Jesus calls Himself the bread of life (John 6. 33, 35, 41, 48, 50, 51) and his Gospel bread (6. 35; cf. Mark 7. 27 par.)[4] and water (John 4. 10, 14; 6. 35; 7. 37–8), are to be understood similarly in an eschatological sense. Mark too knows of the comparison of Jesus with the bread of life: the "one loaf" which the disciples had in the boat during the crossing (Mark 8. 14) is meant to be Jesus, the bread of life. Jesus is the giver of the water of life in 1 Cor. 10. 4; 1 Pet. 2. 4–5.[5] In whatever way the metaphor is presented, the meaning is always that divine gifts are imparted in eating and drinking.

These eschatological metaphors of the bread and water of life are closely connected with the widespread allegorical interpretation of bread and water which developed particularly in the Wisdom literature. Thus Amos speaks in forceful words about hungering and thirsting after the Word of God (8. 11 sq.); Jeremiah calls God's commands his food (15. 16); Deutero-Isaiah (55. 1–3) calls the promises of God water and bread which are given freely; the Psalmist says that Jahwe is "the portion of my

[1] G. Dalman, *Worte Jesu*, 2nd ed. (1930), 96.

[2] Cf. Joach. Jeremias, *Jesus als Weltvollender* (Guetersloh, 1930), 46–53, 74–9; Enoch aeth. 62. 14, "they shall eat with that Son of Man".

[3] A similar view, but without sufficient emphasis on the eschatological element, has been propounded by A. Hoffmann, *Das Gottesbild Jesu* (Hamburg, 1934), 153, "Jesus who, for instance, saw the nourishing bread as symbolizing Himself (cf. Matt. 15. 26, and the Eucharistic Words over the bread) . . . ", 176.

[4] Jesus is at the same time the giver and the gift.

[5] *λίθος ζῶν*, i.e. the rock which gives forth the water of life, cf. Joach. Jeremias, *Golgotha* (Leipzig, 1926), 84–5.

cup" (16. 5);[1] in the Book of Proverbs (3. 18) Wisdom is called "tree of life", and Wisdom herself exhorts "come eat ye of my bread and drink of the wine which I have mingled" (9. 5; cf. 9. 2). Ecclesiasticus speaks of the ἄρτος συνέσεως,[2] which Wisdom offers to her disciples (Ecclus. 15. 3), and makes her say: "they that eat me shall yet be hungry; and they that drink me shall yet be thirsty" (24. 21). Lastly, in the rabbinical literature comparisons of the Torah with bread and water[3] or bread and wine[4] are frequent.[5] Jesus Himself used this metaphor calling the Word of God His bread of life (Matt. 4. 4 par.), and the Will of God His daily food (John 4. 32, 34).[6] All these examples show how familiar was the metaphor of bread and water (or wine) which gave the true life, and that it was by no means limited to the eschatological sphere.

The idea that eating and drinking imparts divine gifts is also expressed in the interpretation of history. From Ps. 78. 25; Wisd. 16. 20, we know that the Manna was regarded as the food of the angels,[7] an idea which is fancifully said in the Midhrāsh to mean that Manna adapted itself to everyone's taste and "tempered itself to every man's liking" (Wisd. 16. 21).[8] Paul had a more profound conception of the idea, when he spoke of the spiritual food and drink which were offered to the wandering Israelites by the miracles of the Manna and of the water at Mount Horeb (1 Cor. 10. 3–4). It follows both from the description of Christ, "that spiritual rock that followed them", 1 Cor. 10. 4, as the giver,

[1] Cf. on this R. Otto, *Reich Gottes und Menschensohn* (Munich, 1934), 238–9.

[2] לֶחֶם דַּעַת

[3] P. Billerbeck 2. 433 sq., 483 sq., 485, 492, 752.

[4] Ibid. 2. 482c, 484, 614.

[5] On the comparison between the Torah, wisdom, insight and righteousness on the one hand and the "living water" on the other cf. the wealth of material collected by H. Odeberg, *The Fourth Gospel* (Uppsala-Stockholm, 1929), 152 sq. On the comparison of the Torah, etc., with the bread of life, cf. ibid. 238 sq.

[6] Cf. Enoch aeth. 69. 24, saying of God's creatures, "their food consists of incessant thanksgiving".

[7] Cf. Exod. 16. 4; Ps. 78. 24; 105. 40; Neh. 9. 15; Wisd. 16. 20; 19. 21; John 6. 31–2: "bread of heaven", and b. Yoma 75b: the Manna is "the bread eaten by the ministering angels".

[8] Rabbinical sources in P. Billerbeck 2. 481–2.

and from the parallel drawn with the Eucharist of the Church, that he is thinking of actual spiritual gifts here. A second example from a much earlier period may be found in Exod. 24. 11, where it is said of Moses and the Elders when they ascended Mount Sinai: "and upon the nobles of the children of Israel He laid not His hand; and they beheld God and did eat and drink". In these last words the thought is of a covenant meal: the fact that God grants to the envoys the fellowship of His table, is the pledge of the covenant.

There is, furthermore, the cultic aspect to be considered: "Behold Israel after the flesh: have not they which eat the sacrifices communion with the altar?" (1 Cor. 10. 18), says Paul; and the subsequent verses show that he intends to say that the eating of sacrificial meat brings the priests and participants in sacrificial meals into a very close relationship to God. Especially instructive is a passage which positively ascribes an atoning effect to the cultic meal: "Where (is it said) that the eating of the sacred sacrifices brings atonement to Israel? The Scripture teaches: 'And He (Jahwe) hath given it (the sin-offering) to you to bear the iniquity of the congregation, to make atonement for them before the Lord', Lev. 10. 17. How so? The priests eat, and for the masters (who provide the sacrifice) atonement is made."[1]

As a last instance of the idea that eating and drinking impart "spiritual" gifts, we may quote a passage from the Slavonic book of Enoch, to which R. Otto has drawn attention.[2] It is particularly instructive, because it contemplates a situation similar to the Last Supper. It concerns the farewell meal which Enoch's sons intend to hold with their father before he leaves this world. "Then Methusalem answered his father and said: We will do what is well-pleasing in thy sight, O father, and prepare food before thy face, that thou mayest bless our houses and our sons and all thy household, and that thou mayest glorify thy people, and then depart".[3] The last common meal is meant to impart to those who are left behind, at their request,[4] the blessing of the departed.

[1] Siphra Lev. 10. 17 (ed. princ. Venice, 1545), 24d. 38–40.

[2] *Reich Gottes und Menschensohn* (Munich, 1934), 261–2.

[3] Enoch slav. 56. 1 rec. B.

[4] Enoch, however, refuses to partake of earthly food, ibid. 56. 2.

Jesus' actions at His farewell meal belong to this circle of ideas: by their eating and drinking the disciples are not only to be given a share in the blessing pronounced by Jesus as the Paterfamilias, but also to receive a share in the redemptive work of the Saviour. This is Christ's last and greatest gift: He can give nothing greater than a share in the redeeming power of His death.

The fact that Paul also understood the Eucharist in this way is an important confirmation of our exegesis. In 1 Cor. 10. 16, he says that the benefit received in the Eucharist is the *κοινωνία τοῦ αἵματος τοῦ Χριστοῦ* and the *κοινωνία τοῦ σώματος τοῦ Χριστοῦ*. Verse 17 makes it clear that he uses the expression *τὸ σῶμα τοῦ Χριστοῦ* in its specifically Pauline sense, signifying the Church. Accordingly it may be assumed that he understood the expression *τὸ αἷμα τοῦ Χριστοῦ* in its frequently repeated and specifically Pauline sense (Rom. 3. 25; 5. 9; Eph. 1. 7; 2. 13; cf. Col. 1. 20) of the saving death of Christ. To have part in the community of the redeemed, to have part in Christ's atoning death—that is, according to Paul, the benefit received in the Eucharist. This interpretation tallies with our exegesis even in detail.

(*d*) . . . *that God may remember me.*

The command to repeat the rite is found only in Paul (with reference to both bread and wine) and in Luke (with reference to the bread only). As we have seen, it probably did not belong to the earliest form of the account of the Last Supper. Nevertheless, this alone is not a sufficient reason to regard it as unhistorical, for the command to repeat the rite did not necessarily form part of the liturgical formula, since the celebration itself was its fulfilment. "On ne récite pas une rubrique, on l'exécute."[1] The command to repeat may be regarded as a separate tradition which was given a place only in the Antiochene tradition. In any case Jesus said more at the Last Supper than the few words which have been preserved in the ancient liturgical formulæ. There is, however, another fact which tells more heavily against the historicity of the command to repeat the rite: its wording has affinities with the formulæ used for the foundation of

[1] P. Benoit, *Rev. Bibl.* 48 (1939), 386.

ancient ceremonies of commemoration of the dead;[1] in many cases these are explicitly called *ἀνάμνησις*.[2] Particularly close is the relation to the deed of such a foundation preserved in an epitaph from Nicomedia, where we read: . . . *δίδωμι δὲ καὶ καταλείπω τῇ κώμῃ ʽΡακήλων ἀργυρίου δηνάρια . . . ἐπὶ τῷ ποιεῖν αὐτοὺς ἀνάμνησίν μου, ἣν ποιήσουσιν <ἐν τῇ συγγ>ενε<ίᾳ> Δραδιζανῶν*[3] and to the will of Epicurus in which a meeting of remembrance on the twentieth day of each month is provided for *εἰς τὴν ἡμῶν τε καὶ Μητροδώρου <μνήμην>*.[4] These meetings of remembrance, it is true, were generally held on the anniversary of the birth of the dead person and not every Sunday or every day, as was the Eucharist in the Primitive Church;[5] moreover, they belonged to the funeral rites, and thus to an entirely different environment

[1] This has been specially stressed by H. Lietzmann, *An die Korinther*, 3rd ed. (1931), 58, 93–4; id., *Messe und Herrenmahl* (1926), 223. Cf. also J. Weiss, *Das Urchristentum* (1917), 506; C. Clemen, *Religionsgesch. Erklaerung d. N.T.*, 2nd ed. (1924), 179; H. Windisch, *Paulus und Christus* (1934), 53; J. Finegan, *Die Ueberlieferung der Leidens- und Auferstehungsgeschichte Jesu* (1934), 66; A. Fridrichsen, "Église et Sacrement dans le N.T." in *Rev. d'hist. et de philos. relig.* (1937), 35; P. Benoit, op. cit. 386 n. 2, etc. Cf. *ad rem* B. Laum, *Stiftungen i. d. griech.-roem. Antike* (1914), who deals with the foundation of memorial celebrations in vol. 1. 74 sq. The second volume contains the texts. Foundations of meals of remembrance with the words "in memory of" are found in the following: 2. 16 sq., No. 14, *εἰς τὴν ἡμῶν τε καὶ Μητροδώρου <μνήμην>*; 141, No. 203, *<ἐπὶ τῷ> ποιεῖν αὐτοὺς ἀνά<μ>νη<σ>ίν μου*; 180, No. 61, a meal in honour of the dead: *in memoriam eorum*; 181, No. 68, ditto: *ob memoriam*; 181, No. 69, ditto: *in memoriam sui*; 184, No. 86, ditto: *ad <memoriam cole>ndam*; 195, No. 125: *ob memoriam fratris sui*. Meals in memory of the dead in Asia Minor, ibid. 2. 88, No. 75; 97, No. 91; 135, No. 175; 136–7, No. 178; 141, No. 203, cf. supra.

[2] Many sources for *ἀνάμνησις*, meaning "a meal in memory of the dead" in F. J. Doelger, *Ichthys 2, Der heilige Fisch in den ant. Religionen und im Christentum* (1922).

[3] Text in B. Laum, op. cit. 2. 141, No. 203. It is uncertain whether the "memorial" instituted in this bequest was a meal to be held at regular intervals in honour of the deceased; Laum, 1. 74, believes, however, that it probably was, especially in view of the fact that the last words of the text seem to provide for the participation of all the relations of the deceased; but these last words are conjectural.

[4] Text in Laum, op. cit. 2. 16–17, No. 14.

[5] E. Lohmeyer in *Theol. Rundschau* 9 (1937), 192–3; id. in *Journ. of Bibl. Lit.* 56 (1937), 244–5.

(funeral guilds) from that of the Eucharist. It is most improbable that there is any relationship. However, even if that were the case, the command to repeat the rite is not necessarily unhistorical. It did not, as we have seen, belong to the earliest liturgical formula, and therefore its wording was not so strictly fixed and was more susceptible to the influences of its Hellenistic environment.[1]

On the other hand, the phrase *εἰς ἀνάμνησιν*, which—perhaps fortuitously—has not yet been found in any of the Hellenistic formulae, is very common in Palestinian usage.[2] In particular it is said of the feast of the Passover that it should be celebrated *lezikkārōn* (Exod. 12. 14, cf. 13. 9; Deut. 16. 3; Jub. 49. 15), and in the festival *Ḳiddūsh*, the one spoken by Jesus at the passover meal, God is praised as He "who has given to His people Israel festal seasons for joy and *lezikkārōn*"[3]—as indeed the entire feast of the Passover is a feast of remembrance, and the passover meal a meal of remembrance. "He has made His wonderful works to be remembered", says Ps. 111. 4 of the Passover. The large part played by *ἀνάμνησις* in the ideas of late Judaism concerning the history of salvation is shown in the liturgy of the New Year. Among the special prayers (*mūsāph*-prayers) of this feast are the *malkhiyyōth*, the *zikhrōnōth*, and the *shōphārōth*. The *zikhrōnōth*[4] are prayers which enclose Bible passages treating of "remembrance", exclusively God's gracious remembrance of His covenant-promises both in the past and in the future. The closing prayer of the *zikhrōnōth* ends with the doxology: "Praised be thou, O Lord, that rememberest the covenant (*zōkhēr habberīth*)". Of special importance is the old Passover prayer which beseeches God for "the remembrance of the Messiah".[5]

The ultimate verdict on the historicity of the command to repeat the rite will depend upon its interpretation, which is fraught with difficulties. The first word *τοῦτο* cannot refer to the recital of the words of interpretation (that is ruled out by *ποιεῖτε*, which contemplates action) and therefore must mean the rite of

[1] P. Benoit, *Rev. Bibl.* 48 (1939), 386 n. 2, cf. supra, p. 113 n. 4.

[2] LXX Lev. 24. 7; Ps. 37 (38) tit.; 69 (70) tit.; Wisd. 16. 6. The analogy to this in the Gospels is *εἰς μνημόσυνον*, Mark 14. 9; Matt. 26. 13.

[3] b. Ber. 49a.

[4] Text e.g. in P. Fiebig, *Rosch-ha-schana* (1914), 53–8.

[5] Said at the Passover after the third benediction of Grace after meat.

breaking the bread and blessing the cup, i.e. the rite of Grace before and after the meal.[1] It is difficult to assume that this refers only to the repetition of the usual Grace—that required no special command—it refers rather to the special Grace[2] by which the table fellowship of the Messianic community was established and which prayed for its consummation.[3] It has to be done *εἰς τὴν ἐμὴν ἀνάμνησιν*. The expression is ambiguous. One thing is certain: *ἐμός*[4] here, as nowhere else in the New Testament,[5] stands for an objective genitive,[6] meaning "that remembrance should be made of Me", "in remembrance of Me" (A.V.). The question remains, however, who is to remember Jesus? The usual interpretation that the disciples should keep His memorial is not the only one which is possible, nor even the most probable. For the expression לְזִכָּרוֹן, Aram. לְדִכְרָן, Greek *εἰς ἀνάμνησιν*, *εἰς μνημόσυνον*, although it means both man's remembering and the merciful remembrance of God in the Old Testament, has in the Palestinian religious texts of the pre-Christian era much rather the second meaning than the first. Thus in the LXX we find *εἰς ἀνάμνησιν* used three times of God's remembrance,[7] and only once of human memory,[8] and *εἰς μνημόσυνον* means in Ecclesiasticus (45. 9, 11, 16; 50. 16) and in the newly discovered Greek fragments of Enoch (in the Chester-Beatty papyri[9]) always God's

[1] This was also Paul's interpretation: *τὸ ποτήριον τῆς εὐλογίας ὃ εὐλογοῦμεν* and *τὸν ἄρτον ὃν κλῶμεν* 1 Cor. 10. 16; *εὐλογοῦμεν* and *κλῶμεν* means the fulfilment of the command *τοῦτο ποιεῖτε*. [2] Cf. Did. 9. 1–10. 5.

[3] M. Barth, *Das Abendmahl* (1945), 18, would like to refer *τοῦτο* to the entire meal. This is equally possible.

[4] From the emphasis put on the possessive pronoun by giving it the first place, many have concluded that the remembrance of Jesus is here opposed to the remembrance of the Passover, as e.g. O. Procksch, "Passa und Abendmahl" in *Vom Sakrament des Altars* (1941), offprint p. 13. It is, however, very doubtful whether the Aramaic original put any stress on the pronoun (by using *dīlī*).

[5] E. Lohmeyer in *Theol. Rundschau* 9 (1937), 193.

[6] The use of the objective genitive with *ἀνάμνησις* is firmly established, cf. Mark 14. 9; Wisd. 16. 6; Ecclus. 10. 17; 23. 26; 38. 23; 39. 9; 41. 1; 44. 9; 45. 1; 46. 11; 49. 1, 13; add. ad Esth. 8. 12u; 1 Macc. 3. 7; 3. 35; 8. 22; 12. 53; 2 Macc. 6. 31.

[7] Cf. LXX Lev. 24. 7; Ps. 37 (38) tit.; 69 (70) tit. [8] Wisd. 16. 6.

[9] Aeth. Enoch 99. 3 (twice) ed. C. Bonner, "The Last Chapters of Enoch in Greek", *Studies and Documents* 8 (1937). *Μνημόσυνον* also occurs ibid. 97. 7; 103. 4, where it means once more God's remembrance.

remembrance. The same applies to the expression דכיר לטב in inscriptions recording the dedication of a synagogue,[1] and of the analogous Hebrew expression זכור לטוב.[2] In the New Testament too *εἰς μνημόσυνον*, which is the equivalent of *εἰς ἀνάμνησιν*, means God's merciful remembrance in both passages where it occurs, Mark 14. 9 (par. Matt. 26. 13) and Acts 10. 4. This is obvious in Acts 10. 4 *εἰς μνημόσυνον ἔμπροσθεν τοῦ θεοῦ*, and at least highly probable in Mark 14. 9.[3] These facts make it very probable that *εἰς τὴν ἐμὴν ἀνάμνησιν* in 1 Cor. 11. 24–5 and Luke 22. 19 should be understood in the same way, "that God may remember Me". God's remembrance, however, has always a quite definite meaning in Holy Scripture: it never means a mere recollection on the part of God; but when God remembers somebody, He acts, He does something, He sits in judgment and grants His grace, He fulfils His promise.[4] In what way, therefore, is God expected to "remember", when the Messianic community meets and prays to Him that He should "remember His Messiah"?[5] The only answer possible is: God remembers the Messiah by bringing about His kingdom in the parousia.

This understanding of *εἰς τὴν ἐμὴν ἀνάμνησιν* (that God remember Me) agrees with 1 Cor. 11. 26 and the Didache. In 1 Cor. 11. 23–25 Paul gives the liturgical formula, and from verse 26 onwards he adds his own notes. In verse 26, as appears from

[1] For this point I am indebted to K. Galling.

[2] P. Billerbeck 1. 987.

[3] E. Lohmeyer, *Das Evangelium des Markus* (1937), 295–6. Two short remarks on Mark 14. 9 may be added: (1) sy^{sin} understands *ὅπου* as a temporal conjunction (*kadh*), cf. Mark 9. 18, where *ὅπου ἐάν* with the aor. subj. also has a temporal meaning; (2) the *εὐαγγέλιον* which will be proclaimed in all the world should be compared with Rev. 14. 6, where the angel proclaims to every nation, kindred, tongue, and people the *αἰώνιον* eternally valid *εὐαγγέλιον*, that the *ὥρα τῆς κρίσεως* has come. This leads to a strictly eschatological interpretation of Mark 14. 9, whose original meaning is, "Amen, I say unto you, when the news (of victory) will be proclaimed, what this (woman) has done will be reported (before God), that (He) may remember her (at the Last Judgment)." Cf. Joach. Jeremias, Mark 14. 9, *Z.N.W.* 44 (1952/3), 103–7.

[4] O. Michel in *Theol. Woerterb. z. N.T.* 4. 678 sq.; F. J. Leenhardt, *Le Sacrement de la Sainte Cène* (1948), 19. Cf. e.g. Luke 23. 42, "Lord remember me, when Thou comest (again) as king", or Luke 1. 54, "He remembering His mercy, hath holpen His servant Israel, as He promised to our forefathers."

[5] Cf. the Passover prayer, supra, p. 161.

γάρ and the repetition of *ὁσάκις* from verse 25, he intends to explain in what sense the celebration of the meal by the congregation is an *ἀνάμνησις* of the Kyrios: *ὁσάκις γὰρ ἐὰν ἐσθίητε τὸν ἄρτον τοῦτον καὶ τὸ ποτήριον πίνητε, τὸν θάνατον τοῦ κυρίου καταγγέλλετε, ἄχρι οὗ ἔλθῃ* (11. 26). From the linguistic point of view we can say, (1) that *καταγγέλλετε* is indicative and not imperative, because of *γάρ*, and does not visualize preaching to those outside (who indeed are not even present), but the "proclamation of something already accomplished".[1] By — or at — each celebration of the meal the death of the Lord is proclaimed—not as a happening of the past but as an eschatological event, i.e. as the beginning of the New Covenant.[2] Every Eucharist proclaims the beginning of the time of God's salvation. (2) *ἄχρι οὗ ἔλθῃ*, is not simply a definition of time, but *ἔλθῃ* is a prospective subjunctive in which, as appears from the omission of *ἄν*, an element of finality is contained.[3] A free rendering would be: "until (the goal is reached that He comes". As a matter of fact, *ἄχρι οὗ* with the subjunctive of the aorist and without *ἄν* in the New Testament always opens up the prospect of the attainment of the eschatological goal: Rom. 11. 25; 1 Cor. 15. 25; Luke 21. 24. *ἄχρι οὗ ἔλθῃ* is an obvious allusion to the *maranatha* of the liturgy,[4] by which the congregation prays for the coming of the Lord. That means the Eucharist is an *ἀνάμνησις* of the Kyrios, not because it reminds the Church of the event of the Passion, but because it proclaims the beginning of the time of salvation and prays for the inception of the consummation. In the eucharistic prayers of the Didache God is expressly asked for His remembrance: *μνήσθητι, κύριε, τῆς ἐκκλησίας σου τοῦ ῥύσασθαι αὐτὴν ἀπὸ παντὸς πονηροῦ καὶ τελειῶσαι αὐτὴν ἐν τῇ ἀγάπῃ σου, καὶ σύναξον αὐτὴν ἀπὸ τῶν τεσσάρων ἀνέμων, τὴν ἁγιασθεῖσαν, εἰς τὴν σὴν βασιλείαν, ἣν ἡτοίμασας αὐτῇ* (10. 5). The celebrating congregation prays God to remember His Church by granting her fulfilment and by gathering her into His kingdom which He has prepared for her. Here it is unambiguously God who is asked for His remembrance.

[1] J. Schniewind in *Theol. Woerterb. z. N.T.* 1 (1933), 70. 5.
[2] A. Schlatter, *Paulus, der Bote Jesu* (1934), 325.
[3] Blass-Debrunner, *Gramm. d. N.T. Griechisch*, 7th ed. (1943), § 383, 2.
[4] J. Schniewind, *Theol. Woerterb. z. N.T.* 1 (1933), 70 n. 25.

If we understand the command to repeat the rite like that, it makes sense only if Jesus Himself gave it. He desired that His disciples should continue to meet together daily as the table fellowship of the Messiah during the short interval between His departure and the parousia, and thereby beseech God to remember His Messiah by bringing the consummation to pass.

(3) *The Vow of Abstinence*

(Luke 22. 15–18 par. Mark 14. 25)

The words of interpretation do not exhaust the elements of surprise in what Jesus did at the Last Supper, and which were indelibly impressed upon the minds of the disciples. "And He took the cup and gave thanks and said: Take this and divide it among yourselves", Luke 22. 17. The cup was normally passed round in silence: at the most *λάβετε* would be appropriate. The unusual[1] instruction *λάβετε τοῦτο καὶ διαμερίσατε εἰς ἑαυτούς* can hardly be otherwise understood than as implying that Jesus did not share in the cup.[2] The disciples must already have been surprised by the fact that, contrary to custom, although Jesus blessed the cup, He did not share in it, and their surprise must have increased still more at the words with which He accounts for His non-participation: the so-called eschatological looking forward. The words of Jesus that He would eat the passover meal and drink wine again only in the kingdom of God, are generally understood as a prediction of His death. But such an interpretation by-passes the greatest difficulty of the text, which is that the words of Jesus are in the form of an oath.

(1) Reference has to be made first to *οὐ μή* (Luke 22. 16, 18; Mark 14. 25; Matt. 26. 29). Previous examination of this (classical) emphatic form of negation has shown that it is far more common in the New Testament than in classical or contemporary Greek, but that this disproportionate use is due solely to its frequency

[1] P. Fiebig, *Neues Saechs. Kirchenblatt* 42 (1935), 376.

[2] This is almost generally accepted: cf. the commentaries by Th. Zahn, E. Klostermann, and A. Schlatter ad h.l.; G. Dalman, *Jesus-Jeschua* (1922), 144–5; P. Fiebig in *Theol. Lit.-Zeitg.* 60 (1935), 343; E. Lohmeyer, *Journ. of Bibl. Lit.* 56 (1937), 246–7; C. H. Dodd, *The Parables of the Kingdom*, 4th ed. (1938), 60; M. Dibelius, *Jesus* (1939), 114; G. Dix, *The Shape of the Liturgy* (1944), 54.

in the quotations from the LXX, and in the Sayings of Jesus before and after His resurrection. For these two groups account for almost 90 per cent. of the cases in which *οὐ μή* occurs in the New Testament.[1] Moulton has explained this unusual frequency by the assumption that inspired speech tends to use words with a strong emphasis.[2] However, we must go a step farther. Of the nine Marcan passages in which *οὐ μή* occurs, no less than five (including Mark 14. 25)[3] are linked up with the oath-word *ἀμήν*,[4] and the other Gospels provide further instances of the same[5] or similar[6] pairings. Moreover, if we examine the passages from the Gospels where someone other than Jesus or the angel of God (Luke 1. 15) uses *οὐ μή*, we always find it in oath-like assurances (Mark 14. 31 par.; Matt. 16. 22;[7] John 13. 8; 20. 25), with the one exception of John 11. 56. In 1 Cor. 8. 13, we find *οὐ μή* in a (hypothetical) vow of abstinence. Of the 98 passages in the New Testament all the rest consist—with but few exceptions—of oath-like assurances, promises, or threats by God[8] or Jesus. Noteworthy in our passage is the connexion of *οὐ μή* with the oath-substitute *ἀμήν* and the intensifying *οὐκέτι* (Mark 14. 25). (2) The same result follows from the examination of *γάρ* at the beginning of Luke 22. 18. Jesus explains in verse 18 why He himself does not drink: *λάβετε τοῦτο καὶ διαμερίσατε εἰς ἑαυτούς· λέγω γὰρ ὑμῖν, οὐ μὴ πίω ἀπὸ τοῦ νῦν ἀπὸ τοῦ γενήματος τῆς ἀμπέλου ἕως οὗ ἡ βασιλεία τοῦ θεοῦ ἔλθῃ*, verses 17b–18. The translation which takes *οὐ μὴ πίω* as a mere future gives no reason for Jesus' not drinking. Only a resolution would

[1] J. H. Moulton, *Einleitung i. d. Sprache des N.T.* (1911), 296–303.

[2] Ibid. 303.

[3] Mark 9. 1, 41; 10. 15; 13. 30; 14. 25.

[4] "'*Āmēn*: therein lies oath, therein lies agreement, therein lies confirmation", b. Shebu' 36a par. In late Judaism *'āmēn* is exclusively used as response to either an oath or a benediction. Jesus used it instead of an oath, cf. G. Dalman, *Die Worte Jesu*, 1st ed. (1898) = 2nd ed. (1930), 187.

[5] With *ἀμήν*: Matt. 5. 18; 5. 26; 10. 23; 18. 3; 24. 2; Luke 18. 30; John 8. 51; 13. 38.

[6] With *λέγω γὰρ (δὲ) ὑμῖν*: Matt. 5. 20; 23. 39; 26. 29; Luke 13. 35; 22. 16, 18; with *λέγω δὲ ὑμῖν ἀληθῶς*: Luke 9. 27; with *λέγω σοι*: Luke 12. 59; with *ἰδού*: Luke 10. 19.

[7] The horrified exclamation of Peter, Matt. 16. 22, has the force of an oath-like entreaty.

[8] By a quotation from Holy Scripture or by the word of an angel.

provide a reason here. It is a fact that the Aramaic imperfect underlying the Greek *φάγω, πίω* (Luke 22. 16, 18; Mark 14. 25; Matt. 26. 29) is used with future meaning in Galilean Aramaic only occasionally, but almost invariably jussively, finally, or modally.[1] In our passage it is used to express intention: "divide it amongst yourselves, for (Luke, here as elsewhere, omits the oath-substitute *ἀμήν* found in Mark 14. 25) I say unto you, I have no intention from now on of drinking wine any more, until God[2] establishes His kingdom".[3]

In other words: Jesus makes a twofold (Luke 22. 16, 18) vow of abstinence.[4] "I will not eat of it (the Passover), till God[5] fulfils it in the kingdom of God . . . I will no more drink of the fruit of the vine till God[5] establishes His kingdom" (Luke 22. 16, 18).[6]

[1] W. B. Stevenson, *Grammar of Palest. Jewish Aramaic* (1924), §18. 8; H. Odeberg, *The Aramaic Portions of Bereshit Rabba* 2. *Short Grammar of Galilean Aramaic* (1939), §§408, 410, 411, 552 sq. Jewish Aramaic (the Targums) is different, for there the imperfect more often assumes a future meaning (influenced by Hebrew).

[2] The expression "the kingdom of God comes", which ascribes an activity to the abstract "kingdom of God", indicates God's activity.

[3] Notice that the determination of the time (*ἕως*) is characteristic for the vow of abstinence. He who makes the vow states for what length of time his abstinence is to last. Cf. עַד in 1 Sam. 14. 24; *ἕως* in Acts 23. 12, 14, 21; *donec* in the vow of James, the Lord's brother, infra, p. 171.

[4] The first who made this point clearly is Ch. P. Coffin, *Indications of Source for the Accounts of the Last Supper as given by the Synoptists and by St. Paul* (1937), 6. Earlier: Th. Zahn, *Das Evang. d. Lukas*, 3–4th ed. (1920), 673. Correct is M. Barth, *Das Abendmahl* (1945), 42, the words of Jesus have "the form and significance of an oath". G. Dalman, *Jesus-Jeschua* (1922), 141–2, also recognises that Jesus excludes Himself from the drinking of the wine (141), expresses a renunciation (141), and so gives it a declaration of renunciation, i.e. an *'issār* (142). However, as in the case supra, p. 140 n. 3, doctrinal considerations intervene—"can we attribute to Jesus such a renunciation?" (142)—and prevent D. from drawing the correct conclusion.

[5] The passive is used to signify God's action, cf. supra, p. 122 sq. No. 13.

[6] This was the reason why Jesus refused the wine mingled with myrrh, which was offered Him as a narcotic before the crucifixion, Mark 15. 23; Matt. 27. 34. If our thesis is correct, Luke 22. 15–18 does not belong to the beginning of the meal: esp. v. 16 would only—because of v. 15—suit the end of the meal. Mark is therefore correct: the two cups of Luke 22. 17 and Mark 14. 23 par. are probably identical. P. Benoit, *Rev. Bibl.* 48 (1939), 381, has come to the same conclusion, though from entirely different considerations.

What then was the intention of Jesus when He made this strange twofold vow of abstinence? An attempt to answer this question can be made only when the contemporary sources have been examined.

The basic regulations of the Law concerning vows of abstinence (אִסָּר) are found in Num. 30. 2-17. Instances of such vows are found in the Old Testament. 1 Sam. 14. 24b, "Saul adjured the people saying: Cursed be the man that eateth any food until it be evening, and I be avenged on my enemies"; Ps. 132. 2–5, where David is said to have vowed not to sleep in a bed or in a house, indeed to forgo sleep altogether, till he had found a place for God's house; 2 Sam. 11. 11 (Uriah's vow of abstinence), etc.

In later Judaism such renunciations played a large part.[1] They referred to all kinds of food—for a limited or an unlimited period[2]—drinks of all kinds,[3] especially wine,[4] certain clothes,[5] sexual intercourse,[6] sleep,[7] speaking,[8] bathing,[9] business with and profits obtained from others (e.g., by buying or selling),[10] entering a house[11] or a city[12] etc. (1) As may be seen from the enumeration of instances such as these, renunciations were connected with religion only in so far as they had the binding power of vows; the motives for them were rather, in everyday life, of a very secular kind: they were often caused by anger[13] or hatred,[14] in which case they expressed a refusal to have any

[1] In the following remarks only vows of abstinence (in which somebody renounces the use of something) will be considered; the vows of interdiction (by which somebody compels another person to renounce something, as in Mark 7. 11), which also belong to the *'issārim* (renunciations) are discussed by P. Billerbeck 1. 713–17.

[2] Nedh. 1. 1, 3–4; 2. 1–2; 4. 1, 5, 7–8; 6. 1–10; 7. 1–2, 6–8; 8. 6; 9. 8; 11. 2; Ḥull. 8. 1, cf. 1 Sam. 14. 24 (supra).

[3] Nedh. 3. 2; 6. 5, 7, 9; 8. 1, 5; 9. 8; 11. 8.

[4] 6. 7–9; 8. 1, 5; 9. 8; Mi. Naz., esp. 2. 3. The vows of the Nazirite constitute a special case of these renunciations. Abstinence from wine alone does not make a man a Nazirite, for he was also bound not to have his hair cut and to beware of defilement.

[5] Nedh. 7. 3, 8.

[6] Nedh. 2. 1–2, 5; 3. 2, 4; 8. 7; 9. 5; 11. 12; Keth. 5. 6, cf. 1 Sam. 21. 6; 2 Sam. 11. 11; 1 Cor. 7. 5.

[7] Nedh. 2. 1, cf. Ps. 132. 2 sq. (supra).

[8] 1. 4; 2. 1.

[9] 11. 1.

[10] Philo, *Spec. Leg.* 2. § 16 (5. 89. 9); Nedh. 3. 6–11; 4. 1–7; 5. 1 sq.; 9. 2, 7, 10; 11. 3, 5–6, 11.

[11] 7. 4–5; 9. 2–3.

[12] 7. 5.

[13] 4. 6; 7. 3.

[14] 9. 4.

more dealings with someone (wife, father, or business partner).[1] They were meant to reinforce such a resolution as by an oath.[2] When bargaining, buyer and seller used them to force the other party to yield.[3] They were generally attempts to put pressure upon another person, e.g. to make him accept[4] or present[5] a gift—almost everywhere they signified that the resolution made was irrevocable.[6] The same intention is found in the vow of abstinence of more than forty men, not to eat or to drink until they had killed Paul (Acts 23. 12, 14, 21). It probably explains Acts 18. 18, provided that Paul is here the subject of *κειράμενος*,[7] for, as the cutting of his hair took place at Cenchreae, immediately after his departure from Corinth, we may conclude that by the vow not to have his hair cut before his departure, Paul had made it plain to the Corinthian Church that his decision to go was irrevocable, although they had pressed him to stay. (2) But there are many examples to show that these renunciations had by no means quite lost their religious significance. The fear of committing sin when drunk, the fight against the evil impulse e.g. (vanity), the resolution to mortify the flesh, are all mentioned by rabbinical writers as reasons for the renunciation of wine or the taking of the Nazirite vows so frequent[8] in the time of Jesus.[9] Paul says that if by eating meat he would be in danger of inducing a brother to sin, he would willingly renounce the eating of meat for ever (1 Cor. 8. 13). The Nazirite dedicates himself to God.[10] The same intention of dedicating themselves to God is found in those who for the sake of the kingdom of God renounce married life (Matt. 19. 12).[11]

[1] Philo, *Spec. Leg.* 2. § 16 (5. 89. 7); Nedh. 4. 6; 7. 3; 9. 4.

[2] 3. 2, 4. [3] 3. 1. [4] 3. 4. [5] 8. 7.

[6] Of a refusal, 8. 7; 9. 2; of the resolution to be divorced, 9. 9, etc. Cf. from ancient times: Gen. 24. 33; Ps. 132. 2 sq.

[7] So P. Billerbeck ad h. l.; K. Lake-H. J. Cadbury, *The Beginnings of Christianity* 1. 4 (1933), 229. Aquila is held to be the subject by Wendt, Zahn, and Bauernfeind ad h. l., but has the accuont such an interest in Aquila?

[8] Historical evidence has been collected by P. Billerbeck 2. 87–8, 748–9, 755–6; I. Heinemann, *Philon's griechische und juedische Bildung* (1932), 92; A. Schlatter, *Die Theologie des Judentums* (1932), 117. Acts 21. 23–4; Luke 1. 15; Euseb., *H. E.* 2. 23. 4.

[9] Evidence in P. Billerbeck 2. 748. See also Test. Jos. 3–4, 9–10.

[10] *Αὑτοὺς καθιερῶσιν*, Jos., *Ant.* 4. 4. 4 §72.

[11] Cf. Rev. 14. 4.

No different is the case when Anna the prophetess, like Judith,[1] renounces a second marriage and serves God with prayer and fasting, Luke 2. 37. The Christian couples who for a time refrain from marital intercourse do so in order to devote themselves without distraction to prayer, 1 Cor. 7. 5.[2] Similarly, when John the Baptist repudiated the eating of meat and the drinking of wine (Mark 1. 6; Luke 7. 33) his reason was most probably that he wanted to devote himself altogether to his mission. (3) To these motives for taking a vow of abstinence may be added a third. "For thou, O God, hast heard my vows", says Ps. 61. 6. The word "vow" is used here with the meaning of "prayer". The Psalmist is thinking of vows which are spoken in combination with a petition. The suppliant promises a sacrifice or a dedication to the Temple, should his prayer be heard. Such a vow reinforcing a prayer need not be the promise of a gift, but could—from very early times—just as easily be a vow of abstinence. Saul made his warriors swear that none of them would eat before the evening, until complete victory should be won, 1 Sam. 14. 24—their renunciation was meant to gain God's grace. David fasted in order that God should spare the life of his sick child, 2 Sam. 12. 15 sq., esp. v. 22. There is a good deal of evidence to show that in New Testament times vows of abstinence were made to secure God's hearing. Josephus says that it was customary that "those who were plagued with a grave disease or with another serious distress" took upon themselves a thirty days Nazirate,[3] and numerous rabbinical sources record vows of fasting, sometimes for long periods, which were made on behalf of sick persons[4] or because of personal or national emergencies, or because assurance was wanted that the prayers should be heard.[5] "He who prays

[1] Judith 8. 4–6.

[2] Jewish scholars used to renounce marital intercourse for a time for the sake of their study of the Torah, cf. P. Billerbeck 3. 372.

[3] Jos., *Bell.* 2. 15. 1 §313. Queen Helena of Adiabene undertook to live as a Nazirite for seven years if her son would safely return from the war, Naz. 3. 6. We also hear of husbands vowing to be Nazirites if their wives should have a child or a son, ibid. 2. 7.

[4] Tos. Ta'an. 3. 3 (219), cf. Ps. 35. 13.

[5] P. Billerbeck 4. 94 sq. The usual wording of a fasting vow, ibid. 97 note e. Cf. Ps. 109. 24; Dan. 9. 3; Tob. 12. 8; Test. Benj. 1. Prayer and fasting in the N.T.: Mark 9. 29; Luke 2. 37; Acts 13. 2–3; 14. 23.

without being heard, must fast."[1] The Gospel according to the Hebrews reports that the risen Lord appeared first to His brother James: *iuraverat enim Jacobus se non comesurum panem ab illa hora qua biberat calicem Domini, donec videret eum resurgentem a dormientibus.*[2] James expected for certain—that much follows from *donec*—that Jesus would rise again, and vowed that he would take no food until then; the fasting is obviously meant as fasting prayer. In all the cases which have been enumerated under (3), the vow of abstinence gives expression to the insistency of the prayer.

We repeat the question: Can we venture a conjecture as to Jesus' intention in making His vow of abstinence? All the main reasons we have mentioned could have played their part, for they are not exclusive of each other, but rather merge into each other. Jesus may have intended to make clear to His disciples that His decision to open the way for the kingdom of God by His vicarious suffering was irrevocable: He burns His bridges, forswears feasting and wine, and prepares Himself with a resolute will to drink the bitter cup which the Father offers Him. Beneath His resolution there is already something of the dreadful tension of the struggle at Gethsemane, and of the depth of His dereliction on the Cross. At the same time, Jesus may have wished to make plain to His disciples how completely His life was detached from this world: His life is dedicated wholly to God (John 17. 19), and belongs wholly to the coming kingdom of God, the Passover of fulfilment. Lastly, Jesus may have desired to give to His disciples by a symbolic and urgent prayer for the speedy fulfilment of the Passover, almost by a wrestling with God for it, the certainty that the kingdom of God was at hand. The eschatological element in the ἕως-clause brings this last motive to the fore—the prayer for complete fulfilment which is sure of being heard.

The glory of God has drawn very near. The Passion of Jesus will be the beginning of the last great hour of temptation for the whole earth, Mark 14. 38, which will usher in the dawn of the day of salvation, ibid. 14. 58. So the hour is at hand when the celebra-

[1] j. Ber. 4. 8a. 1.

[2] Jerome, *De vir. ill.* 2 (E. Klostermann, *Apocrypha* 2, 3rd ed., 1929, 10–11). Klostermann suggests, probably rightly, that the words quoted are a comment by Jer. on of the text of the Gospel according to the Hebrews.

tion of the Passover year after year will cease, and God will instead inaugurate the eternal Passover of fulfilment (Luke 22. 16: πληρωθῇ) for which God's people look so longingly in their earthly passovers. The next meal which Jesus will hold with His disciples will be the Messianic meal on a transfigured earth. The word of the apocalyptic seer will come true: "The Lord of the spirits shall dwell above them, and with that Son of Man shall they eat, lie down and rise up for ever and ever" Enoch aeth. 62. 14. Jesus will drink the wine "new", adds Mark (14. 25). To be "new" is the mark of the redeemed world and of the time of salvation, of the transfigured creation. And when Matthew, in a correct interpretation, adds his μεθ' ὑμῶν (26. 29), he makes it clear that the Passover of fulfilment means the perfection of communion between the redeemed community and its Redeemer. On a transfigured earth, where the perfect communion with God will have become a reality through corporal transfiguration, Jesus will once more, as at the Last Supper, act as the Paterfamilias: He will break for His own the bread of blessing and give to them the cup of thanksgiving—He Himself once more the giver and the minister, and His own once more the recipients who, through eating and drinking, receive the gift of God's salvation, eternal life.

The disciples are specially in need of such assurance, in view of the immediately impending events of the Passion. Jesus wishes to fix it as firmly in their minds as He possibly can. Therefore He is not content with a spoken promise, but translates it into the language of the senses for them by His actions. He does not share in the cup. He does more: by a solemn vow of abstinence He forswears all feasts and wine for the future, so as to set before His disciples and impart to them His own complete certainty that the final consummation is near at hand.

(4) *The Hymn of Praise*

The saying of Grace after meat was followed immediately by the singing of the Hymn of Praise, Ps. 114[1]–118 (Mark 14. 26 par.). It was antiphonal: one member of the table fellowship recited the text, and the others responded to each half-verse with "Halle-

[1] Cf. supra, p.31 n. 1.

lujah".[1] Jesus' great knowledge of the Bible warrants the assumption that He Himself sang the *Hallēl*.[2] However that may be, whether He recited it or whether He only joined in the prayer and the responses, we know the prayers with which Jesus concluded the Last Supper. They are all prayers of thanksgiving. They praise the Deliverer from the power of the Egyptians, before whose presence the earth trembles (Ps. 114). They praise Him as the one, the only living God in whom His chosen people put their trust, who blesses those who fear Him, and who will be blessed for evermore (Ps. 115). They promise to the merciful Redeemer who has delivered their soul from death, sacrifices of thanksgiving and the payment of vows in the presence of all His people (Ps. 116). They call upon the heathen to join in praise (Ps. 117). And they close with a prayer expressing the thanksgiving and the jubilation of the festal community: "O give thanks unto the Lord; for He is gracious; for His mercy endureth for ever" (Ps. 118. 1). Out of my distress the Lord has heard me. Now the songs of jubilation resound: "I shall not die, but live, and declare the works of the Lord" (v. 17); the rejected stone has become the keystone through God's action (v. 22-3); "blessed be He that cometh in the name of the Lord" (v. 26); "thou art my God, I will exalt thee; O give thanks unto the Lord, for He is good: for His mercy endureth for ever" (v. 29). Jesus prayed in these very words.

We know that especially the last verses of the *Hallēl* had been much in Jesus' mind: the Hosanna (Ps. 118. 25–6), the jubilant shout of the people going in procession round the altar with palms in their hands at the Feast of the Tabernacles, was sung to Him by the crowd at His entry into Jerusalem (Mark 11. 9–10); in the saying about the rejected stone which God has made the keystone (Ps. 118, 22) He saw a prophecy of His death and subsequent exaltation (Mark 8. 31, cf. 12. 10–11; Luke

[1] Sukka 3. 10, cf. Soṭa 5. 4; j. Soṭa 5. 20c. 9 sq.; b. Soṭa 30b (Bar.). This resulted, according to j. Sheq. 16. 15c. 39, in a 123-fold Hallelujah. The response with Hallelujah seems to have been the earliest, I. Elbogen *Der juedische Gottesdienst*, 2nd ed. (1924), 496. Tos. Pes. 10. 7 (172. 22), ordaining the repetition of the last words of each line, is applicable only in the case of children reciting.

[2] It often happened that no member of the table fellowship was able to recite the *Hallēl*, Tos. Pes. 10. 8 (172. 24).

17. 25); He described the exclamation "blessed is He that cometh in the name of the Lord" (Ps. 118. 26) as the salutation with which Israel, that now rejects Him, will greet Him as king (Matt. 23. 39 par.). Like many contemporary commentators,[1] Jesus also gave an eschatological-Messianic meaning to Ps. 118, and applied it to Himself: He found in this psalm a description of how God would guide His Messiah through suffering to glory and of the ceaseless Divine praises of the age to come. When He arose to go to Gethsemane, this psalm was on His lips.

Jesus' understanding of Ps. 118 gives us a decisive pointer to the interpretation of His eucharistic words. The alternative: "the Eucharist a re-enactment of the death of Jesus or an eschatological feast of joy?"[2] must not be decided exclusively the one way or the other, for the two are closely inter-related. Jesus Himself celebrated the Eucharist singing the jubilant psalm of thanksgiving which gives praise to Him who leads His Messiah through chastening to the opened door of salvation.

In this way the manifold ideas combine into a very simple unity. This Messianic meal is distinguished from the series of Messianic meals which began with Peter's confession by the fact that it is the passover meal, and at the same time the last, the farewell meal. The Messiah will die, and His death will be the opening act of the eschatological πειρασμός, the great time of temptation which shall come over the earth, Mark 14. 38. In this situation all the actions and words of Jesus have only one aim, to assure the disciples of their possession of salvation. Everything is embraced in this one purpose of assurance. When He not only announces His death to His disciples and interprets it as the atonement, but also makes them partakers of its atoning power by their eating and drinking, and when He forswears all future Passovers and all further

[1] Instances for the eschatological-Messianic interpretation of the psalms of the *Hallēl* are: j. Ber. 2. 4d. 47–50 (Ps. 116. 1 = the days of the Messiah; 118. 27 = the days of Gog and Magog; 118. 28 = the world to come); Midhr. Ps. 118 §22 (Ps. 118. 24–9 = the jubilations of the redeemed people of God in the last days). Cf. also b. Pes. 118a, b. 119b (Ps. 115. 1 = the sufferings of the Messianic era; 116. 1–2 = the prayer for salvation; 116. 4 = the salvation of the souls of the righteous from Gehenna; 116. 9 = the resurrection of the dead; 116. 13 = the eschatological meal of salvation); b. Pes. 117a; 132a; Pesiq. 132a. Cf. P. Billerbeck 2. 256.

[2] Emphasized by E. Schweizer, *Theol. Zeitschr.* 2 (1946), 81–101.

wine and so assures them of the imminence of the consummation—all this is a pledge and an assurance, a summons to thanksgiving for the gift of God. As surely as they eat the bread which Jesus breaks for them and drink the wine over which He spoke the word about His outpoured blood, so surely holds good for them too the "for many" of His dying and the "with you" of the future eucharistic fellowship in a transfigured earth when Jesus keeps His promise to drink wine "new with you in my Father's kingdom."

BIBLIOGRAPHY

The view that the Last Supper was a passover meal is taken by: JOHN LIGHTFOOT, *Opera Omnia* 2 (Roterodami, 1686), 378 sq.; 670–1. —CHR. SCHOETTGEN, *Horae Hebraicae et Talmudicae in universum Novum Testamentum* (Dresden-Leipzig, 1732), 226 sq.; 400–1.—FRANZ DELITZSCH, "Talmudische Studien 4. Der Passaritus zur Zeit des zweiten Tempels", in *Zeitschr. f. d. ges. lutherische Theologie und Kirche* 16 (1855), 257–8.—JOH. WICHELHAUS, *Versuch eines ausfuehrlichen Kommentars zu der Geschichte des Leidens Jesu Christi* (1855), 185 sq.—L. J. RUECKERT, *Das Abendmahl* (Leipzig, 1856).—TH. KEIM, *Geschichte Jesu von Nazara* 3 (1867 sq.), 237.—G. BICKELL in *Der Katholik* 51 (1871), 129–56; 257–91; 385–425; 513–47.—Id., *Messe und Pascha* (Mainz, 1872).—D. F. STRAUSS, *Das Leben Jesu fuer das deutsche Volk bearbeitet*, 3rd ed. (Leipzig, 1874), 533 sq.—AUG. WUENSCHE, *Neue Beitraege zur Erlaeuterung der Evangelien aus Talmud und Midrasch* (Goettingen, 1878), 329 sq.—TH. ZAHN, *Forschungen zur Geschichte des N.T. Canons* 3 (1884), 297.—H. SCHULTZ, *Zur Lehre vom heiligen Abendmahl* (Gotha, 1886).—ALEX. BRANDT, "Die Einsetzungsworte des heiligen Abendmahls", in *Zeitschr. f. wiss. Theologie* (1888) 31.—P. LOBSTEIN, *La doctrine de la Sainte Cène* (Lausanne, 1889).—J. WATTERICH, *Das Passahmahl des neuen Bundes* (Baden-Baden, 1889).—D. CHWOLSON, *Das letzte Passahmahl Christi und der Tag seines Todes* (Leipzig, 1892, 2nd ed. with extensive additions and corrections: Leipzig, 1908).—C. v. WEIZSAECKER, *Das Apostolische Zeitalter der christlichen Kirche*, 2nd ed. (Leipzig, 1892), 575.—AD. JUELICHER, "Zur Geschichte der Abendmahlsfeier in der aeltesten Kirche", in *Theologische Abhandlungen fuer Karl Weizsaecker* (Freiburg i. Br., 1892), 233–4; 245.—N. SCHMIDT, "The Character of Christ's Last Meal", in *Journal of the Soc. of Bible Literature* 11 (Boston, 1892). —BOVON, *Théologie du Nouveau Testament* (Lausanne, 1893), 1, 337.—FRANZ DELITZSCH, art. "Passah" in Riehms *Handwoerterbuch des bibl. Altertums* 2 (Bielefeld und Leipzig, 1894), 1160–1 ("anticipated paschal meal", p. 1161a).—F. SCHULTZEN, *Das Abendmahl im N.T.* (1895).—A. RESCH, *Ausserkanonische Paralleltexte zu den Evangelien* 2, T.U. 10. 3 (Leipzig, 1895), 612–18.—R. A. HOFFMANN, *Die Abendmahlsgedanken Jesu Christi* (Koenigsberg, 1896).—R. SCHAEFER, *Das Herrenmahl nach Ursprung und Bedeutung* (Guetersloh, 1897).—A. RÉVILLE, *Jésus de Nazareth* 2 (Paris, 1897), 351 sq.—E. STAPFER, *La mort et la résurrection de Jésus-Christ*, 2nd ed. (Paris, 1898), 114.—A. EICHHORN, "Das Abendmahl im N.T.", *Hefte zur christl Welt* 36 (Leipzig, 1898), 21–2, 28.—C. CLEMEN, "Der Ursprung des heiligen Abendmahls", *Hefte zur christl Welt* 37 (Leipzig, 1898), 26.—P. W. SCHMIEDEL, "Die neuesten Ansichten ueber den Ursprung des Abendmahls", in *Protestantische Monatshefte* 3 (1899), 128; 140 sq.—A. LICHTENSTEIN, *Des Apostel Paulus Ueberlieferung von der Einsetzung* *des hl. Abendmahls* (Berlin, 1899).—TH. ZAHN, *Einleitung in das N.T.*, 2nd ed., 2 (Leipzig, 1900), 526.—W. BERNING, *Die Einsetzung der hl. Eucharistie* (Muenster, 1901).—H. J. HOLTZMANN, *Handkommentar zum N.T.* 1. 1: *Die Synoptiker*, 3rd ed. (Tuebingen-Leipzig, 1901), 99. —AD. MERX, *Das Evangelium Matthaeus* (Berlin, 1902), 377 sq.—Id., *Die Evangelien des Markus und Lukas* (Berlin, 1905), 416–48.—J. C. LAMBERT, "The Passover and the Lord's Supper", in *J.T.S.* 4 (1903), 184–93.—H. E. D. BLAKISTON, "The Lucan Account of the Institution of the Lord's Supper", in *J.T.S.* 4 (1903), 548–555.—P. W. SCHMIDT, *Die Geschichte Jesu* 2 (Tuebingen-Leipzig, 1904), 369 sq.—WABNITZ, *Histoire de la vie de Jésus. La passion, la mort et la résurrection de Jésus* (Montauban, 1904), 100.—J. SCHNEID, *Der Monatstag des Abendmahles und Todes unseres Herren Jesus Christus* (Regensburg, 1905).—Fr. WIELAND, *Mensa und Confessio. Studien ueber den Altar der altchristlichen Liturgie* 1 (Munich, 1906), 17 sq.—P. VOLZ, "Ein heutiger Passahabend", in *Z.N.W.* 7 (1906), 247–51.—R. SEEBERG, *Das Abendmahl im N.T.* (1905, 2nd ed. 1907).—W. HESS, *Jesus von Nazareth in seiner geschichtlichen Lebensentwicklung* (1908), 109–10.—D. CHWOLSON, *Das letzte Passahmahl Christi und der Tag seines Todes*, 2nd ed. (Leipzig, 1908).—J. RÉVILLE, *Les origines de l'Eucharistie* (Paris, 1908).—F. DIBELIUS, *Das Abendmahl* (Leipzig, 1911), 93.—H. L. STRACK, *Pesaḥim* (Leipzig, 1911), 10*, a proleptic celebration.—J. SICKENBERGER, in *Bibl. Zeitschrift* 10 (1912), 412.—J. LICHTENSTEIN, *Kommentar zum Matthaeus Evangelium*, in Hebrew, 2nd ed. (Leipzig, 1913), 122 sq.—P. W. SCHMIEDEL, "Das Abendmahl Jesu und das Kiddusch", in *Protestantische Monatshefte* 21 (1917), 225–39.—TH. ZAHN, *Das Evangelium des Lukas*, 3rd and 4th ed. (1920), 672 sq., *Das Evangelium nach Johannes*, 5th and 6th ed. (Leipzig, 1921), 499; 631–3, etc.—E. B. ALLO, "La synthèse du dogme eucharistique chez St. Paul", in *Revue Bibl.* 30 (1921), 324 n.—B. FRISCHKOPF, "Die neuesten Eroerterungen ueber die Abendmahlsfrage", *N.T. Abhandlungen* 9. 4–5 (Muenster, 1921).—O. GERHARDT, *Der Stern des Messias* (Leipzig, 1922), 117–8; "Das Datum der Kreuzigung Christi", in *Astronomische Nachrichten* 240, No. 5745–6 (1930), 137–62; additions, ibid. 242, No. 5790 (1931), 127–8 and 5801 (1931), 305–10.—P. BILLERBECK, *Kommentar zum N.T.* 2 (Munich, 1922–6), 812–53, excursus "Die Angaben der vier Evangelien ueber den Todestag Jesu unter Beruecksichtigung ihres Verhaeltnisses zur Halakha"; 4, 41–76, excursus, "Das Passahmahl".—G. DALMAN, *Jesus-Jeschua* (Leipzig, 1922), 80 sq.; 98 sq.—Id., *Ergaenzungen u. Verbesserungen zu Jesus-Jeschua* (Leipzig, 1929), 8 sq.—H. LAIBLE, *Theol. Literaturblatt* (1923), 130–1.—JACOB MANN, Rabbinic Studies in the Synoptic Gospels, 4. "The Last Supper as a Paschal Meal", in *Hebrew Union College Annual* 1 (Cincinnati, 1924), 341–8.—C. CLEMEN, *Religionsgeschichtliche Erklaerung des N.T.*, 2nd ed. (Giessen, 1924), 177.—H. RASCHKE, *Die Werkstatt des Markusevangelisten* (Jena, 1924), 291–2.—W. BAUER, *Das Johannesevangelium*, 2nd ed. (Tuebingen, 1925), 209; id., 3rd ed. (1933), 215.

—R. EISLER, "Das letzte Abendmahl", in *Z.N.W.* 24 (1925), 161–92; 25 (1926), 5–37, cf. the criticism of H. LIETZMANN, "Juedische Passahriten und der ἀφικόμενος. Kritische Randnoten zu R. Eislers Aufsatz ueber 'Das letzte Abendmahl'," in *Z.N.W.* 25 (1926), 1–5, and of A. MARMORSTEIN, "Miscellen 1: Das letzte Abendmahl und der Sederabend", in *Z.N.W.* 25 (1926), 249–53.—H. KRENGEL in *Monatsschrift fuer Gesch. und Wiss. des Judentums* 70 (1926), 422.—A. OEPKE, "Ursprung und ursprueglicher Sinn des Abendmahls im Lichte der neuesten Forschung", in *Allg. ev.-luther. Kirchenzeitung* 59 (1926), 12–14; 37–40; 54–9; 79–86.—K. VOELKER, *Mysterium und Agape* (Gotha, 1927), 11; 17 sq.; 19, 3; 21.—O. CASEL, "Das Mysteriengedaechtnis der Messliturgie im Lichte der Tradition", in *Jahrbuch fuer Liturgiewissenschaft* 6 (1927), 113 sq.—J. E. CARPENTER, *The Johannine Writings* (London, 1927), 374 sq.—J. BORNSTEIN in *Encyclopaedia Judaica* (1928 sq.), art. "Kiddusch", vol. 9, 1201.—J. SCHAUMBERGER, "Der 14. Nisan als Kreuzigungstag und die Synoptiker", in *Biblica* 9 (1928), 57–77.—TH. ZAHN, *Grundriss der N.T. Theologie* (1928), 53.—A. KOEBERLE, *Rechtfertigung und Heiligung* (Leipzig, 1929), 89–90.—J. KLAUSNER, *Jesus von Nazareth* (Berlin, 1930, 2nd ed. 1934), 448 sq.—JOACH. JEREMIAS, *Jesus als Weltvollender* (Guetersloh, 1930), 75.—P. JOÜON, *L'Évangile de Notre Seigneur Jésus-Christ* (Paris, 1930), 432.—A. MERX, art. "Abendmahl", in *Lexikon fuer Theologie und Kirche* 1, 2nd ed. (Freiburg, 1930), 17 sq.—G. SCHRENK, "Zwinglis Hauptmotive in der Abendmahlslehre und das N.T.", *Zwingliana* Heft 2 (1930), 176–85.—A. SCHWEITZER, *Die Mystik des Apostels Paulus* (Tuebingen, 1930), 245.—CHARLES C. TORREY, "The Date of the Crucifixion according to the Fourth Gospel", in *Journ. of Bibl. Lit.* 50 (1931), 227–41.—W. GOOSSENS, *Les origines de l'Eucharistie. Sacrement et Sacrifice* (Gembloux-Paris, 1931), 110 sq.—F. HAUCK, *Das Evangelium des Markus* (Leipzig, 1931), 166–7; id., *Das Evangelium des Lukas* (Leipzig, 1934), 261 sq.—E. KALT in *Bibl. Reallexikon* 1 (1931), 8.—J. SICKENBERGER, *Leben Jesu nach den vier Evangelien. 6. Der Abschluss* (Muenster, 1931), 74.—JOACH. JEREMIAS, *Die Passahfeier der Samaritaner und ihre Bedeutung fuer das Verstaendnis der A.T. Passahueberlieferung* (Giessen, 1932).—J. SCHNIEWIND in *Das N.T. Deutsch* 1. 1 (Goettingen, 1933), 171: the Last meal of Jesus is connected with the Passover tradition; 250–1 an anticipated Passover meal.—P. FIEBIG in *Theol. Lit. Zeitung* 59 (1934), 416.—CH. C. TORREY, *The Four Gospels* (London, 1934).—J. PICKL, *Messiaskoenig Jesus* (Munich, 1935), 72; 247–8.—W. NIESEL, "Das Abendmahl und die Opfer des Alten Bundes", in *Die Freiheit der Gebundenen, Theol. Aufsaetze f. Karl Barth*" (Munich, 1936), 178–90.—JOH. SCHNEIDER in *Z.K.G.* 55 (1936), 383.—A. ARNOLD, "Der Ursprung des christlichen Abendmahls im Lichte der neuesten liturgiegeschichtlichen Forschung", *Freiburger Theol. Studien*, Heft 45 (Freiburg i. Br., 1937, 2nd ed. 1939).—J. BEHM, art. κλάω in *Theol. Woerterb. z. N.T.* 3 (Stuttgart, 1937), 726–43.—CH. P. COFFIN, *Indications of Source for the Accounts of the*

Last Supper as given by the Synoptists and by St. Paul (Evanston Ill. s.a. — 1937 —).—JOACH. JEREMIAS, "Das paulinische Abendmahl, eine Opferdarbringung?" in *Theol. Stud. u. Krit.* 108 (1937), 124–41.—K. H. RENGSTORF in *Das Neue Testament Deutsch* 1 (Goettingen, 1937), 221 sq., an anticipated paschal meal.—I. ZOLLI, *Taljā*, in *Biblica* 13 (1937), 401–4.—H. SASSE in *Allg. ev.-luth. Kirchenzeitung* 71 (1938), 90 sq.; id., *Kirche und Herrenmahl* (1938).—I. ZOLLI, *Il Nazareno. Studi di esegesi, etc.* (Udine, 1938), 178–227: *La pasqua nella letteratura antico- e neotestamentaria.*—P. BENOIT, "Le récit de la Cène dans Lc. XXII, 15–20. Étude de critique textuelle et littéraire", in *Revue Bibl.* 48 (1939), 357–93.—J. GEWIESS, "Die urapostolische Heilsverkuendigung nach der Apostelgeschichte", *Breslauer Studien zur histor. Theol.*, new ser. 5 (1939), 167 sq.—L. GOPPELT, *Typos. Die typologische Deutung des Alten Testaments im Neuen* (Guetersloh, 1939), 132.—W. FOERSTER, *Neutestamentliche Zeitgeschichte* 1 (1940), 104.—O. PROCKSCH, "Passa und Abendmahl", and H. SASSE, "Das Abendmahl im N.T.", in *Vom Sakrament des Altars. Lutherische Beitraege zur Frage des heiligen Abendmahls*, ed. by H. SASSE (Leipzig, 1941).—E. STAUFFER, *Die Theologie des N.T.* (Stuttgart, 1941), 141–2 and note 546.—E. GAUGLER, "Das Abendmahl im N.T.", in *Internat. kirchl. Zeitschr.* 32 (1942), 97–164, published separately (Basel, 1943).—P. J. HEAWOOD in *Exp. Times* 53 (1941–2), 295 sq.—W. MICHAELIS, *Der Herr verzieht nicht die Verheissung* (1942), 28-9.—C. C. RICHARDSON, "Early Patristic Evidence for the Synoptic Chronology of the Passion", in *Angl. Theol. Rev.* 22 (1942), 299–308.—N. JOHANSSON, *Det urkristna nattfartsfirandet. Dess religionshistoriska bakgrund dess ursprung och innebörd* (Lund, 1944).—M. BARTH, "Das Abendmahl. Passamahl, Bundesmahl und Messiasmahl", *Theol. Studien* Heft 18 (1945).—E. GAUGLER in G. DELUZ-J. PH. RAMSEYER-E. GAUGLER, *La Sainte-Cène* (Neuchatel-Paris, 1945), 53–89.—K. BORNHAEUSER, *Die Leidens- und Auferstehungsgeschichte Jesu* (Guetersloh, 1947), 62, paschal meal without the paschal lamb.—F. J. LEENHARDT, *Le Sacrement de la Sainte Cène* (Neuchatel-Paris, 1948).

The view that the Last Supper was not a passover meal is taken by: E. RENAN, *La vie de Jésus* (1865), 385 sq.—G. W. PIERITZ, *The Gospels from the Rabbinical Point of View. The Lord's Last Supper* (Oxford and London, 1873).—HALLER, "Das Heilige Abendmahl und das Passahmahl", in *Theol. Studien aus Wuerttemberg* 8 (1887), 65–78.—Fr. SPITTA, *Beitraege zur Geschichte und Litteratur des Urchristentums* 1 (Goettingen, 1893), 205–337.—W. BRANDT, *Die evangelische Geschichte und der Ursprung des Christentums* (Leipzig, 1893), 304.—E. HAUPT, *Ueber die urspruengliche Form und Bedeutung der Abendmahlsworte* (Halle, 1894).—JOACHIM, "Die Ueberlieferungen ueber Jesu letztes Mahl", in *Hermes* (1895), 39 sq.—C. STAGE, "Die neueren Forschungen ueber das Abendmahl", in *Prot. Monatshefte* 1 (1897), 268–9.—P. DREWS in Haucks *Realenzyklopaedie*, 3rd ed., 5 (1898), 563 sq.—G. HOLLMANN, *Die Bedeutung des Todes Jesu* (1901), 151.—H. H.

WENDT, *Die Lehre Jesu*, 2nd ed. (Goettingen, 1901), 569.—G. H. BOX, "The Jewish Antecedents of the Eucharist", in *J.T.S.* 3 (1902), 357–69, and ibid., 10 (1909), 106–7.—JOH. HOFFMANN, *Das Abendmahl im Urchristentum* (1903), 86.—O. HOLTZMANN, "Das Abendmahl im Urchristentum", in *Z.N.W.* 4 (1903), 89–120.—A. ANDERSEN, *Das Abendmahl in den zwei ersten Jahrhunderten nach Christus* (Giessen, 1904), 22–3; id., "Zu Matth. 26. 17 sq. und Lukas 22. 15 sq.", in *Z.N.W.* 7 (1906), 87–90, cf. ibid. 172–5.—E. v. DOBSCHUETZ, *Probleme des Apostolischen Zeitalters* (Leipzig, 1904), 17.—K. G. GOETZ, *Die Abendmahlsfrage in ihrer geschichtlichen Entwickelung* (Leipzig, 1904, 2nd ed. 1907).—P. BATIFFOL, *Études d'histoire et de théologie positive, deuxième série. L'eucharistie la présence réelle et la transsubstantiation* (Paris, 1905, 9th ed. 1930), 139–40, and esp. IX.—E. v. D. GOLTZ, "Tischgebete und Abendmahlsgebete in der altchristlichen und in der griechischen Kirche", *T.U.* 29 (N.F. 14), 2b (Leipzig, 1905), 5.—E. SCHWARTZ, "Osterbetrachtungen", in *Z.N.W.* 7 (1906), 22 sq.—J. WEISS, *Die Schriften des N.T. neu uebersetzt und fuer die Gegenwart erklaert* 1 (Goettingen, 1906), 187.—J. WELLHAUSEN, *Ἄρτον ἔκλασεν*, in *Z.N.W.* 7 (1906), 182; id., *Das Evangelium Marci*, 2nd ed. (Berlin, 1909), 108 sq.; *Das Evangelium Johannis* (Berlin, 1908), 88–9; *Einleitung in die drei ersten Evangelien*, 2nd ed. (Berlin, 1911), 130 sq.—F. C. BURKITT, "St. Luke 22. 15, 16: What is the general meaning?" in *J.T.S.* 9 (1908), 569–71.—W. HEITMUELLER, art. "Abendmahl im N.T.", in *R.G.G.*, 1st ed. 1 (1909), 26/7; id., art. "Jesus Christus", ibid. 3, 369.—A. HARNACK in *Theol. Lit. Zeitung* (1909), 49.—M. GOGUEL, *L'eucharistie des origines à Justin Martyr* (Paris, 1910), 59 sq.—F. WESTBERG, *Die biblische Chronologie nach Flavius Josephus und das Todesjahr Jesu* (Leipzig, 1910).—G. BEER, *Pesachim* (Giessen, 1912), 92–109.—F. JACKSON, *The Problem of the Fourth Gospel* (1918), 56.—B. W. BACON, *The Fourth Gospel in Research and Debate*, 2nd ed. (1918).—A. LOISY, *Le quatrième évangile*, 2nd ed. (Paris, 1921), 384; 465.—P. BATIFFOL, *Leçons sur la Messe*, 2nd ed., 5 (Paris, 1919).—K. BORNHAEUSER, "Zeiten und Stunden in der Leidens-und Auferstehungsgeschichte", *Beitr. zur Foerderung christl. Theologie* 26 (Guetersloh, 1921).—KENNETT, *The Last Supper. Its Significance in the Upper Room* (Cambridge, 1921).—E. MEYER, *Ursprung und Anfaenge des Christentums* 1 (Stuttgart-Berlin, 1921), 173 sq.—P. FEINE, *Theologie des N.T.s*, 4th ed. (Leipzig, 1922), 123.—A. SCHLATTER, *Die Geschichte des Christus*, 2nd ed. (Stuttgart, 1923), 492.—W. O. E. OESTERLEY, *The Jewish Background of the Christian Liturgy* (Oxford, 1925), 156–93.—O. HOLTZMANN, *Das N.T. nach dem Stuttgarter griech. Text uebersetzt und erklaert* 1 (Giessen, 1926), 63.—H. LIETZMANN, *Messe und Herrenmahl. Eine Studie zur Geschichte der Liturgie* (Bonn, 1926), 211 sq.; id., art. "Abendmahl", IV. Liturgiegeschichtlich, in *R.G.G.*, 2nd ed., 1 (1927), 34.—E. KLOSTERMANN, *Das Markusevangelium*, 2nd ed. (Tuebingen, 1926), 125–6; 163; 3rd ed. (1936), 111–2.—P. FEINE, *Der Apostel Paulus* (Guetersloh, 1927), 620.—K. L. SCHMIDT, art. "Abendmahl", I. Im N.T., in *R.G.G.*, 2nd ed., 1 (1927), 10.—C. G. MONTEFIORE, *The Synoptic Gospels*, 2nd ed., 1 (London, 1927), 308 sq.; but cf. the addition on p. 328, where M. expresses himself more cautiously; 2. 332.—A. LOISY, "Les origines de la Cène eucharistique", in *Congrès d'histoire du Christianisme* 1 (Paris-Amsterdam, 1928), 80.—G. H. C. MACGREGOR, *Eucharistic Origins. A Survey of the N.T. Evidence* (London, 1928), 37 sq.—K. G. GOETZ, *Der Ursprung des kirchlichen Abendmahls* (Basel, 1929), 28.—H. HUBER, *Das Herrenmahl im N.T.*, Diss, Berne (Leipzig, 1929), 70 sq.—M. GOGUEL, "La relation du dernier repas de Jésus dans 1. Cor. 11", in *Rev. d'hist. et de philos. rel.* 10 (1930), 61 sq.—R. BULTMANN, *Die Geschichte der synopt. Tradition*, 2nd ed. (Goettingen, 1931), 286–7; 300.—F. GAVIN, *The Jewish Antecedents of the Christian Sacraments* (London, 1928, 2nd ed. 1933), 96–7.—T. W. H. MAXFIELD, *The Words of Institution* (Cambridge, 1933).—M. DIBELIUS, *Die Formgeschichte des Evangeliums*, 2nd ed. (Tuebingen, 1933), 181 sq.—R. OTTO, *Reich Gottes und Menschensohn* (Munich, 1934), 235.—M. DIBELIUS and W. KOEHLER, "Der Todestag Jesu", in *Theol. Blaetter* 13 (1934), No. 3, 68–9.—J. FINEGAN, *Die Ueberlieferung der Leidens-und Auferstehungsgeschichte Jesu* (Giessen, 1934), 61 sq.—M. DIBELIUS, *Die Botschaft von Jesus Christus* (Tuebingen, 1935), 137.—C. H. DODD, *The Parables of the Kingdom* (London, 1935, 4th ed. 1938), 56 n. 1.—K. G. GOETZ, "Der Einfluss des kirchlichen Brauches auf die Abendmahlstexte des N.T.", in *Vom Wesen und Wandel der Kirche, Festschrift fuer E. Vischer* (Basel, 1935), 21.—R. HUPFELD, *Die Abendmahlsfeier, ihr urspruenglicher Sinn und ihre sinngemaesse Gestaltung* (Guetersloh, (1935).—A. SCHLATTER, *Markus. Der Evangelist fuer die Griechen* (Stuttgart, 1935), 255.—F. BUECHSEL, *Das N.T. Deutsch* 1. 2, 163.—L. FENDT, *Der Christus der Gemeinde. Eine Einfuehrung in das Evang. nach Lukas* (Berlin, 1937), 224.—K. G. GOETZ, "Zur Loesung der Abendmahlsfrage", in *Theol. Stud. u. Krit.* 108 (1937), 81–123.—E. KAESEMANN, "Das Abendmahl im N.T.," in Abendmahlsgemeinschaft? Beih. 3 zur *Evang. Theol.* (Munich, 1937), 60–93.—J. LEIPOLDT, *Der Gottesdienst der aeltesten Kirche* (Leipzig, 1937), 12.—E. LOHMEYER, *Das Evangelium des Markus* (Goettingen, 1937), 309–10; id., "Vom Urchristlichen Abendmahl", in *Theol. Rundschau* 9 (1937), 168–94; 195–227; 273–312, ibid., 10 (1938), 81–99; id., *Journ. of Bibl. Lit.* 56 (1937), 217–52.—J. M. NIELEN, *Gebet und Gottesdienst im N.T.* (Freiburg i. Br., 1937), 260.—R. H. LIGHTFOOT, *Locality and Doctrine in the Gospels* (London, 1938).—F. L. CIRLOT, *The Early Eucharist* (London, 1939).—M. DIBELIUS, *Jesus* (1939), 110.—E. BARNIKOL, "Die nachapostolische, dogmatische Passahdatierung des Todes Jesu durch den Markusevangelisten im Anfang des 2. Jahrh.", in *Theol. Jahrbuecher* 8 (1940), 3–17.—W. KUEMMEL, "Jesus und Paulus", in *Theol. Blaetter* 19 (1940), 226 n. 57.—E. HIRSCH, *Fruehgeschichte des Evangeliums* 1 (1941), 143 sq.—L. S. THORNTON, *The Common Life in the Body of Christ* (Westminster, 1941), 325; 347.—TH. PREISS, "Le dernier repas de Jésus fut-il un repas pascal?" in *Theol. Zeitschr.* 4 (1948), F 84–111.

Wholly sceptical are e.g.: M. GOGUEL, *Das Leben Jesu* (Zürich, 1934), 290: "all that seems to be proved, is that Jesus died round about the time of the feast of the Passover".—G. BERTRAM, *Die Leidensgeschichte Jesu und der Christuskult* (Goettingen, 1922), 32: "we neither know the day of the last meal of Jesus nor the date of His death".

Undecided as to whether the Last Supper was a passover meal are: V. ZAPLETAL, "Der Wein in der Bibel", *Bibl. Studien* 20. 1 (1920).—L. v. SYBEL, "Das letzte Mahl Jesu", in *Theol. Stud. u. Kritiken* 95 (1923/4), 118.—W. v. LOEWENICH, *Vom Abendmahl Christi* (Berlin, 1938).—G. DIX, *The Shape of the Liturgy* (Westminster, 1944), 50 n. 1. Dix had first in the text expressed himself against the paschal character of the Last Supper, but in the note quoted he adds the remark that this view has been disputed of late in Germany, "and it is only fair to say that the question is not yet finally settled".

The Talmudic texts are quoted from the following editions:

Mishna: from the editions of H. L. Strack, or else from the edition (Stettin, 1865).
Tosephta: ed. by M. S. Zuckermandel (Pasewalk, 1877 sq.).
Talmud jer.: ed. princ. (Venice, 1523/4).
Talmud bab.: (Frankfurt a. M., 1721).
Mekhilta: ed. secunda (Venice, 1545).
Siphra: ed. princ. (Venice, 1545).
Siphre: ed. princ. (Venice, 1545).
Midhr. Rabba: (Stettin, 1864).
Targum Onkelos: ed. A. Berliner (Berlin, 1884).
Targ. Ps.-Jonathan (Jer. I): ed. M. Ginsburger (Berlin, 1903).
Fragmentary-Targum (Jer. II): ed. M. Ginsburger (Berlin, 1899).
Targum to the other writings of the O.T.: (Wilna, 1893).

INDEX OF BIBLICAL QUOTATIONS

OLD TESTAMENT

NEW TESTAMENT

GENERAL INDEX

PRINTED IN GREAT BRITAIN BY
BILLING AND SONS LTD.
GUILDFORD AND LONDON
G4697